Sphere of Russian influence

The West at Bay

by
Barbara J. Ward

"When bad men combine,
the good men associate"
BURKE

ALLEN AND UNWIN
Ruskin House, Museum Street
London

Printed in Great Britain
in 11 on 12-point Times Roman type
by Bradford and Dickens
London

TO MY
FATHER AND MOTHER

AUTHOR'S NOTE

This book attempts to give some background to the related topics of the Marshall Plan and of Western Union, and if the treatment of the two vital subjects seems at times hurried, sketchy and incomplete, this small excuse can perhaps be made. It was not certain until the opening of the debates on the Marshall Plan in the American Senate whether such a Plan had a real chance of coming into being. The writing of the book could not therefore begin much before January 20th. On the other hand, a book on the Marshall Plan and on Western Union should, if possible, appear in 1948. Yet under present conditions of book production, no book delivered after March 15th has much chance of seeing the light this year. These two dates left little over six weeks for the whole venture, which must therefore be presented strictly for what it is—a hasty attempt made without any research or detailed study to present a few of the major issues.

B. W.

CONTENTS

INTRODUCTION:

THE DOLLAR CRISIS

No corner of the world—except perhaps ancient Greece—has contributed as much as Western Europe to the development and enrichment of mankind. There is quite simply no sphere of life to-day that does not owe its origins and its impetus to the countries which together with Western Germany formed the first Committee of Sixteen to consider the Marshall Plan. Catholic Christianity flowered in Western Europe, Protestantism has its roots there. Democratic society and parliamentary government evolved in the West. The industrial revolution began in Britain. The colossal forces of modern science began modestly in the studies and workshops of Western Europe and its most shattering discovery—the release of atomic energy—was in the first place the work of European scientists—Lord Rutherford and the Curies. Communism was Marx's amalgam of German philosophy, French politics and British economics and Fascism was Europe's disastrous reaction to it. Some of the greatest works of art in the history of all civilizations were created in the West, and what superlatives should one use to describe the vitality of a society which within a few hundred years produced Dante, Shakespeare, St. Francis of Assisi and St. Teresa of Avila, Leonardo da Vinci and Michael Angelo, the music of Bach and Beethoven, the masterpieces of Gothic and Baroque architecture? Nor was all this vitality confined to the limits of the Continent. From the fifteenth to the twentieth century, new societies, European in origin and structure, were created overseas—in North and South America, in the Dominions—and in the nineteenth century, the prodigious commercial activity of Britain laid the foundations for the first coherent worldwide economic system in the history of man.

Yet to-day, this area of Western Europe, until quite recently the intellectual, artistic and economic hub of the universe, needs to be baled out of its embarrassments to the tune of some 4 billion dollars a year. It has become one of the world's distressed areas, one of its problem children. Of all the revolutions of our day, this change of fortune is the most astonishing and the most fateful, and the sense of fatality is increased by the speed with which it has come about. Roman civilization took centuries to decline and fall, but Western Europe's nineteenth century apex and its apparent downfall in the twentieth are separated by barely seventy years.

The chief external symptom of Europe's present crisis is the paralysis that has overtaken its foreign trade.[1] In this century, until the outbreak of the late war, the volume of world trade suffered disastrous fluctuations—falling, for instance, by two-thirds during the Great Depression—but its pattern remained relatively constant. Western Europe (including Western Germany) was in the main an exporter of industrial goods and an importer of food and raw materials. The foodstuffs and the materials were bought from Eastern Europe, from the Far East, from the Dominions, and from parts of North and South America—Argentina and Canada were especially important in the mass export of grain. Trade with the United States was becoming a greater and greater problem, for that vast economy had a persistent tendency to export more than it imported and thus to create a permanent dollar problem. Nevertheless, Western Europe had good non-American sources of supply and did in any case carry on with the highly industrialized United States that large exchange of manufactured goods which one productive, well-developed and industrialized area can always maintain with another. The Americans were also massive buyers of colonial products such as tin and rubber and Europe's Far-Eastern dependencies—British Malaya and the Dutch East Indies —were effective dollar earners. Under these conditions multilateral trade worked, more or less, and was the means of providing Western Europe with a standard of life second only to that of the United States.

It is this pattern that has been shattered by the events of the last nine years. In the first place, West European productivity was crippled by the war. France first suffered the slow blood-letting of the German occupation and then saw some of its best land turned into battlefields. Great Britain worked its machines to a standstill without thought of obsolescence and replacement. Italy at one time endured four governments and four economic systems simultaneously. Holland was starved and flooded. Even countries where material damage was less savage—Belgium and Norway —were cut off from their traditional markets and forced into the strait-waistcoat of Hitler's war economy. In 1945 the pro-

[1] The predicament is well summarized in the Introduction to the General Report produced by the Committee of Sixteen in Paris in the autumn of 1947.

ductivity of Western Europe was probably less than one-third of the level prevailing in 1939. Nor was it only a question of the loss of productivity at home. Many of the combatant nations threw their accumulated savings into the struggle. Great Britain in particular lost most of its great foreign assets and acquired in addition over £3 billions of war debts.

The worst decline in West European productivity occurred, however, in the area which had formerly been the Continent's principal power-house—the Ruhr. First, the Nazis were partially successful in a policy of scorched earth. Then the battle raged across the West of Germany. Then the agreement at Potsdam stabilized German industry at a low figure—left for precise definition later —and decreed the removal of a large part of industry as reparations. In addition, the British and the Americans acquiesced in the Russian policy of settling the German frontier on the Oder-Neisse line and removing some 9 million Germans permanently westward. The new Germany thus lost about one-third of its old territory—which incidentally included its bread and potato basket —and acquired some 9 million new mouths to feed. The point here is not to describe the resulting confusion but to underline the loss of productivity to Europe as a whole. Coal and steel provide the most striking indices. In 1938 the production of coal and steel in Western Germany (including the Saar) was at the rate of 220 million tons of coal and 17.9 million tons of steel. In 1947 the figures were 143 million tons of coal and 3.5 million tons of steel.

With the exception of Western Germany, where production remained feeble and disorganized, the West European nations did begin in 1946 to climb painfully back to their pre-war levels of productivity, but when the end of the ladder appeared in sight the weather took a hand. First, the coldest winter in a hundred years struck at two of the chief pillars of reviving industrial activity—fuel and transport. The summer of 1947 brought a blow for the third—food. Droughts reduced the French harvest to only 50 per cent. of the previous year and played havoc with the root crop everywhere. It is hardly surprising to find, after such a chain of disaster, that one of the chief factors in the present economic crisis is quite simply the inability of Western Europe to produce enough goods. One of the bases of the old pre-war trading system —the general economic vitality of Western Europe—has been seriously undermined.

The Western countries' dependence upon other sources of supply has by the same token been very greatly increased, but some of the most important of these sources have also gone under the harrow of war.

The war surged over the whole of Eastern Europe and Western Russia while the drought of 1946 undid the effects of the first year of recovery. Temporarily at least, land reform in the Soviet Zone of Germany, in Poland and in Hungary destroyed the old food surpluses and the new political orientation of those nations towards the Soviet Union leaves a question mark over the future direction of their trade. Between 1945 and 1948 at least their surpluses were small and not necessarily available for their old customers. The picture in the Far East was not much more encouraging. The rise and fall of Japan's Co-prosperity Sphere in four brief years disorganized the entire productive system of South-East Asia and left behind political troubles so violent that in 1948, nearly three years after the Japanese surrender, large areas of the Dutch East Indies and French Indo-China were still in a state of war, while civil war continued the ruin of China. And these continued disturbances in the Far East reduced the availability of Australasian supplies for Europe. Some effort was made after the war—for the first time in history—to see that the masses in India and China and South-East Asia did not starve and most of the Australian grain surplus was allocated to the Far East.

In this way the European nations were thrown into almost complete dependence upon the Western Hemisphere, the area with which, even in times of their fullest productivity and prosperity, they never succeeded in balancing their trading accounts and with which they had managed to trade only by bringing in all the resources of worldwide multilateral trade. Now, with their own capacity to produce drastically reduced and almost all non-American sources of supply closed to them, they were forced into a virtually complete bilateral dependence upon North and South America.

Happily for the world, the wartime experience of the Western Hemisphere was on the whole one of expansion and increased productivity. Far distant from the battlefields of the world and stimulated by the unlimited demand created by war the economies of North and South America expanded and, in the case of the United States, the expansion was on a gigantic scale. Between 1939 and 1944 the United States' economy doubled. The national income (the total annual output of goods and services) which was running at the level of some $90 billions in 1939 had reached $180 billions by the beginning of 1944. In other words, on top of the old American economy which it had taken some eighty years to produce, the Americans planted another, almost as big, in the space of four years—a fantastic achievement. When war ceased and the new factories and the new machines could be switched from war to peace, there was inevitably a surplus upon which the rest of the world could draw. It was not quite such a big surplus as the figures might suggest, for the rise in production had been accompanied by a great rise in purchasing power and in the American standard of living. Nevertheless, from 1945 to 1947 vast amounts of food, coal and manufactures poured out of the United States to the rest of the world and when in 1947 the crisis came it was not primarily a crisis of supply. It was a crisis of payment.

The problem of paying for American supplies in a world in which there were virtually no non-American surpluses and in which Western Europe's power to produce and earn had been cut to pieces, resolved itself—inevitably—into a problem of finding the dollars.

The problem might have arisen in the war for, during its course, the Allies became increasingly dependent upon American food, American transport and American weapons. But at that time Western Europe was guaranteed all the dollars it required by the device of Lend-Lease or mutual aid, which for the first time in the world applied the principle of "to each according to his need and from each according to his capacity" to national and international needs. In the first eighteen months after the war the scale of Western Europe's dependence upon dollars was still masked. The dollars made available to Italy and to Central and Eastern Europe by the United States contribution (some 2,700 million) to the United Nations Relief and Rehabilitation Administration (UNRRA) entered into the flow of inter-European trade. Some Western nations, France and Belgium and Holland, for instance, had reserves of dollars and gold. Belgium found in addition a profitable dollar-earning export in the shape of uranium from the Congo. Finally, Great Britain received, at the beginning of 1946, a loan of $3\frac{3}{4} billions from the United States and with all these new and old reserves of dollars, Western Europe began an attempt at reconstruction which by the end of 1946 did not look too unpromising.

The economic crisis in Western Europe in 1947 was above all a dollar crisis. By the middle of the year it was obvious that the stop-gap provision of dollars—under UNRRA, under the British Loan—was proving insufficient. The goods and supplies the world most wanted—wheat, meat, coal, steel, machinery—were only to be found in the Western Hemisphere and as the nations bought them eagerly, their dollars drained away. They disappeared all the more speedily in that the pressure of both domestic and foreign demand forced prices in the United States to increase by a third in nine months. France ran out of dollars in the early summer, Italy a little later. Sweden was compelled to reduce its imports, so were Denmark and Holland. The crisis even affected some of the supplying countries. Australia and New Zealand began to cast round for means of reducing their dollar-imports. Two of the chief subsidiary suppliers in the Western Hemisphere—Canada and Argentina—could find the supplies they themselves needed only in the United States. And in the summer of 1947 they, too, began to experience an acute shortage of dollars.

But the most dramatic effects of the crisis were felt in Great Britain. When the British received the American Loan early in 1946 it was hoped that it would last until the early 1950's, by which time the British economy would be earning enough dollars by normal means of trade. The causes already outlined—failure of the Western European economy to revive fast enough, the cutting off of non-American sources of supply—compelled the British from the start to spend the Loan more rapidly than they had anticipated. The desperate winter speeded the process, for the fortnight's closing down of industry was a serious setback to the drive for exports and at one point Great Britain—that island built on coal, that former pillar of the world coal trade—was actually reduced to buying coal for bunkering from the United States.

The *coup de grâce* was delivered in the summer. When the British Government signed the Loan Agreement one of the conditions it agreed to was that in two years' time it would make sterling convertible. In other words, it would on demand supply dollars in return for sterling. In July, 1947, the British Treasury duly announced that anyone with sterling could now exchange it for dollars. But by this time every nation in Europe had run out of dollars and each of them began the process of asking London to give them dollars in exchange for their holdings in sterling. There was only one reserve from which these dollars could

PART I

A VANISHED WORLD

CHAPTER I

THE END OF THE NINETEENTH CENTURY

The surest way of testing the theory that the present dislocations in Western Europe are only temporary is to ask whether in fact the war is a *sufficient* explanation for each of them. And quite a superficial examination shows that it is not. The nineteenth-century supremacy of Western Europe—and of Britain in particular—in the economic field had been challenged by the United States at least twenty years before the second World War. Behind the cutting off of Eastern Europe lies not only the hazards of war but the steady growth of Communism as a world force. Behind the confusion and dislocation in the Far East lies the resurgence of Asiatic nationalism and the secular revolt against the colonial systems of the West. Behind our present difficulties, there seems to lurk the dissolution of the chief forces moulding the nineteenth century—the industrial and commercial predominance of Western Europe, the dissemination of liberal ideas and the colonization of non-European peoples. There is thus at least a presumption that any adequate explanation of our crisis must go deeper than the last war. What is at stake may prove to be the passing of a whole era of human effort and achievement.

The nineteenth century was, more than any other, a British century. In the field of economics and politics most of the dominant ideas and developments boiled up from the small compact and furiously active island "moored" as André Siegfried once said "in European waters but always ready to sail away." Everyone knows that Britain owed this predominance to the fact that it was in this island that the most profound revolution in human behaviour—comparable to the discovery of fire and the wheel or to the taming of the horse—had its origins. The industrial revolution had a thirty to forty year start in Great Britain and for a time made it, as every schoolboy learns, "the workshop of the world."

What is perhaps less generally realized is that the peculiar structure and character of Britain had almost as much influence

13

on the development of the industrial system as the invention of
steam itself. Knowing what we know to-day about the advantages
to industrialization of large internal markets (which make worth-
while the techniques of mass production) and of secure access to
raw materials, we should not have picked an island off the coast
of Europe as the most favourable spot for beginning the industrial experiment. Geography would always set limits to the
growth of a large internal market (by the 1940's it was clear that
48 million was a tight squeeze), and although the country has been
described as "built on coal and surrounded by fish," few of the
raw materials necessary to modern industry can be found within
Britain's frontiers.

But these factors, which in the twentieth century have proved
to be serious problems in the maintenance of industrial strength,
determined the whole development of the world economy in the
nineteenth and determined it really very favourably not only for
Britain but for the world. There could never be any "capitalism
in one country" for Britain. Apart from coal, all the raw materials
of industry had to be purchased abroad, and almost from the
start the classical economic exchange grew up—Britain exporting
its manufactured goods and importing the raw materials to be
worked up into manufactures. The repeal of the Corn Laws in
1846, followed later by the opening up of vast cheap sources of
wheat in Russia and the New World, extended the classic exchange
to food and Britain abandoned the production of bulk foods at
home and bought them abroad in return for its goods.

But not only for goods. The British Isles were too confined to
absorb the great accumulations of capital made possible by the
new industrial system. Britain was too small a community and
too compact an island to offer sufficient opportunities of investment for the larger and larger accumulations of capital the new
thrifty hardworking class of industrialists were acquiring year by
year. It did not take much more than a couple of decades to
provide the country with a very adequate network of railways—
that first and most typical enterprise of the Industrial Revolution
—and once Britain was supplied, the enterprising railwaymen
went abroad. In the 1860's, there was hardly a country in the
world where you might not have found Scottish engineers building
British railways. They went to South America. They went to
North America. They built railways in Europe which to this day
retain the British gauge. They went to Africa and India and the

Far East. Nor were railways the only investments. From halfway through the nineteenth century, a flood of capital streamed out of Britain—to steelworks in America, to mills in India, to plantations in Africa and Malaya and to every sort of undertaking and enterprise everywhere. In return for these investments the various communities paid interest mainly in the shape of the raw materials and foodstuffs Britain either could not or had ceased to produce at home.

The development of this system had momentous consequences for the rest of the world. If industrialism had started in the United States it might have been possible for the system to reach a high stage of development without affecting other nations at all. It could have been virtually self-contained. But the necessity compelling the British to go outside their own frontiers in search of raw materials, coupled with the development of transport and the far-wandering habits of a community of men who had been merchants, explorers, colonizers and adventurers before they turned to industry, conspired to involve the whole world in the British experiment. In the course of the nineteenth century mankind achieved for the first time in history an economy which embraced the globe.

British economic ideas were as potent as British economic practice. There is no need to examine the philosophical basis of free trade. It is a combination of belief in a natural harmony underlying the world and confidence that unfettered competition will reveal where it lies. Let everyone compete, so the argument ran, and the nation most suited to the production of any one commodity will produce that commodity most cheaply and will therefore be able to compete on the markets of the world. The economic foundation of British free trade was its forty-year industrial start. No other nation could compete with Britain in the production of industrial goods, and British manufacturers had everything to gain in pressing for the removal of all obstacles to the sale of their goods abroad. They were prepared to concede the equal right of goods from abroad—raw materials and food—to enter freely into the home market (and as a consequence British agriculture all but disappeared at the end of the century under the successful competition of wheat and meat from the New World) as long as their manufactures and their export of capital could find unimpeded entry wherever they sought to go. The defence of free trade—the most passionate political issue of the mid-nineteenth century—was not, however, consciously based on Britain's interest in opening every market to British goods which could undercut those of every other competitor. It was a moral issue and the principles of free trade were held to have intrinsic rightness, to be part of the structure of the universe. We shall have occasion to notice the development of a similar attitude in the United States when some seventy years later it was American and not British manufacturers who could undersell every competitor.

Few other nations accepted the British thesis. Most of them had interests they wished to protect from the relentless pressure of British manufactures. Many of them wanted to begin their own process of industrialization and realized that, at least at the beginning, their young factories would have to be protected against the competition of Britain's mature industrial system. Tariffs to protect "infant industries" were imposed in most countries. They were particularly high in the United States and long after the infant industries had grown into such mammoths as United States Steel, the tariffs were maintained and steadily increased. One consequence of this protective behaviour—it was known appropriately enough as a policy of Protection—was to turn the nineteenth century mind to the question of tariffs when any question arose of improving trade relations. The reduction of tariffs was *par excellence* the nineteenth century method of increasing trade—logically so, for the barriers set up on each national frontier were the chief obstacle at that time to the free flow of goods and the chance of each nation to discover, by reasonable competition, the goods it was most fitted to produce. Utterly uneconomic ventures—for instance, a heavy steel industry in a country such as Italy which had neither coal nor iron ore nor easy access to either—were impossible so long as the system of free trade and moderate tariffs survived.

One device used to reduce tariffs and increase trade deserves especial attention since it is still the centre of bitter controversy. When one nation agreed with another to a mutual reduction of tariffs—the French, shall we say, reducing the tariff on Swedish ore and the Swedes in return reducing the tariff on French wine—there was normally included in their agreement a "Most Favoured Nation clause" by which the advantages of the agreement were extended to every other nation. Not only Swedish but American iron ore would now benefit by the new level of tariffs. German wine as well as French would enter Sweden at the new low rate. If such an extension were not made, the French and the Swedes would have been guilty of the economic practice most objectionable to nineteenth century minds—the practice of conceding to one nation advantages not conceded to others, in other words, of "discriminating" against them. According to the trading dogmas of the nineteenth century, tariffs were a permissible evil (some people, particularly owners of "infant industries," did not even think them evil) but discrimination was anathema. Tariffs must be at the same level whatever nation was seeking to trade, and no nation could be permitted to receive advantages not open to every other. One of the United States' first excursions into active world diplomacy was to insist at the end of the nineteenth century to the "Open Door" in China, through which every trader of whatever nationality should go in on an equal footing to exploit the Chinese.

To this rule there was only one exception. A group of nations could "discriminate" totally against others by forming a customs union between themselves. By reducing their tariffs to zero for themselves and keeping them at 100 per cent. for others, they slipped under the ban against discrimination. This rider is not, however, as illogical as it seems. Since tariffs were in the nineteenth century virtually the only barrier to the creation of a completely unified economic area, it was generally realized that to form a Customs Union was to form or serve notice of forming a single state. So it had proved after 1787 between the Confederated States of America. So it proved between the separate states of Germany after the Customs Union of 1833. And clearly the same rules could not apply to the creation of a new national economy as to the normal economic relations between separate states.

The apparently automatic working of the system of free trade in the nineteenth century and the economic advantages that seemed to flow from adopting it led most people to believe that in some way its principles were universally valid and quite independent of the accidents of time and place. It is therefore not surprising that they did not notice how much its smooth working depended on the peculiar nature of the British economy.

The fact that had sent British manufacturers overseas and involved most of the world in the British experiment—Britain's lack of raw materials and need to buy them abroad—also had a profound effect upon the financial basis of world trade. Nations bought and sold from each other in spite of using different currencies by giving each currency a fixed value in relation to gold and allowing any merchant to change any one currency into any other at the fixed rate of exchange. If a trader wished to buy British goods he would find, through a discount bank, a "bill on London" provided by some British trader who had bought goods abroad. Only in the exceptional circumstance of the supplies of a national currency falling below the demand for that currency were transactions settled in gold. Gold was a marginal factor, a payment used only, for instance, if the demand for French goods had become so acute that all the francs earned by all the nations engaged in selling goods to France had become exhausted. Yet theoretically such a state of affairs might have been arising all the time. There is no law written into the foundations of the universe that the trading accounts of the nations of the earth shall automatically balance—and in our own century they do not. What was the reason, then, for the old stability? It was quite simply that Britain, the most powerful and vigorous exporter of goods and capital among trading nations of the nineteenth century, was at the same time the most rapacious importer of food and raw materials. As the century developed, far from exporting more than they imported—thus creating a shortage of sterling—the British little by little began to import more and more and export rather less, the balance being adjusted by goods bought with the interest on British capital investments abroad or with the payments earned on British shipping. Underlying the steady and apparently frictionless working of free exchanges in the nineteenth century lay not so much the gold standard as the "sterling standard"—the fact that the greatest single currency in demand for world trading was never out of balance, never ran short, never confronted nations with the inability to buy the goods they needed most—British goods—or to pay interest on the capital of which they had borrowed the greatest amounts. Sterling went out from London in the shape of exports and capital. It came back to London in the shape of food and raw materials. This was the real blood stream of nineteenth-century trade, the real circulation which kept all the parts supplied and the body economic in steady health.

It is not surprising that the economic system of the nineteenth century should have cast such a spell over men's minds or that even to-day many people should look back to it with nostalgia and believe that it can and should be restored, since, in their view, it represents the norm from which mankind has disastrously departed. It brought about a fantastic increase in wealth in most parts of the world. It created a sense of expanding horizons and limitless possibilities for human development. It coincided with a long period of peace and with the spread round the world of the ideals of freedom and democratic government. It was not difficult to believe under these conditions that man had come of age at last and discovered the most efficient, the most natural and the most rewarding method of conducting his affairs. It was on the contrary almost impossible to believe that the whole system was to a remarkable extent fortuitous, that it depended upon the accident of history which had made a small island the starting point of the industrial revolution and that even as the system was expanding to embrace new markets and new techniques, the condition upon which much of its frictionless success had been based—the hegemony of Britain—was being steadily undermined.

As we have seen, Britain by the nature of things could not keep its industrialism to itself. The capital which poured out of London and Manchester and Birmingham went to start enterprises abroad and to stimulate all round the world the growth of the industrial system. Before long, industry took root in countries which did not share the limiting conditions imposed by geography on the British system—its relatively small internal market and its lack of home-produced raw materials. Two new industrial systems in particular began to make their competition felt as the century advanced. Germany's challenge developed quickly, but since it was as much political as economic it will be mentioned in another context. The chief economic challenge came from the United States.

In the United States there existed every advantage for the building of a powerful industrial system. The country was as large as a continent and the growth of its own population, increased by the nineteenth-century immigration of some 19 million people from abroad, quickly made it the largest single internally unified market in the world. Within the continental area was an abundance of every raw material needed for industry (except rubber and tin) and the rich plains of the Middle West and the magnificent climate of California produced the food for one hundred million hungry people. There were few feudal remnants in the structure of property or traditions of behaviour to inhibit the drive of the middle classes to produce and make money and the Civil War wiped out the last remnant—the threat that slavery, that least mobile and least productive form of "property," would survive in the South and spread to the new frontier lands in the West. This was the background—physical and social—to the immense expansion of industry in the United States after 1860 and this was the background that made possible the revolutionary innovations in industrial technique associated with the name of Henry Ford. It is hardly likely that the value of mass production and of small returns on a vast turnover could have been proved so conclusively in any but a mass market without internal inhibitions to the free sale of goods, but once the advantages had been established and the practice extended to more and more lines of business, the United States was able to produce industrial goods in the main more cheaply than any other competitor. Climate, geography, history, and technique conspired to give the United States the advantages which a thirty-year start in the industrial revolution had given Britain some seventy or eighty years before. America was now the country whose goods could enter most markets of the world unchallenged and it was beginning to be the largest creator of surplus capital. Other things being equal, it seemed at the turn of the century that the United States was destined to take over the central role Britain had fulfilled in the first stages of the development of the world economy.

But other things were not equal. Close as they were in politics and in social and moral outlook, the two countries had little in common in the economic sphere. The United States having started its industry in the wake of Britain's, had felt the early competition of British goods and raised tariffs against them. The industries swelled and strengthened and needed no protection, but the tariffs remained. There was at no point any question of non-American goods flooding the American market as agricultural supplies had flooded away British agriculture. On the contrary, the nations found it far from easy to do business with the United States at all. Although, as its industrial strength increased, the United States began to trade more freely with the outside world, the increase was not in proportion to the actual growth in American power. The bulk of the exchanges remained in the home market.[1] Thus the

[1] In 1939, a reasonably typical year, American exports represented just over 3 per cent. of the gross national production of goods and services.

first obstacle to an American lead in the world economy was the weight of American tariffs coupled with the fact that goods of almost every kind were produced in abundance inside the country.

The next was more grave. Although as the century advanced America became an increasing exporter of certain goods which the world was only too eager to buy and at the same time grew to be the largest producer and exporter of surplus capital, there was no sign of any greater tendency to buy abroad and thus provide the foreigner with the dollars to pay for American goods or pay interest on American capital. The essential disharmony of the position was masked during the twenties by the readiness of the Americans to lend sufficient dollars to the outside world to pay interest and to meet the deficit in trade. But in 1929 the collapse in America put a sudden end to most overseas lending and to a calling in of many outstanding short-term loans. Shortly afterwards the Smoot-Hawley tariff was introduced which raised to still more fantastic heights the fortress of tariffs behind which America's giant industries "sheltered." With all the dollars drained out of their economies and a virtual wall thrown up between them and the chance of selling in the American market, the rest of the world had its first taste of the dollar problem.

In these conditions the old rules concerning "non-discrimination" and "convertibility" proved essentially irrelevant. When the dominant factor in an economic situation is a desperate shortage of the currency which has behind it the largest market in the world and is thus basically—in spite of temporary fluctuations—the most stable currency, the application of nineteenth century rules only adds to the general economic confusion. If a nation is to treat all its trading partners on a basis of absolute non-discrimination, the decision not to buy from any one of them—for whatever reason—ought, in logic, to be extended to the others. A recent example may be quoted. In the autumn of 1947, so severe had the dollar shortage become in Canada that the Government was obliged to place a ban on some 300 articles of import from the United States. Among others, the list included chocolate. But, conforming to the rules of non-discrimination, the Canadian government—with sterling to burn—felt obliged to ban the import of chocolate from Britain as well. In other words, applied to a situation in which the basic difficulty is a breakdown in the supply of the strongest currency, the rule of non-discrimination increases and spreads the breakdown of trade and thus acts in an exactly opposite sense from its reasonably beneficent working in the nineteenth century.

The working of "convertibility" has similar effects. Increasingly in the twenties and the thirties the dollar became the currency in greatest demand. It was needed to pay interest on American loans. It was needed to buy American goods. It was needed as an end in itself, as a stable investment, as a form of property as reliable as gold itself. But the supply did not keep pace with the demand since Americans perpetually bought less than they sold and foreign goods could not clear the hurdle of the American tariff. Under these conditions businessmen and investors in their search for dollars could use "convertibility" as a means of draining all the reserves of dollars and gold away from the central bank of their own country. By presenting francs or sterling or lire to be converted into dollars and then all too often salting the dollars down as a prudent reserve in the United States, they produced that "flight" from the local currency which was a recurrent disturbance of financial stability in certain European countries between the wars. Only by imposing exchange control and by instituting the blocking of currencies—in other words, by abandoning the practice of convertibility—could governments prevent the fatal drain of their financial reserves. Before the last war the chronic weakness of the franc and the desire of a great mass of private investors to transfer their wealth into dollars placed France's financial stability under constant fire. But the most striking example of the impossibility of practising convertibility against an impossible economic background has already been described in the British experience of convertibility in the summer of 1947.[1]

It would, however, be misleading to place all the blame for Europe's dislocation on the changed relationship between America and Europe. This was only one factor—although the most important—in a general shift in the world's economic relations. Over the years, countries which had formerly enjoyed all the advantages which come from pioneering in a new field lost their lead and began to experience the disadvantages which spring from older equipment, older technique, and especially, older ideas. It is an irresistible temptation to believe that the methods which

1 Page 6

brought overwhelming success in the past will continue to do so. But with the introduction of industrial development and its close alliance to scientific research, a force had been launched on the world which permitted nobody to stand still. Each decade brought forward improved methods of industrial production and the revolution wrought by coal and steam was followed by an electrical revolution, a chemical revolution and—who knows?—an atomic revolution. As these new means of power and the new techniques based on them flooded industry the problem of obsolescence—of plants which were no longer competitive, of capital sunk in machinery made out of date by a new idea from the research laboratory—became a permanent one and adaptability and capacity for innovation grew to be a hall-mark of industrial survival.

These qualities are more difficult to achieve in long-established industries, particularly if these industries have records of phenomenal early success. Britain, which had been the pioneer in the whole field of heavy industry, was particularly vulnerable to this difficulty. In the sixties and seventies of last century its coal and its textiles and its steel products had gone all over the world almost without competition and the aura of this early success remained. No drastic reorganization, no tremendous drive for modernization occurred in such basic industries as coal mining and cotton spinning and weaving. Even after the first World War, when the writing on the wall appeared in the shape of permanent depression in the old export industries—in South Wales and Lancashire—little was done to bring about the necessary reconstruction. When in the course of the second world war experts studied British coal-mining and British textile production in relation to American methods, they found an astonishing lack of modernization and mechanization in Britain's two basic industries.[1] The iron and steel industry kept better pace with modern needs but here, too, the progress was not uniform nor was it sufficient. At the end of the war—in 1945—it was estimated that the need for new capital investment in the industry would be, at a minimum, of the order of £22 millions a year for the next seven years. Yet in the 1920's the average new investment was about £1 million a year, in the 1930's about £6 million. Even

[1] Two Reports—the Reid Report on coal mining and the Platt Report on the cotton industry—give a devastating account of the extent to which these British industries had fallen behind in the competitive race.

allowing for the fact that the post-war figure has to take into account the wear and tear to plant and the lack of investment during the war, the pre-war figures are nevertheless quite insufficient and it is a fact that behind the screen of the protective tariff administered by the Import Duties Advisory Committee after 1931, a number of British steel products came to be as much as four times more expensive than those of their Belgian competitors.

Perhaps the most revealing pointer is the figure for capital investment in general. Most economists agree that to secure a steadily expanding level of production in an industrial community 10 to 15 per cent. of the national income should be invested in new capital development. The average yearly figure for Great Britain between the two wars was only 3 per cent. These facts do not mean that Britain was a stagnant community. On the contrary, some striking industrial developments were achieved, such as the creation of an entirely new centre of modern and successful light industry in the neighbourhood of London and a consequent shift in industrial population from north to south, but all the time the basis of the industrial pyramid—the older industries and the basic export industries—were losing their strength and the community was impoverished year by year to the extent of two million idle men.

France is another country to fall behind in certain branches of industry. Like the British, the French had an early start in the industrial race but increasingly in the twentieth century their scale of development and modernization proved insufficient. When after the second world war a complete survey of French industry was drawn up by M. Monnet and his assistants and the calculations made of what France would need to re-equip its economy, it was discovered that between 1929 and 1939 a process of disinvestment or decapitalization had taken place in France. Not only had the country not recovered from the depression, its national income was at a lower level than that of the previous decade.

This tendency towards economic stagnation in parts of Western Europe has been combined with a great increase in industrial activity in other parts of the world. The phenomenal industrial expansion in the United States (which is now said to contain two-thirds of the industry and three-quarters of the investment of the world) has already been mentioned, but the spread of industrialism was virtually universal. Western and Central Europe, some of the British Dominions, Japan, European Russia had all achieved a measure of industrialization before the first World War. Parts of India and China and Asiatic Russia followed suit. The second world war stimulated industrial production enormously not only in the United States but in Canada and Australia, while the demand for South American materials created reserves which such countries as Brazil and Argentina decided to divert to industrialization. Since the war expensive plans have been laid down for the development of industry in Eastern Europe. All these moves may mean a decisive turning away from the production of foodstuffs and raw materials and a trend towards some self-sufficiency in manufactured goods. This trend has already had its effect on British export figures. In 1938, the British were importing 20 per cent. more and exporting 40 per cent. less than in 1913—the balance was paid for by British shipping and by the interest on British overseas investments.

The change might also affect not only the volume of imports and exports but also their cost. The fundamental relationship between the old manufacturing nations in Western Europe and the nations overseas was one of exchanging industrial goods for raw materials and food. One of the cornerstones of European prosperity was the fact that manufactures were more expensive than primary materials. The standard of living in Britain in particular was built up on the fact that it took comparatively few man hours of work to produce the industrial goods necessary to buy sufficient food for reasonable health. It was only after the first World War that what is known as "the terms of trade" became a difficulty. These terms simply express the amount of exports necessary to buy a given volume of imports. When primary materials—food, cotton, ores, rubber—are cheap, the terms of trade are "favourable" since fewer exported manufactures buy more imported raw materials. After the dislocations and shortages of the first World War, the terms of trade were noticeably unfavourable for the first time. However, the depression knocked the bottom out of the price of many primary materials and the terms of trade moved so strongly in Britain's favour (in other words it could secure its imports so cheaply) that it was possible to achieve a large measure of internal revival without much recovery in the basic export trades, where unemployment continued year after year above the two million mark. After the

c

second World War, the terms of trade became so unfavourable owing to the inflated costs of wheat and meat and other primary products that the rise in import costs alone was almost enough to account for Britain's disastrously unfavourable balance of trade. Of the £500 million deficit in 1946 and 1947 at least £250 million is due to the change in the terms of trade.

And the point must be grasped that the terms of trade may be less liable to favourable fluctuations after this war. The possibility is connected with the steady increase in industrialization all over the world which is likely to create a greater variety and volume of manufactured exports (a fact which will bring their price down) and a greater pressure of demand for the basic raw materials (which will force their price up). It is impossible under these conditions to assume that anything like the old nineteenth century division of labour between an industrialized Europe and an unindustrial outside world can ever be restored, and with it may vanish the old chance of securing the terms of trade which were once such a pillar of European prosperity.

These changes—the growth of American supremacy, the decline, absolutely and relatively, of Western European strength and the disappearance of the old division of labour—are the principal factors underlying the permanent shift in the economic balance of the world. But each of the changes has been accelerated and confirmed by the two World Wars. A tremendous stimulus was given to the American economy by the first World War. During the second, as we have seen, its national income was actually doubled and its output of steel and grain and meat all reached the highest level ever achieved. And while America was the chief example of wartime expansion, the development of arms manufacture in Canada and Australia was remarkable enough. In Europe, on the contrary, all was confusion and dislocation. Only the neutrals kept their economies intact. As we have seen, Italy had at one time four governments and four divergent economic systems in its narrow peninsula. France suffered the enforced stagnation of four years of occupation, in Holland flooding was added to the other dislocations of war. Britain, although it was spared invasion and could expand sections of its industry, lost most of its overseas assets, acquired £3 billion of war debts, used its plant to capacity and its working force almost beyond endurance and emerged—as did every other country involved in the war—with the financial load of inflation.

But the critical collapse came in Germany. The German disaster was in two phases. First came the actual destruction of war itself. Not a city in the industrial West was left standing. The ports were half destroyed. Eastern towns—Berlin and Leipzig and Dresden —were in ruins. The Nazis also attempted in their retreat to wreck as many bridges, railways and public installations as possible. Some five million men ended the struggle as prisoners of war. Such was the absolute dislocation which faced the victors in 1945. Then came the second phase, the confirmation of disaster by the decisions taken by the Allies themselves.

The Potsdam decrees are still too fresh in people's minds to require detailed description. Yet they need to be recalled, for they have affected the whole economy of Western Europe. The first was the decision to have no German Government and to divide the country into Zones directly governed by the occupying powers. This decision not only disturbed the balance of whatever economy remained—Eastern Germany had been the great supplier of bulk foodstuffs. It also proved in a very short time that lack of government can be as potent an instrument of economic disintegration as lack of food. The Western Allies had not the manpower to govern effectively 40 million people. It took two years to begin to form even the skeleton of a German administration. In the interregnum the normal processes of economy all but disappeared. In the vast German black market chaos became organized and anarchy became the norm.

The second decision has already been recorded. The lands beyond the Oder, largely food-producing areas, were transferred to Poland while their millions of German inhabitants fanned out over the remaining Zones. More people had to be fed on smaller reserves—and this at a time of world-wide shortages. The inevitable result was standards of nutrition so low as to be obstacles to any sort of economic revival.

The last decision was to place limits, in any event, upon that economic revival. Germany was deprived of a large part of its heavy industry, its steel output was fixed at 5.7 million tons a year (the last "normal" output—in 1928—was about 18 million tons for all Germany, including Silesia), its merchant navy and its aircraft were abolished and its future was planned on the basis of coal mining, agriculture and light industry. Thus a far smaller area producing much less food would have to support a larger population on diminished industrial resources.

It is necessary to understand the Allies' policy. The results proved totally impracticable but the starting point was a genuine dilemma—a dilemma which still confronts the West to-day. Twice in a generation the Ruhr had been the arsenal of the German armies and it was not altogether illogical to argue that the Germans had now proved their utter unworthiness to be entrusted with a heavy industry capable of making war. Last time disarmament had failed. This time let there be nothing to disarm. Let the Germans become a pastoral people, not simply beating their swords into ploughshares (for they could always beat them back again) but losing the capacity to make either shares or swords. But then came the other horn of the dilemma. If such a policy were to be adopted, how could Germany live? Worse still, what prospects could there be for a highly industrialized, urbanized, densely populated Western Germany? Something like 60 per cent. of Germany's pre-war exports had been the products of heavy industry. Now at a time when more exports would be needed to buy the food formerly secured from Eastern Germany, the German export trade would have to stand on its head in a search for new markets. The Allies at Potsdam evaded the dilemma. They accepted the policy of a wide measure of de-industrialization and assumed that the German economy would be viable.

It was not. A highly integrated system such as the heavy industry of the Ruhr could not be partially dismantled while leaving the remaining parts in full working order. The decision in the first months of the occupation to revive nothing but the mining of coal meant that even the limited production of steel lagged behind and as stocks and spare parts ran out there was no new output from which to replace the vanished materials. Coal production itself suffered for lack of machines and equipment and after two years had risen to only 400,000 tons a day (before the war it was over 600,000 a day). Transport suffered. Production generally remained at about 30 to 40 per cent. of the pre-war level. And little by little, Germany's old trading partners—Holland and Belgium in particular—began to realize what a 50 per cent. drop in German production meant to their economic position. At a time when coal and steel were Western Europe's chief industrial need German output remained at the low level of some 140 million tons of coal and 3 million tons of steel.

Potsdam to-day is to a large extent a dead letter in the Western

Zones of Germany. The level of industry has been revised, reparations have virtually ceased, something approaching a German Government exists at Frankfurt. But three years' production has been lost. After World War I, the output of the Ruhr was barely interrupted. Wealth continued to be created on a massive scale. After this war, the smokeless chimneys, the empty canals and the shattered houses of Germany are concrete symbols of Europe's impoverishment. The war and its aftermath have thus reinforced the most dangerous tendency already existing in Europe—its tendency towards declining productivity and industrial stagnation. They have widened the gap between American wealth and European penury. They have delayed—we do not yet know by how long—the whole mighty task of rebuilding a prosperous Continent. The German dilemma—the question whether the Germans, who cannot live without a revived industry, can be trusted with one—will recur later. Here it is only necessary to point out the part played by the war and by the Potsdam decisions in deepening Europe's economic crisis.

Taking the secular change in industry and production, the shift of power from the Old to the New World, the loss of European supremacy and the aggravation of these factors by two disastrous wars and laying them together in the scales of history, one is hard put to it to believe that the present crisis is simply a passing phenomenon, a product of wartime dislocation and nothing more. Behind the chief feature of the present crisis—the lack of balance between Europe and America—there lies a century of economic change and of world-wide industrial development. The causes are not of to-day or yesterday. They go back at least a hundred years.

CHAPTER II

FAR-EASTERN REVOLUTION

What of the other features of the crisis—the loss of Eastern Europe as a secure source of agricultural surpluses and the dislocation of the Far East? Are they, too, the product of forces long developing in the womb of history? Or can they be put down to the disturbances of the war alone?

These pages are mainly concerned with the European problem and the place of the Far East is in a sense incidental. But a few words are necessary to place the problem in some perspective, since Far Eastern products have played an important part in the European balance of payments and the extension of Western Europe into South-East Asia through the colonizing activities of the Dutch, the British and the French was one of the elements in the nineteenth century supremacy of the "Western fringe." The question is: can it be restored either economically or politically in its old form?

The story of Western colonization is soon told. The Europeans came as traders and only where the organization of the local community was entirely primitive—as in many of the East Indies for instance—did they take over political control immediately. Otherwise they established trading posts and treaty relations with the local rulers. In the late eighteenth and the nineteenth century, however, the gradual coming of industrialism and the sudden growth both in West European power and in its economic demands led to a new situation. Local rulers were superseded or reduced to nominal power. Direct European rule was established and the resources of the area were developed to provide raw materials for the European market. Oil and rice from Burma, Malayan tin and rubber, oil, rubber and sugar from the East Indies—these were some of the East's contributions to European prosperity.

A word must be said of the effect of this development on the natives. European control gave them a measure of internal security. Some of the advantages of civilization—roads, drainage, public health services—reached them, at first incidentally but later more and more as a matter of policy. Some groups were positively enriched. An even smaller percentage were able to acquire a modern education in Europe. On the other hand, the wealth created by the development of local resources went to an overwhelming extent to Europe. The natives were richer by their wages and salaries, but the raw materials produced and the profits they earned were despatched abroad. The social consequences were even more equivocal. Old tribal methods of government and cultivation were destroyed and a large proportion of the natives became plantation labourers under European administrators. Without understanding in the least the processes in which they were involved, their well-being fluctuated with the fluctuation in the world price of the products they helped to produce. Old habits of obedience and belief dwindled. In their place was the organized uncertainty of Western colonial exploitation and the infinitely remote ideas of technical Western civilization—itself in a state of considerable uncertainty about what it did in fact believe. As Professor Toynbee once pointed out, Western Europe achieved its greatest physical expansion at a time when it had lost many of its great certainties and could offer men with confidence only its economic techniques. Under such conditions the growth of a genuinely new community of interests between governors and governed was handicapped at every turn. The Western Powers could hope to bring up a minority to an educated acceptance of their ideas and men from Burma and Indo-China and the Dutch East Indies appeared in the schools and universities of Western Europe. But what did they learn? The claims of nationalism, the right of self-determination, the complete equalities of democracy. Later they learnt the evil of exploitation, the shortcomings of capitalists, the claims of dependent peoples. They learnt Western ideas but they were calculated to undermine the experiment of Western rule.

Morally and intellectually, the hold of the West on the East remained precarious. At the turn of the century it was submitted to a new strain—the adoption by an Eastern Power of Western ideas *without* Western intervention. The rise of Japan gave a tremendous impetus to Asiatic nationalism, for Japan was the first non-European nation to inflict defeat upon a European Power. The year of Russia's defeat by Japan—1905—must be counted a turning point in the Far East. But Japan's moral influence was limited by the speed with which it adopted the conquering and exploiting habits of the West. The Chinese soon

learnt that they had more to fear from expansive Asiatic nationalism than from the Western variety. The rest of South-East Asia
went through a similar experience when between 1941 and 1945
the Japanese established their "Co-prosperity sphere" from the
Philippines to Burma. A more lasting stimulus to the ideal of
national independence will probably be found to have come from
Communism since, in theory at least, it proposes to substitute
for Western imperialism not an Asiatic variety but an association
of free and equal peoples. Communist parties are active in Burma,
on the left wing of the Republicans in Java, in Indo-China where
Ho Chi Minh, the leader of the Viet Nam (the Annamite independence movement) is a Communist and in China itself where
large areas in the North and in Manchuria are under Communist
control.

The Western Powers have in fact recognized that the old
relationship of governor and governed cannot be exactly restored.
Britain has given full independence to Burma. The French and
the Dutch are trying to incorporate their colonial territories into
a federal union as autonomous communities on a footing of
equality with the Mother Country. But whatever they do, the
political pressure towards complete independence will remain
unless and until the new structures prove that they can call forth
a new loyalty.

It is not only the old political relationship that has disappeared.
Hand in hand with Asiatic nationalism has advanced the problem
of Asiatic industrialization. Japan led the way. By a prodigious
feat of imitation and adaptation the Japanese turned themselves
from a closed medieval community of knights and farmers into
a modern industrial state in a few decades. Their output of textiles
and of light manufactures of all kinds grew steadily in the first
thirty years of the century. Japan, even shorter of basic raw
materials than Britain and even more densely populated, was
under the same compulsion to export and once its exports reached
the world they challenged with all too great success the old-
established European industries. After the first World War the
Lancashire cotton markets were crippled by a double invasion—
Japanese and Indian textiles. Both countries, relying on a far
cheaper labour force, could undersell the European producers.
The threat spread to light manufactures of all sorts. In the early
'thirties Japanese ships were visiting Africa offering bicycles at £2
and motor-cars at £60. It was to defeat this competition that the

British Government first reverted to discrimination and placed a very heavy tariff on all Japanese goods entering the colonial empire.

Naturally, the industrialization of Japan was not all loss to other industrial nations. As a general rule, the exchange of goods between industrialized communities is at a higher and more valuable level than the exchanges between advanced and primitive economies—certainly Australia benefited greatly by Japan's expansion. But the point is that the nineteenth century relationship between East and West began to disappear and might have vanished altogether if Japan had realized its plans of becoming the universal provider in the Far East on the basis of its domination and development of China's resources.

Has the war reversed this trend? Hardly. Japanese industrial revival is already recognized as essential if its eighty million people are to survive. Indeed, deprived of some of their dependencies, and cut off from China, the Japanese will need to export more, not less, and already the scale of the export of textiles planned for them has caused alarm in Britain. Exports of manufactures are therefore likely to recover and even surpass their old scale.

At the same time, two new factors may influence the old supply of raw materials from the Far East. The first is quite simply that for the first time the world's conscience has been a little stirred by the fate of Asia's millions and has taken a timid step towards the idea that possibly in times of shortage they should not be allowed to starve. The diversion of Australian wheat to India to save the ration, the work of UNRRA in relieving distress in China may, it is true, be no more permanent than, say, Mr. Hoover's efforts to feed Europeans after the 1914 war. But possibly the changed attitude is not an incident but a precedent. Certainly that is how such new international bodies as the Food and Agriculture Organization would conceive it. In which case the world's supplies of basic foodstuffs would be radically changed.

The other new factor is also uncertain but important none the less. It is this. As a result of the tremendous slump in the prices of primary products in the early 'thirties much economic misery was imposed upon colonies which had destroyed the old native subsistence economy in order to concentrate on one or two bulk products for the export market (rubber in Malaya for instance, or oil and sugar in the East Indies). Enlightened colonial administrators began to question the wisdom of over-concentration and to advocate the diversification of agriculture in the interests of the native, a modification of the system of plantations and a lessening if necessary of the amount of bulk products thrown upon the world market. Little was done to press this change of view but the events of 1941 and 1942 brought it once again to public notice. The almost total apathy of the native populations in face of the Japanese advance, their scant loyalty to their European administrators, their readiness to settle down under the Japanese suggested the small extent to which the European colonial system impinged upon their lives and the paucity of the advantage they seemed to feel they derived from it. The argument was once more put forward that as a wage earner on a foreign plantation, subject to the remote and infinitely unfamiliar fluctuations of the world market, the native had really no positive part whatsoever in his own community and therefore could hardly be expected to show loyalty of any kind. The need was to give him an intelligible stake in it and this should be done not only by better health and educational and technical services—though they were important—but by recreating peasant agriculture and settling the native on the land (even if such a policy entailed a distribution of some of the estates). If these ideas were to become settled policy, then clearly the scale of exports of Far Eastern materials might decline.

It should be mentioned, in passing, that the change of mood in Europe, of which the concern for the dispossessed native is one manifestation, has affected British colonial policy vitally and will certainly spread to the other colonial Powers. The change of mood is simply that colonies are not for exploitation in the interests of Europe but for development in the interests of the native. Whereas in the old days one man and a gunboat could provide all the European services necessary to see that the natives of the district worked in the mines and fields of their employers (more often than not some large European concern), to-day the health, the education, the technical training, the rehousing of the native demand an army of skilled officials. The colonial empires no longer appear as a credit sign in the balance sheet (with the exception perhaps of the Belgian Congo). They are no longer expected even to pay their way. The British colonies, for instance, are now the beneficiaries under various development funds raised by the taxpayer at home and running to hundreds of millions of pounds sterling.

It is true that in the last two years new hopes have been pinned on Africa as a source of raw materials for Western Europe and undoubtedly in the long run much can be done to develop not only groundnut schemes, but the mining of coal and minerals in Central Africa, the construction of transport from the industrial areas to the coast and the building up of local industry to support the new ventures in the way already planned in Southern Rhodesia. These developments will undoubtedly be all the more successful if they are undertaken by the states of Western Europe in co-operation with each other and if they remove, as far as possible, any irrational obstacles to production created by colonial frontiers and mixed sovereignty. Even so, it is doubtful whether new development in Africa can quickly make good the loss of the old European position in the Far East. The new expansion schemes will all take time. They will all involve a care for native well-being and for local welfare and development which were not always apparent in the Far East. Above all, Africa is not so rich a land. Such reservations do not mean that the expansion of African production should not be vigorously pursued, but they do suggest some caution in assessing the wealth it will make immediately available.

If all the factors discussed so far in the colonial situation are put together—the steady growth of Asiatic nationalism, the industrialization of the Far East (still in its early stages), the possible reduction in available exports thanks to greater Far Eastern consumption and a possible reorganization of the Far Eastern export economies, and finally, the tendency all over the world for colonies to cost more than they bring in—if all these factors are put together, it can be said with some certainty that whatever else is re-established in the Far East, it will not be precisely the old relationship between the Western European Powers and their Far-Eastern dependencies.

CHAPTER III

THE POLITICAL BALANCE

There remains one last factor to consider—the changed political and economic conditions in Eastern Europe. Before the war, the East European nations were responsible for a good part of Western Europe's food. Particularly in the case of Germany, the balance between Western industry and Eastern foodstuffs was a permanent feature of the economy. The avowed intention of the new governments in Eastern Europe is to change the old ratio in two ways: by introducing or extending industrialization in their own countries—a project made simpler in the case of Poland by the inclusion in the Polish state of the industrial wealth of Silesia —and by developing closer economic ties with Soviet Russia. But the new situation in Eastern Europe has more than purely economic significance. Its challenge is not so much to the economic bases of the old order as to the political stability and the intellectual and moral values on which it believed itself to be built.

So far, the nineteenth century has been described primarily in economic terms, but the position of world leadership occupied by Great Britain and to a lesser extent by Western Europe was based on more than economic strength. It was underpinned by two military factors—the supremacy of the British Navy and the Balance of Power in Europe. And it derived its driving force from the vigour of its Christian and liberal concept of man and society. It is these latter bulwarks of the old Western European order that the revolutions in Eastern Europe challenge to-day.

The disappearance of the British Navy's unique position need only be mentioned. Even if the United States had not surpassed Britain in naval strength the coming of air power would have revolutionized the situation. In Europe itself the question is primarily that of the Balance of Power. Diplomacy based on this concept has come in for considerable criticism in recent years. Clearly there is nothing ideal in an arrangement whereby a potential aggressor is deterred from making war because his opponent is seen to be equal in strength and victory is therefore uncertain. Yet in a sense it is a species of collective security, for

36

equality of strength is at least one step towards that overwhelming concentration of strength on the non-aggressive side which is the ideal of the old League and the new United Nations. Nor can it be said that it has always worked out badly in practice. Britain's application of the principle has been to ally itself with any European nation in order to redress the balance of power against the rising strength of any other. As a result the various bids made by different Powers at different times to dominate and organize the Continent—the Spaniards, the French, the Germans— have finally been frustrated and the British have always been found at the head of the victorious alliance which brought their pretensions to nothing.

It can perhaps be argued that it is a great pity Great Britain prevented the unification of the Continent and that a great deal of trouble would thus have been avoided. Yet it is not the Swedes nor the Swiss nor the Danes nor the Low Countries nor in our own time the Italians and the French who would argue thus. They have maintained an independence and a diversity which mark them off from the dull backwardness of those on whom prolonged foreign tyranny has been imposed. The Balkans, for instance, were unified for hundreds of years under the Turks and were indeed spared major wars and disturbances. But they emerged from their servitude unorganized, primitive, turbulent, and savage.

It is easy to interpret British policy in Europe as one of "divide and rule"—easy but ridiculous. For while British arms prevented the forcible unification of Europe by others, Britain never attempted the task itself. It may have divided; it made no attempt to rule, and within the empirical but workable framework of the balance of power, Europe flourished and struggled and created and produced as the most dynamic community on the surface of the globe.

There are limiting factors in a policy of balance. The chief is clearly that the elements to be balanced must be roughly of the same size. After 1815 this condition was more or less fulfilled. Inside Europe, Germany and France balanced each other (once Britain in alliance with Germany had extinguished France's Napoleonic ambitions). Outside Europe Britain's growing industrial strength matched the vast extent of the Russian Empire. Between 1815 and the end of the century the only constantly recurring threat to the balance in Europe was that Russia should outflank the Continent by swallowing up the decaying Turkish Empire and establishing itself in the Mediterranean. The British watched this "Eastern Question" with the utmost vigilance, year after year, but only once did the vigilance require armed action— in the Crimea in 1853. Otherwise, vigilance, in other words the readiness to go to war if necessary, was enough—in itself a certain justification of a diplomacy based on the balance of power.

By the end of the century the equilibrium was beginning to vanish. A unified and increasingly industrialized Germany began to dwarf France (inflicting a brutal defeat on it in 1870) and to extend its influence into the Balkans and on towards the Middle East. The growth in disequilibrium called for a new form of balance and after some hesitation the British allied themselves against Germany, first with France, and then with Russia, the alignment which existed at the beginning of the first World War. Germany had, nevertheless, grown so strong that the intervention of America was necessary to give the *coup de grâce*.

After 1918 a new situation was created by the total though temporary disappearance of revolutionary Russia from the scene of European diplomacy and by the instant retreat of America into its traditional isolationism. France and Britain were left as the only large Powers in Europe and either through a passion for playing at the balance of power as an end in itself or through a quite mistaken estimate of France's military strength, the British fell out of sympathy with France's strident but justified demands for security against a revival of German strength and became, if not one of the instruments, at least of the passive spectators of Hitler's seizure of power and his rearmament of the German people.

The second World War is to such an extent a repetition of the first—the same enemy, the same allies, the same alignment of forces—that there is something at once pitiful and grotesque in the spectacle of a continent so totally unable to learn by its own tragic experience. But if the circumstances of the war had all the dreariness of old disasters relived, the conclusion of the war was new. German power received a death blow comparable to the blow delivered by the Thirty Years War and likely to last as long. France's military and economic weakness was fully revealed. Great Britain, the only nation to stay in both world wars from the first day to the last, was overstrained and exhausted. The world woke up to a new fact—that in the order of Great Powers there were probably only two who did not hold that title by courtesy—Russia and the United States. In the European balance it meant a vacuum from the Channel to the Russian frontiers, or would have meant a vacuum if Russia had not advanced at once to the line of the Elbe. Whatever did not vanish in the cataclysm, one factor quite certainly had done so—the old European equilibrium. Two years after the end of the war the balance in Europe lay between an East firmly, if sometimes restively, organized under the control of a single Great Power and in the West—what was there in the West? The observer would be hard put to it to say. Perhaps the position can best be summed up by saying the West contained neither an organization nor an equilibrium nor a balance nor a force—but simply two question marks. Would the Western nations organize themselves in sufficient unity to meet the new concentration of power in Eastern Europe? And would the United States enter into some relationship with this Western fringe strong enough to reinforce it but tactful enough to leave its sovereignty unimpaired?

The profound shift in the balance of power in Europe has disturbed its political structure to the foundations. It would have done so in any case, whatever the character of the states responsible for the change. But the disturbance has been all the more sensational in that the states concerned are not simple nation states comparable to other nation states—as were France and Germany and Britain in the nineteenth century. One of the chief agents is Russia which is not only a state but a religion as well. What has happened is not a mere shift in a pre-existing relationship between comparable Powers. It is the emergence of a division which goes to the political and moral and psychological roots of the European community.

CHAPTER IV

COMMUNIST CHALLENGE

Karl Marx entered history to analyse it and cure it at the same time. His vantage point in time was the turbulent decade of the eighteen-forties. It was during this period that his fundamental theories were born. *Das Kapital* was written later to prove the theses he had already conceived—like other men of genius—in a moment not of research but of inspiration. In pursuing the proof of his ideas he found many occasions for modifying them and for introducing qualifications and refinements. These qualifications, however, have not gone into history as Communism. The Communist Manifesto and Mr. Zhdanov's speech in August 1947 on the revival of the Communist International (the Cominform) are of precisely the same order of ideas. *Das Kapital* has enabled men of critical and distinguished intelligence to remain Marxists. *The Communist Manifesto* has made Communism a mass force in the world.

The society of which Marx wrote was an equivocal society. We have already referred to its vast increases in wealth, its extension round the world of a new international economy, its relative stability, its hundred years of peace. At no comparable period in human history did man's capacity to create wealth and material well-being increase so fast. It was also an age of tremendous intellectual and literary activity—particularly in Great Britain. However remote some of the debates may seem to us now—on free trade, on the corn laws, on Christian doctrine, on ecclesiastical organization—we cannot deny their vigour or their serious intent.

But Marx did not have to look far to see the other side of this world. The decisive social change introduced by the application of science and industry to human production was to bring men —and women and children too—together in factories to work with machines and to bring the factories together in great urban agglomerations scattered along the main lines of traffic, by land and by sea. There had been evils and miseries enough in agricultural society, but there was some security and considerable familiarity with wider economic forces such as weather or harvests (and the temper of the squire). In the new industrial society there was little security and no familiarity whatsoever. Nobody —neither capitalist nor worker—really knew the nature of the forces they had begun to manipulate. The capitalist saw that they created wealth. The workers saw they created wealth too—but not for him. Nor in his poverty and defencelessness was he in a position to secure a larger share. Any Government Blue Book of those times, any evidence given by the factory inspectorate gives one an insight into a human misery so hopeless and revolting that the whole surface of that supposedly prosperous period changes and underneath one sees its foundations in degradation, squalor, injustice and servitude.

This was the world that stirred Marx to revolutionary activity and to this day it is moral indignation that draws many fine souls to accept his creed. But a man may be morally indignant and also wrong. No one would deny the necessity of abolishing the evils Marx denounced. The question is whether the analysis he made and the cure he offered were correct.

It is hardly necessary to restate Marx's philosophy in any detail. The essence of it is his belief that the economic structure of society conditions all the rest. As he put it,[1]

"What individuals are coincides with what they produce; and not only with what they produce but with how they produce. Consequently, what individuals are depends upon the conditions of material production."

History is thus determined by economic developments and the dynamism of history is produced by the unequal division of property. In the battle to acquire property and power class struggles against class and their victories and defeats are the dialectical progress of human evolution. Since, however, the ownership of private property is at once the instrument of domination and the bone of contention, to abolish the property-owning classes and to transfer property to the community would emancipate the workers and abolish class struggle once and for all. The new society, free from the fight for power and possession, would then evolve its own appropriate philosophy and the State itself would wither away since it had existed in the past merely to impose class dominion.

[1] *German Ideology* (p. 7).

Marx believed that in his own day the end of the capitalist era was imminent. Capitalist society was at the mercy of its own inner contradictions, of which the greatest was the refusal (or the inability) of the owners to share sufficient wealth with the workers to create markets for the ever-increasing flood of goods the new techniques were able to pour out. Cycles of so-called "over-production" were already occurring in industrial society— a serious one coincided with the outbreak of the French Revolution of 1848. They would grow worse and in an effort to overcome them by any means save the only efficacious one—the public ownership of the means of production—classes and governments would wage wars to acquire new markets or to divert the masses from the spectacle of their own misery. But out of this deepening time of troubles a class-conscious proletariat would be born. It would include more and more of the community while its share in wealth would decrease (since by yet another iron law, industry would organize itself on increasingly monopolistic lines, big business would swallow the small *entrepreneur* and the "little men" would be thrust down into the ranks of the propertyless proletariat). Finally, the dispossessed, realizing their vast numerical superiority, would take over the State and inaugurate the classless society.

Marx may have thought at first that sheer weight of numbers and the logic of history would transfer power to the workers. But the July Revolution of 1848 changed his views. It came as a protest against elections at which the voters of France had shown their dislike of further revolution and their conservative preferences by a large majority. Marx lost faith in the vote. He accepted Proudhon's dictum: "Universal suffrage is counter-revolution." He now believed that the change would come violently. "Force," he wrote, "is the midwife of every old society pregnant with a new one," and he introduced the idea of a dictatorship of the proletariat which would seize power in the name of the people. And he believed that this seizure of power would not be long delayed.

This, in barest outlines, is the doctrine of the *Communist Manifesto*. It is not difficult to understand its profound impact upon the nineteenth century liberal world, an impact which was to grow stronger as, after the turn of the century, the stability of that world began to disappear. In the first place, Marxism was an aggressive refutation of the dominant and supposedly self-evident beliefs held by nineteenth century society about itself. The fundamental assumptions upon which the economic system was based were twofold: on the one hand, the men of the liberal era believed that they had an absolute inherent right to private property, they "might do what they liked with their own"; on the other, they believed that if each pursued his own interests with vigour, the interests of the community as a whole would best be forwarded and that the profit motive, operating in conditions of free competition, would prove the best guide to the consumers' choice. The early theorists may not have regarded profits as ends in themselves but simply as useful guides to economic action. But to the practical men of affairs the amassing of huge private fortunes was the purpose and justification of their activities and in Britain at least so engrossing was the pursuit of wealth that into popular language crept revealing phrases such as "good as gold" or "sterling worth" or (perhaps the most revealing of them all) "making good" as a synonym not for a high and virtuous life, but for the acquisition of wealth.

But Marx preached with Proudhon that "property is theft." In his curious labour theory of value he sought to prove that, since work alone creates wealth, profits are merely stolen from the workers who created them. Capital, he declared, is not private property but essentially social property since it is created by the co-operation of groups of workpeople from whom the fruits of their labour have been robbed; far from the private control of this social property serving the best interests of the community, it ensures that on the contrary society will be racked at regular intervals by the most appalling economic crises. Private owners never distribute to their workers sufficient purchasing power to absorb the ever-increasing stream of goods coming from the machines. At regular intervals, therefore, a glut of production occurs, workers are turned off, goods are destroyed (while men starve) and poverty and unemployment plunge society into the extremes of misery. Thus Marx refuted, at their very foundation, the optimistic assumptions upon which free enterprise in industrial society was based.

The men of the nineteenth century, as a logical consequence of their confidence in an unregulated private economic system, believed that any government interference in the economic process could only be for the worse. Since government intervention would falsify the workings of the laws of supply and demand it could only do more harm than good, and in the middle of the century men of integrity and profound moral conviction, such as Richard Cobden and John Bright, could argue against attempts by government to regulate working hours in the factories or the employment of children on the grounds that such attempted regulation would falsify the economic laws on whose workings the prosperity of the whole system depended. Marx's reply to such beliefs was the claim that until government not only interfered but actually took over all the means of production, there could be neither prosperity, stability, nor justice. Only under complete public ownership would the economic system be run for the many, not the few. Only then would the crisis of the trade cycle be overcome. Only then would the full possibilities of industrial production be realized by breaking the restrictions imposed by the monopolies and the trusts.

But Marx did not only attack the fundamental economic beliefs of the nineteenth century. He challenged as decisively its political and moral ideas. He denounced the whole conception of parliamentary democracy as a bourgeois sham. Government, he declared, simply exists to forward the aims of the dominant class. In a bourgeois-capitalist society government is simply the "committee of management" of the bourgeois economy. As for the ideas of individual rights, of human personality, of an objective order of truth and justice and above all of Christian morality and belief in God, what were all these but reflections in the ideal world of bourgeois property relations or else of feudal survivals not yet swept aside by the growth of the bourgeois world? In the *Communist Manifesto* he speaks contemptuously of bourgeois morality, bourgeois truth and bourgeois justice, all of them sham, all of them simply reflecting and protecting the class structure and property relations of the bourgeois industrial community.

Marx's turning upside down and inside out of the basic assumptions of the nineteenth century might have proved less frightening if there had not run through his attack so strong a thread of truth. Everywhere in the first decades of the industrial era the workers were exploited and shared hardly at all in the new wealth their labours had helped to create. The worker had no protection in those early days to shield him from the rigours of the free market on to which he was thrown with nothing but his labour to sell and in which anything up to sixteen hours a day was demanded from him in surroundings of squalor and disease. It was not necessary to be a Marxist to recognize the miseries of the working class in those days. It was only necessary to read a novel of Dickens or pick up a Blue Book issued by the factory inspectorate. And if these exploited wretches attempted to combine to protect themselves, they might find themselves, as did the Dorsetshire labourers of Tolpuddle, in Australia for their pains.

Nor was it Marx who invented the trade cycle. The alternation of prosperity and crisis continued throughout the century and although the level of wealth rose steadily it rose in a violently fluctuating line. Marx's prophecies that these crises would in the international field lead to a struggle for markets and to imperialist war could also be said to be borne out by the colonial rivalries between Britain and Germany at the turn of the century and the Balkan tug-of-war between Russia, Austria, and Germany which helped to precipitate the first World War.

Nor were Marx's attacks on the sham democracy and sham idealism of the nineteenth century altogether wide of the mark. The grosser forms of class "justice" such as the game laws and the penalties attached to theft had been removed in Britain in the early nineteenth century and milder laws were spreading throughout Europe; but it remained an evident truth that the man of property was the dominant figure in government as in society and that much of the legislation upon which parliaments were engaged were designed to serve limited interests, not the general good. And keen and deep as were the religious feelings and the moral fervour of the middle classes, say in Britain or in Germany in the nineteenth century, theirs was, on the whole, a blinkered religion in which the sense of personal responsibility hardly compensated for the lack of social conscience. It was no use pretending that free competitive capitalism was Christian. On the contrary, it aggressively followed its own laws—of survival, of acquisition, of supply and demand. Yet the leaders of this new industrial society were Christian and were unable to see any contradiction between their church-going on Sunday and their employment, say, of small children in their mills all the week. There was in a word no organic relation between their practice and their belief, but they were unaware of the gap and talked of their "Christian society" as though its institutions, from counting house to cotton mill, conformed to the spirit of the Gospels.

Marxism was thus inevitably a strong dissolvent of the certainties of the nineteenth century and once its ideas were launched into the world, sooner or later, the old society was bound to disintegrate and give place to something new. Marx attacked the nineteenth century world at its most vulnerable point—its self-confidence—and he sought to destroy its belief in itself just at a time when a new class in society, the industrial workers, were acquiring sufficient education and sufficient political consciousness to ask what their role in society ought to be. The rise of a new class to be integrated into some sort of social harmony would have led in any case to some modification of the nineteenth century order; but Marx made certain that these modifications would have the nature of a profound revolution, both by declaring that this new class alone had genuine social, economic and political value and also by designating to it a Messianic role predestined since the dawn of history—that of initiating the kingdom of heaven on earth, the classless society. For as we have seen, Marx not only sought to undermine the bourgeois world. He sought to build another, and it is not enough to study his criticisms of the old order. It is even more important to assess the value of his predictions of a new.

Marx made many prophecies of the way in which his new order would come about. He made almost none about the nature of the society which would grow from the collapse of the old. It would be happy and peaceful. It would be classless and, since government is only the instrument of class rule, the State itself would wither away. For the rest all is obscurity. But the uncertainty of the goal is only equalled by the triumphant certainties of the way towards that goal. Among many prophecies four concern us here. The first is that the change would be total. No compromise with the bourgeois past was possible. The new order would be a complete reordering of human life. The second prediction is that this change would occur violently in the most advanced capitalist societies (although Marx later admitted that perhaps in Britain the change might come some other way) and that it would represent the uprising of the proletariat against the intolerable and increasing misery imposed by industrialism. The third is that the dictatorship of the proletariat would be the instrument of this violent class revolt but would later wither away. The last is that Marxist ideas alone would be responsible for the radical reordering of society and that any other ideas would not only be inefficacious but would lead the masses away from their true goal. In the *Communist Manifesto*, the first Communist publication, Marx already attacks with virulent dislike any other version of socialism except his own and this claim to have a monopoly of the only gospel of temporal salvation has been the hallmark of Communism ever since.

What is to be said of these predictions? Has history borne them out? Have the events of the last century proved not only that Marxism was the strongest possible dissolvent of the nineteenth century world but also an adequate guide to what would come after? There are two reasons why it is difficult to pass a final judgment. The first is that the point at which Marxist theory foresees the inevitable disappearance of capitalism is indeterminate. Marx believed that the cataclysm would happen soon. He was always ready to see its beginning in any temporary fluctuation and prophesied "the final struggle" all through the eighteen-fifties and -sixties. But there is no reason in his theory to limit its unfolding to one century or two or three. The fact that it has not happened yet does not mean it may not do so.

The second reason is less obvious. It is the difficulty of testing the accuracy of Marxism as an instrument of analysis once Marxism enters history as a political force. Marxism is not only a theory of history. It is a way of making history happen. If it could be shown, for instance, that in comparable economic situations communities with Communist minorities develop in one fashion and communities without Communists in quite another, the "ineluctable economic laws" would at least require further examination. It was one of the difficulties in Marx's thought that his revolutions were inevitable and yet in need of a helping hand. There is a similar ambiguity to be overcome before deciding the accuracy of his general line. How different might the development of the last hundred years have been if it had not been partly moulded by an active Marxist movement? The fact that the world has been involved in frightful convulsions since Marxism entered history predicting those convulsions is not conclusive proof that the Marxist predictions were correct. It might merely mean that Marxism was an effective agent of disintegration. Wrong ideas have after all been as potent in history as right ideas.

Even so, it must be admitted that a part of the prophecy has been fulfilled. Capitalist society has been engaged in two major wars in a generation. The tendency towards monopoly has increased. The trade cycle has continued to reappear and has grown rather worse, no nineteenth century crisis equalling the depth of the Great Depression. In other words capitalism has not apparently overcome its own internal contradictions, and in two European communities, Italy and Germany, the pressure of the Left for radical social change, coupled with the onslaught of depression, produced the violent reaction of Fascism and National Socialism. Meanwhile, in one country—Russia—a proletarian revolution has overthrown the old order violently and completely. Similar revolutions have been imposed on Russia's neighbours in Eastern Europe. In the sphere of ideas, more and more people have accepted, if not the Marxist dialectic, at least the materialism on which it is based. Scientific explanation, the habit of explaining things—or rather explaining them away—in terms of something else has increased. The idea that class (or a wider concept of environment) conditions man's behaviour has received general support. Altogether for a single man's prophecy the results appear uncannily correct.

But are they? If they are examined closely some curious inconsistencies appear. If we go back to the four criteria Marx laid down for the passing of capitalist society—that only total change could succeed, that the change would be violent, that it would lead to dictatorship, and that the force behind it would be the dogmas of Marxism—they do not apply to those countries to which one would have expected them to apply most of all. For instance, the two most highly developed capitalist countries, Britain and America, have been the most pacific. Both have succeeded in changing a large number of relationships and institutions in their countries—introducing social services, and maintaining them out of greatly increased taxation, nationalizing certain industries (even America has its T.V.A., its Grand Coulee Dam and now its public Atomic Energy Commission) recognizing and strengthening trade unions, undertaking public works, controlling foreign trade. Britain has gone much farther along this road, but it would be a mistake to think of the United States simply as a static undifferentiated capitalist economy.

The effects of such changes have been to reverse the second of Marx's predictions—that the masses would grow poorer as the monopolists grew richer. In America and parts of Western Europe the distribution of property varies tremendously between rich and poor, but the share of the poor has tended to rise. This tendency is particularly marked in Great Britain. Thus the worker, who in

1840 had in very truth nothing to lose but his chains, by 1940 was in a fair way to having a great deal more to lose—a house, for instance, savings, insurance and a settled position as a trade unionist. In America, he might have a car. This advance has tended to make the worker as unwilling as the middle class to work for total and violent change and this fact in turn has led to a further contradiction of the Marxist thesis that change could only come by violence. In America and Western Europe change has come about through the continued use of the machinery of parliamentary democracy as an instrument of social reform. The belief in a gradual transformation of society was accepted by the Left—by the Fabians in Britain, for example—and the fact of its gradualness enabled conservatives to adopt over the years a number of their opponents' tenets. Moderate, democratic socialism became a recognizable force between the wars, with governments in Scandinavia and New Zealand. After the war the British experiment was inaugurated by the first Labour Government to gain an absolute majority at the polls.

The third difficulty in the Marxist theses lies in the absolute lack of proof, beyond dogmatic statement, that a dictatorship of the proletariat exercising total economic power would "wither away." In the twentieth century, the Russian Revolution followed by the extension of Russian influence into Eastern Europe has reinforced men's doubts on the democratic character of the solution—State ownership—proposed by Marx. Total State ownership *may* be combined with political freedom, but so far the governments which have undertaken not simply to regulate but to absorb the economic life of their communities have also established total political control. Thus, the gravest difficulty in Marxism and the one which divides it most strongly from the Western world is this contradiction between its supposed aspiration towards a free society from which government would have vanished and the fact of the totalitarian Communist state. Since the Communist seizure of power in Czechoslovakia, the belief that Communism and free government are incompatible has gathered force and conviction. If the experiment could have been made anywhere with some hope of success it was in the traditionally free and Russophil community of Czechoslovakia. The fact that the Communist minority seized power because they feared to lose votes at the 1948 elections only underlines the possibility that Communists can co-operate with others only so long as they believe that the vote will shortly give them complete power. If they are threatened with declining influence they strike first. In such conditions, free government can hardly survive.

The fourth contradiction of Marx's analysis lay in the sphere of ideas, in his belief that Marxist dogma alone possessed the secret both of truth and growth. This belief has not been borne out in the twentieth century. On the one hand, traditional ideas proved infinitely more vigorous than can be justified by a strict Marxist analysis. The influence of Christian thought in the development of British social thought and practice is remarkable. The work of John Wesley and Methodism in the eighteenth century helped to base the trade unions and the Labour Movement of the following century on Christian foundations. Many of the first trade union organizers were lay preachers. To-day, more than one Labour minister appears in the pulpit from time to time and nothing incongruous was found in the Archbishop of Canterbury opening the Labour Party Conference with a service of dedication and worship. On the side of Conservatism it was a great Evangelical, Lord Shaftesbury, who gave the great impetus to factory reform. In Europe, too, after the eclipse caused first by liberalism and later by the emergency of the dictators, Christian parties revived to a surprising extent after the second World War. Their tendency was on the whole conservative, but it was a conservatism which would have seemed wildest radicalism to their grandfathers since it included acceptance of the idea of a measure of nationalization and of land reform. The change in any case was sufficient to make Socialist-Christian coalitions possible in Western Europe—an almost unheard of arrangement at any time before the second World War.

Not only were old ideas more lively than they had any right to be, but new ideas in the sphere of economics and social theory began to modify the current of thought. Men began to grow less interested in ownership—which the development of limited liability and the joint stock company had made more and more shadowy—and much more interested in the question of control and of the general direction and planning of the economy. The idea of planning is at least as integral a part of Left wing thought to-day as nationalization. At the same time acceptance of the idea of some planning—that is to say, of some attempt to master the economic environment—goes far beyond the Left. Much of this new thinking is associated with the name of Lord Keynes. It was he who elaborated a possible cure for the trade cycle, consisting in the regulation of the flow of new capital expenditure. He showed that it was the uneven demand for capital that was in many ways responsible for the cycles of boom and depression and that a legitimate responsibility of government would lie in encouraging and stimulating investment—either directly by public works or indirectly by financial policy—in times of slackening trade, and in curbing it on the upward swing of expanding trade. This theory has been combined with the more old-fashioned "static" socialism of nationalization as an economic panacea in the suggestion that to enable the government to pursue a flexible policy of contraction and expansion in the economy as a whole, it must control a sector sufficient to make its influence effective. Given State ownership of transport and of part of heavy industry and State control of the central financial institutions, it should be possible, so the argument runs, to secure a stable and regular expansion of capital investment and with it a stable and increasingly prosperous economy.

It is tempting to pursue the question farther at this point and to ask whether these new economic ideas stirring in the Western world are not influenced by a certain decline of confidence in the workability of total economic planning—or at least in its compatibility with political freedom—and whether they do not also represent the ideas and aspirations of a growing class in society—the managers—the men with administrative and technical skill but not necessarily much wealth or property. However, enough has been said to show that in the Western world, whatever the future may bring, the pattern of development has not fully conformed to Marx's predictions and society has shown a marked degree of resilience and adaptability.

The most highly developed capitalized and industrialized sections of the world have not developed along the lines laid down by Marx—in itself a remarkable modification, to say the least, of Marx's belief that it was the inevitable development of capitalism that would bring first revolution and then renewal in its wake. But this is not true of the three other Great Powers, Germany, Japan, and Russia. In these countries, revolutions, civil wars, imperialist expansion have fulfilled all his sombre predictions. There is obviously no single explanation of this curious fact—that the less developed economies should have followed the lines laid down for the more advanced. Indeed, the mania for simple,

single explanations is one of Marx's most damaging legacies to
the following century. The reasons for the failure of Russia,
Germany, and Japan to share in the social stability and capacity
for growth exhibited in Britain and America can only be established by examining the concrete reality of their situation in
history.

Russia is clearly in a special position. If ever an economy was
captured by an idea and not an idea thrown up by an economy,
it was the case in Russia. The pre-conditions of Communism—a
developed industrial society—did not exist. Russia was the first
laboratory of Marxism, not because the laws of its internal
development demanded the Communist experiment, but because
in the chaos of total defeat in 1917, Lenin and the Bolsheviks were
the only groups strong enough and confident enough to provide
government and order. A more revealing contrast lies between
Britain and America and Germany and Japan, all capitalist
states, all class societies, all therefore in theory doomed to the
same collapse. But three things distinguished Britain and America
from the two states which did in fact plunge the world into war.
The first is economic. Both Britain and America developed with
sufficient economic elbow-room. At the time of Britain's industrialization, the world lay open to its goods. It is only really to-day
that the problem of markets and of elbow-room has become a.
devastating one. America had and has a whole continent in which
to develop its wealth. But Germany built up its industry in the
wake of Britain and in a continent which was already criss-
crossed with trade barriers. For the tremendous productive power
of the Ruhr the Germany of 1870 was too limited a market, but
beyond the frontiers lay the competition of British goods and the
irrational obstacles of national tariffs. Japan's case was even
more precarious. Its industrial development had to make its way
against the competition of the whole world while the base of its
economy was the razor edge of a small densely populated island
and a single raw material—silk.

The second distinction was political. In Britain, the power of
the feudal aristocracy had dwindled with the growth of the towns
and of the mercantile class ever since the Age of Discovery. The
Civil War was the victory of the merchants and traders and
gentlemen farmers. The Reform Bill of 1832 completed the political process of ousting the feudal aristocracy—a process con-
summated in the economic sphere by the ruin of agriculture after

1870. By the time Britain was an established industrial economy, it was also a profoundly middle class state. In America, a feudal type of society existed for a time in the South but was non-existent in industrial America. In Germany and Japan, on the contrary, the feudal landlords retained their power. German unification was the work of the Prussian Junker, Bismarck, the preservation of the Junker strongholds in Eastern Germany was one of the great issues in German politics even in the twentieth century, and the landlords retained a decisive influence to the time of the Nazis. In Japan, the link was even more direct. The old feudal families became the new industrial magnates in the vast family monopolies, the *Zaibatzu*.

The last difference is that Britain was one of the creators of Western democracy and gave it to the United States. The parliamentary method is in the bones of both peoples. Both, too, have been profoundly influenced by Christian thought and practice. Germany and Japan, on the other hand, had absolutist Governments until late in the nineteenth century, full parliamentary democracy was a brief discredited experiment made between two wars and although Christianity has played a large part in Germany, Lutheranism, the most typical expression of German faith, has in it an element of passivity towards government which made it a weak check on that glorification of the State and of the military class which, beginning in Prussia, spread from it to infect the whole German community. In Japan, the ideals have been to an overwhelming extent the ideals of military strength and warlike achievement.

Given these profound contrasts, it is hardly surprising that the development of Germany and Japan has been totally different from that of Britain and America. When a state whose traditions are military and whose leaders are still imbued with a feudal and absolutist temper finds itself in economic difficulties, what is more natural than that it should embark on the straightforward feudal method of settling economic problems—that of taking someone else's land? Germany and Japan in the twentieth century have simply applied to their economic problems the solution commonly practised in the fourteenth. Britain and America, neither feeling the same pressure nor reacting to economic stringency in the same way, have remained profoundly pacific.

If these contrasts are relevant, they suggest that Marx's error was not in his interpretation of certain events. The contradictions and difficulties of capitalism exist (which is hardly surprising when one remembers how new, how vast and how unpredictable are the forces released by science and industrialization) and under certain conditions—a strong survival of feudalism, extreme economic stringency, lack of a deeply ingrained democratic and Christian tradition—these contradictions lead to Fascism, to war, and possibly to proletarian revolution. Marx's error lay in believing in the absolute and universal validity of this analysis and in bequeathing to his disciples a determination to make the facts fit the theory at whatever cost. Thus the ability of Western Europe and of America to follow different roads, to achieve a different type of "good society" by other means, becomes a challenge to the validity of the whole Marxist idea and to a lesser extent a direct challenge to Russia's claim to occupy a special, Messianic position in an otherwise rotten and collapsing world.

We are now perhaps in a better position to assess the importance of the dividing line which cuts off Eastern Europe from the West. Clearly the old question whether agricultural surpluses from the East will be available to Western Europe is of minor importance. The food surpluses may be recreated and may cross the line—there are signs of them doing so already. The difficulty lies in the ideas that cross that line and the ability or inability of Western Europe to deal with them. It is on this point that the preceding pages may throw some light. The first conclusion is that Western Europe has shown in the past sufficient originality and vitality to develop according to its own needs and ideas. There is thus no reason why this development should not continue in the future. Nevertheless, the "Western fringe" and the United States are far from having solved the contradictions, the frictions and the injustices of highly industrialized capitalist communities and in so far as they have failed—as for instance in France—they have a large active Communist minority in their midst. It follows from this that they are vulnerable to attack and infiltration from the Communist East and now less than ever can they believe that the old ways and the habits of twenty years ago will see them through the second fifty years of the twentieth century. The need to change, to reform, to expand, to improve Western society is absolute and inescapable. Even if it were not desirable in itself, the hostile witnesses on the frontiers and the disgruntled minorities within leave the Western world no choice.

If this account of the deeper disturbances underlying the

present crisis is at all accurate, it must surely follow that Western Europe to-day is living through a difficult interregnum—the gap between the death of an old, comfortable and familiar world and the birth of a new one of whose nature much can be hoped but little predicted. If only one of the old buttresses had been endangered, if industrial predominance alone had changed or the balance of power or the nature of weapons or the climate of ideas, it might still have been possible to believe in the continuance of the old ways. After all, Western society did persuade itself after the first World War that an earlier order could be restored. It was not only in the United States that "normalcy" was pursued. The British, the French, the Low Countries, all assumed that the inter-war world could be a recognizable version of the nineteenth century with a gold standard, with free trade, with national sovereignty (only slightly limited by the League of Nations), with liberal ideas and capitalist economics. The possibility that the first war had torn a gaping hole in the old fabric was not considered. Even the portent of the Russian Revolution was tidied away behind explanations of the backwardness and barbarism of Russian society. Over these days the last light of the Victorian sun still streamed, the light of a safe world of order and progress, the light of great certainties and greater wealth. But the illusion cannot be recreated after this struggle. For this time, it seems, all the pillars have fallen. The last ray of the old sun has been extinguished and if we of the Western world can do nothing but look backwards, then "we are for the dark."

CHAPTER V

THE CASE FOR WESTERN ASSOCIATION

And if we look forward, what then? The aim at least is clear. It is to re-establish in the Western world a framework of stability and prosperity, and the best way, surely, to discover what policies are necessary to create such a framework in twentieth century terms, is to turn back to the reasons why the old order failed. It failed because the political balance of power in Europe vanished leaving a vacuum behind. It failed because Europe's industrial resources and economic organization were insufficiently modern and powerful to meet the competition of those of the United States and Europe's relative decline created an increasing unbalance in the share of Western Europe in the exchanges of world trade. It failed because internally Western industrial society failed to master the social problem of ingrafting the new industrial masses into a coherent social order and the economic problem present in the fluctuations of the trade cycle; and because this failure in turn led to the great challenge offered to Western conceptions of freedom by the Communist system. It may seem an ambitious project to search for a new ordering of Western Europe capable of solving all these difficulties. Equally there is no reason to suppose that the recreation of stability will necessarily be an easy task. But there is one policy which at least holds some promise of meeting all these conditions—and that is the creation of some form of closer association between the nations of the Western fringe.

A single union, association or federation in Western Europe could fill the strategic vacuum. A unified free trade area from Scandinavia to the Pyrenees, from the Elbe to Donegal would include within it all the economic resources that have made the United States an industrial giant and would contain no such vast economic differences as divide the Deep South from the north of America (nor such racial diversity as is created by the American Negro minority). Such an economy would have to support a larger population—over 200 millions in Western Europe compared with over 140 millions in the United States—

and it would not be entirely self-sufficient in raw materials or probably in foodstuffs.[1] But the scale of its internal market should make possible long-term bulk contracts with such large suppliers as Argentina, the Southern Dominions, and even Russia, while the fact that a large part of the African Continent is under the sovereignty of Western Europe might make possible a new united effort to develop African resources for European use and in return to raise the standards of one of the world's hitherto

---

[1] A comparison between the resources of Western Europe and the United States gives the following results :—

PRODUCTION IN 1938
(in thousand metric tons, unless otherwise stated)

	Western Europe (a)	U.S.A.
(A) *Agriculture*		
Bread grains	28,526	20,504
Coarse grains	29,581	71,534
Rice	461	9,563
Fats and oils	2,414	3,517(b)
Raw sugar	3,390	6,307
Milk	68,077	47,816
Cheese	967	292(c)
Potatoes	54,562	10,024
Tobacco	109	59,003
(B) *Industry*		
Coal and lignite	561,431	358,015
Electricity (mn. kwh.)	126,718	113,808
Crude oil	700	164,302
Rayon and staple fibre	118,073(d)	116,859
Woodpulp	4,946(d)	5,382
Cement	32,500(e)	18,279
Lead(f)	196(d)	348
Zinc(f)	416(d)	405
Aluminium(f)	152	130
Gold (in kgms.)	10,570(d)	145,249
Pyrites	3,259(d)	565
Iron ore	27,010	14,435
Copper	114(d)	571
Manganese ore	324(g)	12
Pig iron and ferro alloys	17,722(h)	19,468
Crude and semi-finished steel	44,783	28,805

(a) Comprising U.K., France, Italy, Belgium, Netherlands, Norway, Sweden, Denmark, Eire, Portugal, Luxemburg, and Western Germany.
(b) 1937–41.
(c) Factory cheese.
(d) Excluding Western Germany.
(e) Estimate.
(f) Smelter production.
(g) Including production of dependent territories.
(h) American Zone only, 1937.

depressed areas. A similar policy might also be possible in the remaining European colonies in the Far East (which are virtually contiguous). Within a West European area of so much greater breadth and wealth than any single Western community the planned development of capital resources could counter with much greater hope of success the fluctuations of the trade cycle, since under present conditions of national sovereignty it is almost impossible for any small state dependent upon foreign trade to plan itself out of a general depression. And in the world of ideas, the experiment of free association between different national groups, the working out on a supernational basis of the balance in an economy between planning and freedom, the new opportunities for creating wealth, the new interchange made possible between different national cultures—all these could restore to the Western idea a force, a vitality and a validity it has lost in the first half of this century.

This is simply the most general outline of the case for Western association. More detailed consideration of its possibilities and difficulties will be the main matter of the following pages. But before dealing more closely with the issues it raises we must consider one or two objections which are as general as the outline given above. The first is the criticism of a regional association simply for being regional. The aim in this century, so runs the argument, must be to avoid exclusive arrangements and to work for a general association within the United Nations. Limited associations breed friction and rivalry. World citizenship and world union are the only legitimate objects to be pursued to-day by individual states. To this the answer is surely that associations are harmful to a wider world community only if they are aggressive and exclusive. The existence of a British Commonwealth is not believed now to impair the loyalty to the United Nations of each constituent Dominion. Nor does the regional ideal of Pan-American association prevent various Latin American states from playing their part in the United Nations. As one writer put it "Even in the parliament of man, there is no reason why there should not be different parties" and regional associations of a constructive and pacific character increase rather than diminish the amount of genuine international co-operation in the world community. The compatibility of regional association with a wider international system is particularly obvious when the association is drawn up as a flexible system of co-operation between like-minded states to which other states can adhere if they wish. In the growth of a national community, it has often been the decision of a few communities to work together that has been the core round which unity has finally been achieved. World unity may be forever impossible if no group of different nations can ever enter into a limited experiment for pooling their sovereignty. The part is in this case no enemy of the whole. It may be a condition of the whole ever coming into being at all.

A similar although more specific objection underlies the protests of those who say that a Western Association will divide Europe. In fact, Western Association has come to be considered by statesmen in the West only after the division of Europe had become an unfortunate fact. The extent to which Eastern Europe has been organized as an extension of Soviet state power can perhaps be exaggerated. The unification of the various economies is not complete nor have they all been geared into the Five-Year Plan. Equally, however, the network of pacts which unites the states of Eastern Europe politically, economically and culturally with each other and with Russia tends towards the creation of an Eastern European Union. Nobody in Western Europe would choose the present frontier between East and West. For one thing, it divides the German world in two from the Baltic to the Alps and every lesson of common sense and history suggests that that division cannot be permanent and that the swinging of the frontier to include all Germany in either an Eastern or a Western system is bound to be a dangerous and incalculable business. But this state of affairs is not of the Western nations' choosing. They have been forced to consider the possibilities of Western association only because the degree of organization reached in the East throws their own uncertainties and divisions into ever sharper relief.

There is even a possibility that a movement towards unity in Western Europe would be the means, not of confirming and consolidating the division of Europe, but ultimately of removing it. The Eastern frontier of Europe is, after all, a sufficiently fluid affair. In one sense it lies on the Urals. Yet Russia and the Balkans, both belonging to the sphere of Orthodox culture, and both exposed for varying periods to Asiatic invasion, have never been fully integrated into Western civilization. Again, at various times in European history the advance of Eastern nations—Russia and Turkey—has brought the frontier of Western civilization almost to the centre of the Continent, yet Western society has survived and even flourished when Russian control stretched almost to the Elbe and the Turks stood before Vienna. The present line is not eternally fixed nor is it certain that the Russians will wish, once the aftermath of war has passed, to keep exclusive control over so many non-Russian peoples in Europe. Communist control or no, the burden of empire remains a burden. Any interpretation of the motives of Russian policy is necessarily open to question, but it can at least be argued that much in recent Soviet diplomacy is dictated by fear. One of the consequences of accepting Marxist dogma is to believe that the outside world must necessarily conform to it. Seen through Marxist spectacles the United States, as an advanced capitalist Power, must by definition be aggressive and imperialist, notwithstanding the country's obvious and continuous reluctance in this century to get into any war, let alone start one. Strict Marxist interpretation does not permit the drawing of any but superficial distinctions between capitalist America and national-socialist Germany, since Germany under Hitler was only the advance model of what America would necessarily become. From this supposed resemblance it is only a short step to drawing the conclusion that since Germany has attacked Russia, America sooner or later will do so.

This ideological argument has been reinforced by the discovery and the use of the atom bomb by the Americans and their understandable refusal to share the secret and internationalize its control except under conditions of inspection and authority which the Russians find unacceptable. One must also remember that to the Russians the fact that Britain and America sent troops to Russia to assist the White armies in 1919 is proof that they may do so again. And the Russian Revolution has not wiped out six hundred years of troubled and isolated Russian history during which the invasions of Russia by European Powers were as regular as they were various. The Poles, the Swedes, the French and the Germans, with a variety of allies, have all invaded Russia; and Europe, looked at from Moscow, must seem little more than a turbulent territory from which attack must always be expected.

The Russians have sought compensation for their fear in a sense of superiority to the non-Russian world, in a belief, centuries old, in Russia's mission to renew and save it. Long before Communism, it was an Orthodox priest who saw in Moscow the "third Rome" of a revivified world religion. The creation in

Russia of the first Communist state reinforced this tendency in Russian thought and has helped to produce one of the most baffling elements in Russian diplomacy, the intimate interweaving of fear and suspicion with pride and self-confidence. After the first and brutal efforts to collectivize Russian farmers, Stalin referred to the Russians' capacity for overweening assurance as "dizziness through success." The last war was calculated to inspire such feelings with renewed force. The achievements of the Russian armed forces were such as to earn the Russians the amazed tributes of the rest of the world. At the same time the country emerged from the war ruined, exhausted and without the atom bomb. The combination of pride and fear, of assurance and suspicion, is at least a factor in the development of Russian diplomacy in the last two years.

The mental processes may be understandable, but this fact does not necessarily make them easier to deal with. Their complexity calls for an equally complex diplomatic riposte from the Western world. The arrogance, assertiveness and indifference to such "bourgeois" pretensions as the self-determination of peoples, national independence, personal freedom and objective justice require firm and resolute opposition. On the other hand, the fear, the suspicions, the basic mistrust demand patience and understanding and perpetual readiness to negotiate and compromise on all but principle. It is clearly impossible to give a blue print of such a policy. It is something more than "containment," for it assumes in the long run that some accommodation may be possible. It is something very much more than appeasement, for it establishes a line beyond which the non-Russian world will maintain its interests by force. Clearly, its application will vary from place to place along the immense frontier which stretches from Finland through Europe and the Middle East to the Himalayas and Sinkiang and the confused line of fighting between Communist and non-Communist in China. But in Europe, at least, it can be argued that the policy of building a Western Association fits best into a policy of "unhostile containment." So long as Europe to the West of the Stettin-Trieste line is disorganized, economically unsettled, politically divided and a prey to its own internal difficulties and contradictions, the temptation to Russian arrogance and self-assertiveness to intervene in such a troubled situation may prove overwhelming. The intervention would satisfy Russia's Messianic urge. At the same time, it would give the illusion of security, of breaking down "hostile capitalist encirclement."

On the other hand, the organization of Western Europe in an essentially unaggressive association, and the proof after five or six years that the area was concerned not to organize for a war against Russia but to pursue the pacific policy of internal consolidation and external co-operation, might still Russia's panic fears of a new invasion, a new European attack. If any analogy can be drawn from the events after the first World War, it is remarkable that the early reaction of the new Soviet State was to believe that the revolution in Russia could be defended only by revolutions everywhere else. Thus the policy of fomenting revolution wherever possible was actively pursued and was abandoned only after the rest of the world had proved decisively that on the one hand it would not become Communist, on the other that it was not planning to attack the Soviet Union. Once this double fact reached the Kremlin the advocates of permanent revolution, with Trotsky at their head, lost their power and it was Stalin who more than any other leader identified himself with a policy of "socialism in a single country" and of normal diplomatic relations with other Powers. Admittedly 1948 is not 1924. New aims and fears and ambitions enter into Russia's calculation. Yet the fact remains that once before the proof of the outside world's stability and pacific temper caused Russian policy to put itself into reverse. A similar proof to-day might have a similar effect and to this extent, the consolidation of Western Europe would lessen, not increase, the dangers of a divided Europe.

Of a further hope, that the prospect of a peaceful, wealthy and freedom-loving Western association might exercise a profoundly attractive influence upon nations at present within the Russian sphere of influence, there will be occasion to speak later. It is obviously of crucial importance in the case of divided Germany. Here, the only relevant issue is whether a policy of Western association will increase the risks of conflict in Europe, and it is difficult to avoid the conclusion that on the contrary such risks are unavoidable unless some policy of association and consolidation is successful in the West.

A quite different order of objections lies in the particular difficulties facing individual nations in Western Europe. For instance, Great Britain is already a partner in the free, world-wide association of the Commonwealth. Can it abandon an existing partnership of immense value, warmth and stability for the sake of a political partnership whose outline even is still unclear? Both the Italians and the French face the tragic difficulty that an influential section of their working class—on whose efforts and hard work so much of European recovery depends—are bitterly hostile to the idea of Western association and regard their chief function to be the defence of the interests of Soviet Russia, even where those interests contradict the needs and interests of their own nation. The extent to which Communism is a force in both countries is an obstacle not only to their own participation in a wider union, but also to other more stable nations joining with them. Nor is the danger simply from one form of extremism. Communist extremism in France has already conjured up the spirit of Right-wing extremism and of a saviour in the shape of General de Gaulle. The establishment of an anti-democratic authoritarian regime in France might be as much of an obstacle to French participation in a wider scheme as is the government of General Franco an obstacle to Spain playing any part in the Marshall Plan.

The Scandinavian nations have difficulties of another order. Sweden has a tradition of neutrality to safeguard and both Sweden and Denmark are for the time being the exposed outposts of the non-Russian world. Sweden is, moreover, bound to Russia by a commercial treaty which could require Swedish industry to devote a large part of its production, not to Western Europe, but to the Soviet Union. If Sweden were to participate fully in a Western association, could neutrality be more than a fiction? Might not the eventual result be a further stiffening of Russian control over Finland and even the type of infiltration and pressure to which others of Russia's immediate neighbours have been exposed? Another nation with a problem of traditional neutrality is Switzerland, and Austria faces the cruel dilemma that most of its economic interests lie with Eastern Europe, but its only hope of political independence lies with the West. Meanwhile, the wretched country remains divided and occupied by the Allies, the "four elephants in a boat" to which the Austrian President once referred.

And all Germany's neighbours, neutrals or not, face the problem of the place of the German people in any wider association. Distrust for their political unreliability and national assertiveness remains profoundly and ineradicably ingrained in Western Europe. On the other hand, the need for economic revival in the Ruhr and the restoration of the German market is growing more and more urgent for the nations of the Benelux Union, for France, for Scandinavia. The dilemma is not insoluble, in fact, it is certainly only in some wider association in Western Europe that it can be solved at all, but the formulation of a policy to include economic revival and political control is one of the major difficulties to be overcome in evolving a form of association in the West.

These particular difficulties will recur in the remaining pages of this book. There are others and they are only mentioned here to give a background to what is perhaps the most damaging criticism of all, the criticism not that Western association is undesirable, but that it is impossible, the criticism which returns to all initiatives and proposals the flat reply: it cannot be done.

This criticism is difficult to counter. In the first place, the lessons of history are not particularly encouraging. Unification has many times been imposed upon peoples of different race and language by a conqueror from without. It has rarely been achieved by agreement within. The greatest examples of unification by consent—the federal constitution of the Thirteen States of America, the union of Germany after 1870, the achievement of Italian unity—had behind them the spur of a common language and a common tradition, and in the case of Germany and Italy the tremendous urge of nineteenth-century nationalism. Where, looking further back in the annals of the West, we discover cases where unification might have changed the face of history—for instance, a coming together of the Greek City States—local particularism and petty urban jealousies proved far stronger than the impulse towards unity and another kind of unity, a unity based on outside force, was imposed first by the strongest among them, later by Rome. There is perhaps a particular lesson for Britain in the behaviour of two more recent city states—Genoa and Venice. In the eighteenth century they might have created and led a movement for a united Italy in which their own glory, tradition and commercial strength would have received due weight. By letting the occasion pass and by allowing others to take the lead, they found, in the final unification, their own light extinguished and were forced to sink to the level of provincial towns.

Another difficulty in countering the criticism that union is impossible lies in the fact that Western association can take any number of different forms. Criticisms which are valid against a tight federal structure, with a federal parliament, universal suffrage in presidential elections, strictly worked-out divisions of power between central and State governments are not necessarily valid against the creation of a free trading area, with certain common services, a co-ordinated full employment policy, a regional defence treaty and organs of regular consultation. The British Commonwealth is proof of how little in the way of institutions is required to hold an association together. The experience of the war has shown how many and various are the possible methods of close co-operation between States. So long as the forms of a possible Western association are as ill-defined as they are to-day, it is difficult either to demolish or uphold their possibility. Criticism and support alike slip through the loose net of definition.

But perhaps the greatest difficulty in meeting criticism of the practicability of a Western association lies in the fact that it is impossible to find out whether it can be done until the effort is made to do it. Most great ventures in politics have started with an act of faith and a determination to plunge in. Few have been the result of a painstaking effort to expose all the difficulties and remove all the obstacles before the first step is even taken. There can be no effortless, painless, riskless acceptance of a policy as momentous and fateful as that of associating one nation's destiny with another and with a group of other nations. The decision to begin resembles, in a sense, the decision to marry. No foresight, no careful preparation can insure in advance the success of the venture. Success lies in the manner of living and experiencing the married state.

Three recent instances in European history bear out the over-riding importance of the decision to act—once a reasonable presumption of necessity or success has been established. The first is the case of the economic union between Holland, Belgium, and Luxemburg. When the decision was taken, none of the obstacles had been cleared away. It has been only in the course of negotiation and of practice that the real difficulties have emerged. It is still, perhaps, too early to say whether complete success lies ahead (the relationship of Benelux to a possible Western association raises new problems), but of one thing the negotiators are convinced. It is that to approach difficulties *after* the decision has been made to solve them is a completely different matter from approaching them to see if they can be solved. And this experience of the men who have been engaged on what might be called a smaller edition of the negotiations necessary to achieve a Western Union is obviously of vital psychological importance.

The other example may seem on the face of it less apposite. It is simply this. When in 1939 the need to check the spread of Nazi aggression became inescapable, the leaders in Britain might well have made a calculation of the risks and possibilities and come to the conclusion that unless an assurance of full American support were given, it would be hopeless to think of success and that it would therefore be folly to engage in a war without that assurance. But in fact, what did they do? They threw their reliance on the future. They assumed that if they did their duty, sooner or later, the Americans would do theirs. They made an act of faith, repeating it in 1940. And it was upon that act of faith that the coalition of a whole world could finally be based. (In parenthesis it may be questioned whether, after all, this analogy is really inapposite. In the next four years at least much will depend upon the relationship between the United States and Western Europe. The nations may find repeatedly that their American friends will in fact applaud things to which they are not necessarily committed in theory or in advance.)

But the most telling instance is surely the origins of the Marshall Plan itself. The sequence of events leading to the Harvard speech of June 5th will be considered in a later chapter. Here it is only necessary to underline the fact that Mr. Bevin's instant decision to take up the offer implied in Mr. Marshall's words, to fly to Paris and concert with the French the steps necessary to gather the European nations together and thereafter to put the whole weight of the British Government behind the deliberations of the Sixteen Nations, is the chief reason why to-day there is a chance of America subscribing to a Marshall Plan and Europe subscribing to a Western association.

These, then, are the arguments with which those who doubt the practicability of a Western association can be countered. Admittedly they do not add up to a proof. There is not a jot of mathematical or any other certainty in the whole project. But at least the critics must sustain one counter-attack—and that is the question of what they themselves propose. Do they believe still that the nineteenth-century balance can be restored without effort? Do they believe that British statesmen need take no more thought for to-morrow than they did in the day of Gladstone and Salisbury? Do they honestly believe that individual undiminished political and economic national sovereignty has the same power and validity that it had a hundred years ago? And if they do not accept these theses, how do they propose that Europe should carry on its affairs? It may be that the lack of an alternative is not the best reason for accepting a policy. Certainly, it is a minimum reason only. Yet the cry, "Lord, whither shall we turn?" has been the starting point of more than one noble experiment in human history and the onus lies on the critics to show another way. For the rest of this book at least the assumption will be made that Western association is a desirable objective of British and of European policy and the chapters will attempt to deal with some of the difficulties and obstacles which are likely to stand in the way.

The starting point for any scheme of Western association is clearly the actual economic and political situation of the nations concerned. Politically, they are all parliamentary democracies of a recognizably Western stamp, but in Italy and France political stability is still to seek. In Italy the combined strength of the Communists and Socialists (who alone of the Socialist parties in Western Europe have voted for co-operation with Communism) could conceivably outweigh the coalition of the Centre and the Right. Since the Left is committed with especial emphasis to creating close ties with Russia and to "breaking Italian dependence upon American finance-capital," a Left-wing victory could mean the withdrawal of Italy from the orbit both of Marshall aid and of Western association.

A Western association is conceivable without Italy, although it would be impoverished and incomplete. But it is impossible to hope for one without France. The danger of the emergence of General de Gaulle as the head of an authoritarian regime has been mentioned. It is, of course, possible that the break between Communists and Socialists and the splitting off from the *Confédération du Travail* of the non-Communist group, *Force Ouvrière*, might encourage the General, who has always underlined the social context of his policy, to check the Communists—which is clearly his first objective—without wiping out the rights, the organizations and the effective political life of the working class. Such a development is conceivable, but, in the past, authoritarian regimes with an anti-Communist bias have always ended by violating the most elementary of the workers' rights, and it is difficult to see how such a development in France could fail to create the same barrier as now divides Spain from the other Western states.

With three exceptions—Portugal with its mild dictatorship, Turkey with its new-born Opposition, and Greece with its civil war—the other nations live under settled, old-established parliamentary governments, and political understanding between them presents no insuperable problems. But it would be as well to bring up at the start a difficulty which will recur throughout the discussion of closer economic integration. It is a strong divergence between those nations which have developed their post-war economies on the basis of austerity, control and purposive direction and those which, on the whole, have left their economies more or less to the workings of *laisser-faire*. Britain leads the austerity group which includes Holland and Norway; Belgium is the most successful instance of a community which, after some vigorous initial intervention by the State (for instance, the mopping up of wartime inflation at the end of 1944 by the *Plan Gutt*) has been encouraged to develop without controls. In between these two extremes, Governments have practised both policies in varying degree, Sweden tending to control, Italy and France to its abandonment. There is no space here to discuss the reasons for these variations. They are not all based on a dogmatic attitude to planning and control. They have depended upon such different factors as the weakness of State machinery (making for freedom) and the weakness of the local currency (making for control), but the existence of the divergence make two things certain: the first is that no single dogmatic pattern of economic collaboration can be imposed, the second that the ideas behind a Western association cannot be confined to "democratic socialism" in a narrow technical sense. Social the policies must certainly be and democratic, but not necessarily cast in the British mould of recent years.

Another type of political divergence arises in the sphere of defence. The most obvious and practicable form for organizing the defence of Western Europe would be a regional pact within the framework of the United Nations Charter modelled on the pan-American Defence Pact concluded by the nations of the Western Hemisphere. Not all the Sixteen Nations are as ready as Britain, France, and the Benelux Union to enter into a joint defence scheme. Some fit uneasily into the geographical pattern—Greece and Turkey, for instance. Others by tradition exclude themselves from all arrangements of common defence and rely on neutrality. The Swiss and the Swedes have not been compelled by invasion and occupation to revise their views on active defence. The Irish, too, are committed to neutrality. The only former neutrals to modify their earlier policy are the Norwegians and the Dutch. The desire for neutrality has actually grown stronger in Sweden and Denmark, since for the present they are strung out uneasily along the line dividing Eastern and Western Europe. Thus when Mr. Bevin coupled his support for the idea of Western Union with the offer of defence pacts, the Swedes immediately announced their intention of avoiding all commitments of any sort that might in any way compromise their neutrality. These divergences suggest that any Western association must be prepared to admit nations to varying degrees of membership, involving different kinds of obligation, a proposition disturbing no doubt to the drafters of federal constitutions and awkward, too, when such questions as the location of industry and the source of raw materials are discussed, but not entirely contrary to common sense, as is testified by the continued membership of neutral republican Eire within the framework of the British Commonwealth.

But these differences are dwarfed by a single fact which, with at the utmost one or two exceptions, dominates the economic life of each of the Sixteen Nations. It is the fact that was the starting point of this book, the fact that Western Europe collectively and each of its states individually runs the imminent risk of national bankruptcy. In most cases this risk takes the form of a deficit in the country's foreign trade, but even where the balance is reasonably favourable, as in Belgium and Sweden and Switzerland, the near-bankruptcy of their neighbours threatens finally to involve them in the same difficulties. The reasons have already been referred to, but they deserve rather closer examination.

The destruction in Europe and the disruption in Asia have made the Western Hemisphere in the last three years the chief source of nearly everything that is vital to reconstruction—food, fuel, machinery. At a time when the nations of Europe were in no position to produce much, they were compelled to buy in a spectacular way on the other side of the Atlantic, particularly in the United States. Thus they could neither export enough to the New World, nor yet do without dollar imports. The United States

tidied them over for a period with generous credits,[1] but the hard
winter and disastrous summer of 1947 hastened the exhaustion
of these reserves. France and Italy were spending their last dollars
by the autumn of that year and had cancelled vital orders for raw
materials before they received some $500 million between them
under Mr. Marshall's Interim Aid Act voted by Congress in
December, 1947. Great Britain reached a position by February,
1948, in which only about £600 million of gold and dollars were
left to act as the reserve both for Britain and for the sterling area
—a figure which could pay the deficit in trade for not more than
six months more. Holland and Norway ran almost as short and
both were compelled in 1947 to restrict their imports drastically
and to cut their domestic consumption (the Norwegian food
ration fell from 2,800 calories a day to 2,200).

This general draining away of Europe's dollars affected prosperous communities such as Sweden and Belgium. Neither the
Swedes nor the Belgians had paid for all their very large imports
from the United States by a direct despatch of exports to America.[2]
Indeed, they did not balance their total trade at all and paid for
the deficit ($522.8 million for Belgium, and 890 million Swedish
kroner for Sweden, in 1946) partly with American credits and their
own reserves at the end of the war (which were still more or less
intact) but also with the gold and dollars of other European
nations with which they had favourable balances of trade. Their
neighbours who on the whole emerged from the war in a much
more battered condition could not send them as much merchandise as they wished to buy. Thus Belgium in particular began
to acquire British sterling and French francs and Norwegian
kroner. These currencies could not be automatically converted
into gold or dollars, but in most trade agreements a clause was
inserted to arrange that Norway, for example, or Britain would,
once Belgium's holdings of their currency reached a certain figure,
pay for any excess in dollars or gold. For instance, Belgium had
an agreement with Britain at the beginning of 1948 to hold up to
£27 million in inconvertible sterling. If British purchases in Belgium
forced the figure higher, Britain would pay gold.

[1] Here are some of the figures from 1945 to November, 1947 (they include private
loans) : Norway, $110 million ; France, $2,026 million ; Denmark, $30 million ;
Britain, $3,750 million ; Italy, $1,689 million ; Holland, $261.7 million ; Belgium,
$149 million.

[2] Sweden bought $207 million worth of goods from America in 1946 and sold
only $46 million. In 1947 Belgium and Luxemburg bought from America to the
tune of $389 million and sold only $51 million.

Thus Sweden and Belgium could hope up to a point to balance their adverse balance with America by converting other currencies into dollars. It was particularly easy to do so during the brief period in the summer of 1947 when sterling became convertible. Belgium, for instance, was able to add to its gold reserves quite considerably during those two months. But as the less fortunate nations began to exhaust their reserves altogether, this subsidiary source of dollars vanished. Sweden was compelled to rely more and more on its own reserves to cover its great deficit with the United States and the reserves melted away. Between July, 1946, and October, 1947, gold and foreign exchange were spent to the extent of 1,600 million kroner, leaving the Swedes with barely enough (600 million kroner) to finance their essential foreign trade. Belgium did not feel the pinch so soon, but in the autumn of 1947 it too began to cut its dollar imports drastically.

Thus whether the nations of Western Europe emerged from the war shattered or prosperous, disorganized or commercially sound, the result after three years has been that the spreading contagion of the dollar shortage has engulfed them all. They have managed to export disequilibrium to each other. Nearly all have unbalanced foreign accounts. Nearly all have the worst deficit in the currency they need most—dollars.[1]

And deficits in dollars mean, in the present dislocation of the world economy, deficits in wheat and fodder, in fuel and fertilizer, in machinery of all kinds—in a word of all those things which can restore Western Europe from a jangling, jamming, broken economic machine to a smoothly working, integrated and prosperous system.

The dollar deficit also means that far from moving forward to greater collaboration, the nations are actually moving apart.

[1] Here is the estimated deficit of all the participants in the Marshall Plan for the period April–June, 1948 :—

(in millions of dollars)

Austria	− 33	Norway	− 7
Belgium–Luxemburg	− 80	Portugal	− 10
Belgian Colonies	+ 5	Sweden	− 7
Denmark	− 18	Switzerland	+ 3
Holland	− 10	Turkey	+ 3
France	−255	Great Britain	−241
French Colonies	− 20	British Colonies	+ 70
Greece	− 31	Germany—	
Iceland	− 1	Bi-Zone	−134
Italy	−149	French Zone	− 13
Netherlands	− 96	Saar	− 2
Dutch Colonies	+ 12		

Since they cannot satisfy their vital needs for food and fuel in Europe, they are compelled to buy them in the New World and to try if they can to divert goods thither from old markets in Europe. As their reserves of gold and dollars decline, they begin to restrict trading to bare essentials and, in so far as Europe is not producing them, inter-European trade declines. At the same time, more and more care has to be taken to see that each dollar is spent on urgent imports only. Thus an increasing volume of less essential trade is either cut out or organized on a strictly bilateral basis, goods being exchanged for goods on the basis of direct barter, to ensure that no gold or dollars are needed to balance any disequilibrium or pay off any debt. Now barter is notoriously the most restrictive form of trade and leads to the increasing economic isolation of the nations that practise it. Yet Europe at the end of 1947 was a web of bilateral agreements, each reinforcing the stark economic sovereignty of the bargainers, each adding one more element of rigidity to a trading area on which a sort of *rigor mortis* was beginning to settle. As the Western nations talked of greater co-operation, they were being driven—by necessity—to ever-increasing isolation. This was the economic reality of Western Europe late in 1947.

It is necessary to underline that the phrase "dollar shortage" is a sort of shorthand. The real shortages were wheat and meat and fuel and steel. But the fact that Europe could not produce these necessities in sufficient quantity and that they were only to be procured in the New World made the dollar (or the Argentine peseta) the only means of satisfying Europe's vital needs. And by the middle of 1947, it was clear that Europe's own production would certainly not recover in time to supply all these needs before the available supplies of dollars ran out. In such conditions, far from the situation in Europe leading inevitably and naturally to a development of integration and co-operation in Europe, every economic force was pushing the nations in the direction of a self-centred and desperate policy of *sauve qui peut*. This was the movement which Mr. Marshall sought to arrest in his Harvard speech of June 5th, in which he asked the nations of Europe to consider their needs *jointly* and to find out how, by working to-gether, they could establish not only the scale of their need, but the extent to which they could satisfy it themselves by individual and collective action. It is thus impossible to speak of a Western association without talking first of the Marshall Plan, which offers the nations that minimum degree of elbow room necessary to consider any policy as eminently sane as that of working together to bale out the European boat. So long as each wave threatened to swamp them, the nations were too busy fighting for the life-belts. Mr. Marshall's action produced a sufficient lull for panic to recede and a more human and co-operative approach to return. In this sense, American aid is inseparable from the idea of European co-operation and its scope and purpose must be carefully examined.

Yet it is vital to remember that the two factors—Marshall aid and Western association—are essentially distinct. In the last two years the European nations have received severally almost as many dollars (about 9 billion) as will be necessary for the first two years of the Marshall Plan. But at the end of the two years they were if anything less united than on the morrow of victory. The new American assistance can vanish in the same way. It can be used to feed and warm and clothe the people. It can tide them over four years which would otherwise have seen a German ration scale in Britain and France, closed factories, mass unemployment and political disintegration. But in itself it will not compel the peoples of Western Europe either towards or away from greater co-operation. Only their policy and their will can bring about such a consummation. Marshall aid in a word is a tool which the generosity of the American people places in the hands of the peoples of Europe. But their decision will determine the nature of the job upon which the tool will be employed and whether the job will be finished in the end.

PART II
AMERICA'S ROLE

CHAPTER VI

AMERICAN ISOLATIONISM

Even if there were no Marshall Plan, the influence of the United States on Europe in the next decade would be tremendous. But with the possibility that some $17 billion worth of supplies will enter Europe at American expense, that American administrators and experts will be intimately concerned with the use Europe makes of these supplies and that the behaviour and the achievements of the European nations will be under constant and critical scrutiny in Washington, it is clear that one of the decisive factors in any development of European association—or of anything else—will be the actions and reactions of American policy.

The chief interest of the Sixteen Nations is clearly that their relationship with America should be reasonably stable and consistent. They will have difficulty enough in concerting their own policies and the task will be even more exacting if they have continually to adjust themselves to violent fluctuations in mood and policy across the Atlantic. Yet such fluctuations are precisely what a number of prophets foretell. "Why," they argue, "do you rely on America? You must know that isolationism is the deepest instinct in its political make-up and that all this outside activity is no more than a sort of prolongation of wartime unsettlement. In any case, there is a slump on the way and America will be unable to sustain the proposed scale of foreign giving and lending. And that slump will encourage what is already such a marked feature of American policy, its imperialist tendencies and its drive to war. In any case, even if these other factors fail to come into play at once, do not forget that 1948 is an election year, that there will probably be a change of administration and that the newly elected Republicans will be no more willing to follow the lead of a Democratic President than was the Harding Administration to follow Woodrow Wilson."

There are four different criticisms of American policy contained in this diatribe—that America is fundamentally and unrepentantly isolationist, that its economy is unstable and threatened by a violent depression, that its policy is likely to develop in the next years on increasingly imperialist and aggressive lines and that, last of all, the American elective system puts a premium on discontinuity in the conduct of foreign affairs. It is a formidable indictment. How much of it is true?

No one will deny the deep roots of American isolationism. Every nation is, after all, isolationist at heart. The thing that in the past has distinguished the practical isolationism of America from the would-be isolationism of other nations is that the United States has had the geographical, economic and political means of being isolationist successfully. At the time of its greatest development, the United States had limitless possibilities of expansion within its own territory and an apparently inexhaustible supply of raw materials inside its own frontiers. No necessity of trade and commerce drove the Americans overseas as the British had been driven. They did not need new markets or new fields of investment or new areas to settle. They only needed to extend the line of internal colonization further West.

They did not need to go out—and other nations had little chance of coming in. Two broad oceans kept the rest of the world a convenient 3,000 miles away. They had Northern and Southern neighbours, it is true, but Canada and the West Indies formed part of a British system only less pacific than their own, and South America throughout the nineteenth century was not strong enough to launch an attack itself nor in a position to provide the springboard for anyone else.

Opinions differ on the question why the South American nations were inhibited in this way from becoming embroiled, like so many other weak continents (India, for instance, or Africa), in Europe's expansion in the nineteenth century. The American answer is that after the enunciation of the Monroe Doctrine in 1824, which denied the right of any non-American nations to intervene in the Western Hemisphere, the solidarity of the two Americas, North and South, held the ambitions of Europe in check. But moral solidarity alone has never restrained any determined aggressor— as the League of Nations was to learn some decades later—and the real reason why no nations came to disturb America's isolation in the nineteenth century was that the British Navy kept them away. At that time, as we have seen, the world was organized peacefully on the basis of the "British system"—the balance of power in Europe and the superior power of the British Navy

...system was pervasive, but smooth
...ike the British commercial system
...med to function so effortlessly and
...ught of it as a law of nature and not
...of political and economic power.
...e excuse than others for mistaking a
...ography or even of the natural law.
...a great industrial nation in a world
...without undue strain or fuss, creating
...nd economic environment for that
...grow up believing in isolationism as
...ar and intervention and international
...British system was keeping all these

...d the American belief in isolationism. It was their vision of their own society as in some sense an ideal community dedicated to the freedom and brotherhood of man. The early settlers came out to escape the tyranny of kings and governments. They built the first democratic communities in the modern sense and made the first experiments in religious and political toleration. After the American War of Independence, the ideas of self-determination for peoples and of the rights of man were enshrined in the fundamental documents of the new Republic and to those rights were added the achievement of a successful federal structure which seemed to offer the Republic the ideal method of combining local loyalties and interests with the broad economic interests common to the whole area. This ideal of a "more perfect union," together with the inalienable right of man to "life, liberty and the pursuit of happiness," came to represent in the American mind a general recipe of political salvation and at the same time an integral part of the American way of life.

The only great internal threat to the American republic—the Civil War of 1861—was calculated to increase the hold of these basic beliefs on the American mind. The war was fought to save the Union and to free it of slavery—in other words, to preserve the formula of unity in diversity worked out in 1787 and to extend to all American citizens the rights laid down in the Constitution. When Abraham Lincoln declared that: "Fourscore and seven years ago our fathers brought forth upon this Continent a new nation, conceived in liberty and dedicated to the proposition that all men are created equal," he expressed America's deepest belief about itself, the belief that the federal union, unlike other nations, was founded not on a racial or national community, but on the pursuit and realization of the rights of man.

American nationalism grew steadily in the century which followed the founding of the Union. But the sense of being different from other nations—and superior to them—was reinforced by the stream of immigrants from Europe who came to escape, not as in the old immigration from religious and political persecution, but from Europe's poverty and economic oppression. In fact, the immigrants found very much the same economic system as the one from which they had escaped. After 1860, the industrialization of America was carried through at breakneck speed and to the accompaniment of strife, class war, the accumulation of vast fortunes and the co-existence of frightful poverty. But in America, until the close of the century, the sense of economic opportunity was maintained by the open frontier in the West and American society, unfettered by feudal survivals, did offer the hard-working and acquisitive worker the chance of becoming a captain of industry. The United States was the land not so much of inherited wealth as of self-made men.

The twentieth century, as we have seen, shattered the peaceful world system in which isolationism could provide America with a practicable political system. It also closed the frontier in the West and exposed the American economy to a series of assaults of which the most shattering was the Depression of 1929. But forty years of disappointment and turmoil are not sufficient to erase completely the memories of America's long, golden youth. Habits of mind at once so congenial and so convenient become deeply ingrained and the hankering to return to a "normal world" must inevitably take the form of a backward look to the nineteenth century when the rest of the world gave no trouble and within America itself the dream of limitless expansion and prosperity could still be passionately believed in and passionately pursued. Under such conditions, it is useless to suppose that all desire for isolationism has faded from the American soul. The longing is as deep and as natural as the longing of all mankind for the lost peace and primal innocence of their Golden Age.

But there is no way back into the Garden of Eden, and for the last thirty years America has been making a painful readjustment to a world in which the principal pre-condition of successful isolationism—the existence, supported by someone else, of an orderly world system—has gradually vanished (and vanished during a time of steadily increasing disorder in the world). The Americans' adjustment was inevitably halting. They began the first World War in strict neutrality, but were driven from it by a double reaction—by their realization of what the control of all Europe by Germany would mean to their Atlantic security and by a revolt against the brutal German methods of conducting the war. Their economic stake in an Allied victory—the security of their loans and the markets for their food and machines (the production of which was boosted enormously by the needs of the belligerents)—gave birth later to the widely accepted myth that an unscrupulous conspiracy of Allied diplomats and American bankers had lured the United States into the war. Books were written on the theme and became best sellers—thereby preparing the mood in which a great mass of Americans faced the possibility of a second world conflict. But this mood of cynical disillusion did less than justice to the motive power behind America's decision to enter the war in 1917. A "world safe for democracy" was not a propagandist's lie but a genuine hope.

The story of President Wilson's attempt to turn this hope into a concrete organization of world society on the basis of international law is too well known to need retelling. He succeeded in writing the Charter of the League of Nations into the Peace Treaty with Germany. By it America would have been committed to sharing, with other peace-loving nations, that task of policing and maintaining world society which had been accomplished in a rough and ready and unformalized way by the nineteenth-century *Pax Britannica*. President Wilson's insight into what would be necessary to maintain a peaceful world came, however, too soon for his own people. If he had handled the question of American participation in a world organization with a little more political skill, had he not gone to Paris to become enmeshed in the "old diplomacy" and (as his opponents said) contaminated by it, had he, above all, associated the Republican Party fully with his, a Democratic President's, policy, perhaps he could have succeeded better. But basically what defeated him was the sweeping desire of the Americans to return to the "normal" world they had known, the world of isolationism in foreign policy and economic expansion at home. Not only was the Treaty rejected, together with the Charter. The United States withdrew from specific commitments such as its military guarantee to France. Then the people turned with relief to the comfortable belief, shared incidentally by Britain, that the war had proved a disagreeable interlude for which an irresponsible German Kaiser was largely responsible in the otherwise even development of a stable world.

In the 'twenties, the Americans departed a step or two from the isolationism to which they had thankfully returned in 1920. Almost unnoticed at the time, a fundamental economic change had occurred to them during the war. From being a debtor nation, they had become the world's greatest creditor.[1] As such, they could not be wholly unaffected by the problems of international finance. In any case, they were fairly involved when in 1922 the British announced that they would collect only such reparations from Germany as were necessary to cover their war debt payments to the United States. The Americans were drawn unwillingly in and it was an American, General Dawes, who evolved the scheme in 1924 which made possible five years of German reparations. (The fact that only American loans to Germany made possible the surplus in the German trading account necessary before reparations could be paid was not noticed at the time.)

In the political sphere, America offered no sustained collaboration. It lived in its world apart, but occasionally its growing sense of power and influence encouraged it to make a sally. Such, for instance, was Mr. Kellogg's excursion into the international arena when in 1928 he persuaded the nations to sign a Pact outlawing war. The Great Depression which burst upon America in the following year ended for a time even the mild efforts of co-operation practised in the 1920's. The nation in its troubles turned in upon itself and looked for revival within its own frontiers. Throughout the 'thirties, the Americans played on the whole an inactive role in the attempts to get some order into the international economy. At the Economic Conference in 1933, their role was flatly negative. In the political field, President Roosevelt's attempts to introduce a wider view in international

---

[1] The following table sums up the change :—

	1914	1919	1929
Foreign assets to the United States ..	—$3,686 million	$12,562 million	$19,763 million

Source : *America's stake in International Investment* (The Brookings Institution, 1938).

affairs were only partially successful. The United States co-operated in the International Labour Office and signed the Statute of the International Court of Justice. But as the danger of war in Europe grew more imminent and the shadow of Hitler spread across the Old World, the profound reaction in the United States was to retreat into a complete and legislatively protected isolationism. (It was at this point that the myth about America having been dragged into the first World War was most widely circulated and believed and the word "warmonger" became one of the strongest terms of political abuse.) In November, 1939, the Congress passed the Cash and Carry Act whereby foreign nations could acquire American arms in time of war only if they paid cash and carried them in their own ships, and at the same time an earlier Neutrality Act was revised and strengthened to make the *cordon sanitaire* round the United States as complete as the isolationists could make it.

The next swing of the pendulum came as an earlier swing had come—by the realization of what a German victory would mean to the United States and by a tremendous revulsion against the methods of warfare the Germans used. By 1941, neutrality was a dead issue, the fifty destroyers had been traded with Britain and the most inspired piece of economic statesmanship the world had yet seen—the offer of Lend-Lease, the "taking of the dollar sign" out of war supplies—was on the Statute Book. Nevertheless, the convinced isolationists fought back. In 1940 and 1941, the "America First" movement, headed by such an equivocal figure as Colonel Charles Lindbergh, was a force to reckon with in its violent denunciation of all policies calculated to draw the United States into the war and its tendency to appease the Nazis as an alternative to American intervention. When, however, war came, in December, 1941, it came in a way that silenced isolationist and appeaser alike. The Japanese attacked the American fleet, without warning or declaration of war, at Pearl Harbour.

From that moment, there could be no more isolationism in the old sense. For the first time in a hundred years the great Republic had been attacked from without. It was clear that if any security were to be built in the world, it could not be left to produce itself. The realization that America would now be compelled to take an active part was hastened by a profound psychological change that began to take place in the American mind as the second World War developed. The first war had made them a giant, but nobody noticed at the time on what scale, they themselves because they were too busy to look about and make comparisons, the Europeans because they still maintained intact the sense of their own greatness (France's growing anxiety for security between the wars suggests that that most logical of peoples had a shrewder idea than their neighbours of the change in the world's balance). But in the second World War, America's strength was so pre-eminent, so obvious, so overwhelming that the Americans themselves began to realize the change. They had believed a world system to exist around them which, if they left it alone, would do as much for them. Now they found that a very large part of that world system was apparently made up by themselves. Even if they wished to "cash out," there was nowhere to cash into.

It was clear that they would have a major hand in preparing the peace and one can imagine how their collective unconscious went to work: "At least we will not repeat the mistakes of 1919. This time at least we know what to do." Seen in retrospect, the mistakes of 1919 seemed to be fourfold. The Great Alliance had broken on the morrow of victory. This time, then, the agreement of the Great Powers would be the cornerstone of the peace settlement and the specific arrangements decided on at the meetings of the Big Three at Teheran, Yalta, and Potsdam would be the basis of the peace. Last time the United States had refused to enter into the organization of international society. Now, therefore, America would play a leading part in creating a new United Nations. After 1919 the German aggressor had been allowed and even encouraged to revive, expand, rearm and finally fall on his neighbours again. This time the very means of revival would be removed. As far as possible Germany would become a pastoral country. Lastly, insufficient international effort had been made after the 1914 war to repair its ravages quickly and to restore economies shattered by war. In the difficult years between 1919 and 1924 were sown most of the seeds of future conflict. This time the world economy should be restored speedily and the gap between war and recovery bridged for each needy nation. This second task would be entrusted to an international organization, the United Nations Relief and Rehabilitation Administration. Britain, whose international position and economy had been particularly unsettled, would receive a large loan. The larger task, that of restoring a functioning world economy, would be accomplished by restoring stable exchanges through the establishment of an

International Monetary Fund, world trade would be freed from those fetters particularly identified with Dr. Schacht, such as quotas, import licences, and exchange control by the setting up of an International Trade Organization to lay down and supervise the basic rules of international trade, and tendencies to disequilibrium, failure to develop, backwardness, lack of resources would in part be met by establishing a World Bank of Reconstruction to make capital advances to needy but deserving nations.

This, then, was the coherent programme with which the United States approached the problem of peace-making. Certainly it was not isolationist. On the contrary, it demanded the action and intervention of the United States at every turn. Yet there lurked in it some last fading spark of the old philosophy. For one thing, it looked backwards. It attempted to remedy the old mistakes of 1919 rather than assess the new problems of 1945. For another, in looking back, it made assumptions about the kind of world order which it would be right and legitimate to seek, and this world order began to take on a remarkably nineteenth-century look. No one would deny that free trade and stable exchanges and a functioning world order are all desirable things. But the problem in 1945 was whether the old methods, particularly the old economic methods, would bring about the desired result. If the American attitude—inevitably a complex thing—can be fairly summed up, one might say that after the victory of 1945 the Americans foresaw a period of readjustment followed by the re-establishment of a recognizably "normal" world. The new international organizations would deal with any pressing problems. The occupation of Germany and Japan would be a direct liability, but over a large field Americans would be able to pursue their own affairs as they had done in the past. It would be unjust to call this state of mind isolationist. It is rather the degree of isolationism an old addict brings over with him after a sincere conversion to international co-operation.

But just as the mood of "cash and carry" could not survive the brutal battery of 1940, so the hidden urge for "normalcy" barely lasted through 1946. One by one the policies upon which so much reliance had been placed proved unworkable. Russian intransigence destroyed the political hope, the deepening of Europe's ruin the economic. Four-Power agreement proved well-nigh impossible from the time of the first London Conference in 1945, and even if the Western Powers had been willing to continue their efforts at conciliation longer,[1] it seems obvious that sooner or later they would have been forced to break with Russia over its policy of "defensive aggression" in Eastern Europe and its unilateral policy of stripping the economy of the Soviet Zone of Germany. The breakdown of Four-Power agreement reduced the effectiveness and prestige of the United Nations and made it an increasingly doubtful instrument of international policy. The de-industrialization of Germany decreed at Potsdam became one of the chief factors in Europe's failure to revive. Last of all, winter and summer conspired to hasten the economic disaster of 1947. This crisis would have occurred in any case. The truth was quite simply that the $9 or $10 billion the Americans lent to Europe was insufficient to correct the profound disequilibrium created by the war. The winter cold and the summer droughts of 1947, however, brought the crisis to a head sooner and gave it a more dramatic development.

The first clear warning came at a point where politics and economics overlapped. Since 1944 the British had been holding the line against Communist expansion in Greece. In the summer of 1946 the Americans were warned—privately it appears—that this commitment was proving an increasing strain on Britain's straitened resources. Desultory exchanges continued through the autumn and winter. Then came the great frost and the sudden industrial crisis in Britain. For a fortnight industry closed to prevent the complete breakdown of the electricity grid. Millions of pounds of exports were lost. New depths of economic stringency opened before the British Government. They announced that by March 31st all British troops would be withdrawn from Greece.

It is probably at this point that the Americans' hopes of 1945 and 1946 finally vanished. They woke up in a cold and angry world in which their friends seemed to be on the verge of ruin and their allies to have turned into bitter enemies. It was a moment of considerable alarm and bewilderment and the first reaction of the American Government tended to increase both. President Truman presented a message to Congress asking for $400 million to bolster up the security of Greece and Turkey as part of a programme to check the extension of Communism everywhere. The Americans felt immediately that they were being

---

[1] There is no doubt, for instance, that all the nations save Britain and America would have been willing to see Unrra continue its work another winter. It was vetoed, however, in the autumn of 1946 as an instrument of economic assistance to the Eastern *bloc*.

asked to accept a new direct liability at the end of which might lie a war.

In the long debate that followed, Congress had ample opportunity to show how profoundly distasteful was the new policy proposed to them. They criticized the President for not relying on the United Nations, for risking an armed conflict with Russia, for backing dictatorship, for embarking on unnecessary world crusades, for wasting American dollars and taking the first step towards wasting American men. The figure was finally voted—unwillingly and grudgingly amid a general feeling of drift and indecision.

The critical voices were not the only voices, however. Ever since Yugoslav fighter planes had shot down an American aircraft over Yugoslavia, opinion in the United States had begun to harden against Soviet Russia. Mr. Molotov's various appearances in the United States did nothing to soften it. The belief that there would be no end to Russian ambitions unless somebody took a firm stand began to spread. Americans remembered they had the atom bomb. There was loose talk of a preventive war. All the same, those who criticized and those who applauded felt increasingly that the United States was without a foreign policy and that their Government was at a loss. The nation was filled with the uncertainty, the irritation and the nervous tension of men facing a danger which they feel powerless to master or prevent.

This was the mood of the people when the Secretary of State, Mr. Marshall, made his speech at Harvard on June 5th. This speech will be described in more detail later. Here it is only necessary to give its outline and to explain the extent to which it calmed and guided America's divided mind. Its starting point was the plain fact that there could be no political stability and economic recovery in Europe so long as men hungered and industry was halted for lack of materials and so long as hoarded foodstuffs and the shortage of manufactures produced all the dislocations of increasingly grave inflation. The nations of Europe had not the means to put an end to these dislocations by their own unaided efforts; therefore, if they would concert a programme of what they could do to help themselves, combined with an estimate of the extra assistance they would need from the New World, he would recommend that the United States should provide the needed assistance.

Mr. Marshall's speech restored American confidence. In the first place, it was avowedly peaceful. It declared hunger and poverty to be the enemies, not Communism. It invited all European nations without distinction to join in the consultations. It implied that the restoration of prosperity would prove the most efficacious method of keeping the peace. At the same time, it stressed the fact that the United States would not be carrying the whole burden but rather supplementing where necessary the efforts of other nations to help themselves. Compared with the negative and military character of the Truman Doctrine, the new Marshall Plan offered an outlet for American hopes and idealism, a positive plan for containing Communism and the possibility that within a reasonable time the non-American world would be able to stand on its own feet. The appeal of the new approach was immediate and widespread and in the six months between the enunciation of the Truman Doctrine and the calling of a Special Session of Congress in November to discuss the first phase of the Marshall Plan—Interim Aid to Italy, France and Austria, the three nations nearest to collapse—the attitude of the people changed almost unrecognizably. From a mood of doubt and frustration, they moved to a position of reasonable confidence. For the time being at least, they felt that once again they could see the road ahead and know that it lay towards a more peaceful and prosperous world.

They probably did not even reflect how far they had moved from their former position—of hankering after isolationism. Now they had even abandoned isolation's successor—the belief that an almost automatic revival of normal conditions would restore the old recognizable, familiar world. They stood on the brink of the heaviest and most generous international commitment ever taken by a nation in time of peace and before anyone really had the opportunity of working out an explanation, an isolationist had become a man who thought a 4-billion-dollar gift would be enough for Europe in the first year.

CHAPTER VII

BOOM AND DEPRESSION

The record of the United States which has been traced in some detail for the last fifty years is thus one of a fluctuating but sustained retreat from isolationism. Swings in the pendulum have occurred, but each time the backward swing has not receded as far as its point of departure, and the forward swing has always carried the people a few degrees closer to the idea of active co-operation. In the economic field, too, a definite line of advance has been maintained. Over the years, American prosperity has increased. But there have also been violent oscillations, and difficult as it would be to attempt an exact chart of the future of American thinking on international affairs, it would be a thousand times more difficult to make any sort of forecast about the next phases of America's economic development. As we have seen, the critics stress its "inherent instability" and denounce as folly any reliance upon sustained American assistance. The supporters of America stress its prosperity and claim that no other economy could have produced the surplus which the Americans at the moment are ready to share.

What are the facts? It is quite impossible in a book of this size to attempt an analysis of the American economic system, but the two factors of extreme prosperity and undoubted instability can perhaps be pursued a little further.

It has been pointed out in an earlier chapter that American geography and history provided the nation with unrivalled advantages in the creation of a modern capitalist industrial economy. It was, from the time the West was opened up, the largest free trade area in the world. It had all the necessary resources for industrial development. Starting relatively late in the industrial race, it profited by the accumulated capital and experience of the industrialized European nations which, with Britain at their head, began the industrialization of America, investing in every manner of enterprise. High tariffs protected these "infant industries" and grew with their growth into prodigious economic empires. On top of all this, the United States economy received two vital stimuli from outside—the two world wars. In neither was the territory of the United States involved, and in both, the necessity of providing the food and materials, not only for its own war effort, but for that of all its allies, brought about an economic expansion out of all proportion to the loss of wealth represented by sunken ships and exploded ammunition. Between 1915 and 1918, expenditure on new buildings and equipment rose from $600 million to $2.5 billion, a large proportion of which was clear gain to the country's permanent capital. The gross national product rose 15 per cent. between 1914 and 1918, while manufacturing increased by 37 per cent.

The war had another consequence. It accelerated the processes of standardization and of mass production, its urgency hurried the development of new scientific methods and the invention of new machinery. In the decade which followed—a decade of constantly expanding prosperity in almost every branch of the economy[1]—the productive capacity of the community as a whole and of each worker individually was stimulated by a phenomenal increase in the amount of horse-power put behind each pair of hands. Between 1919 and 1929 the horse-power per worker increased 49.5 per cent. in manufacture, 62.2 per cent. in agriculture and 60.3 per cent. in mining.

The Great Depression put an end for a time to this breathtaking expansion of wealth. In 1939 the levels of production were roughly those of 1929. But the second World War repeated the expansion of the first, this time on an even greater scale. Between 1939 and 1944,[2] as we have seen, the gross national

[1] The National Income increased from $59.4 billion in 1921 to $87.2 billion in 1929.

[2] Increases in American Production, 1939–42 :—

Item.	1939	1941	1943
Farm marketings, volume (1935–39=100), total	109	115	133
Crops	111	111	119
Livestock	108	119	144
Industrial production (1935–39=100)	109	162	239
Manufactures	109	168	258
Durable manufactures	109	201	360
Non-durable manufactures	109	142	176
Minerals	106	125	132
Selected commodities, production :—			
Coal, bituminous (thous. short tons) ..	394,855	514,149	590,177
Crude petroleum (mil. barrels)	1,265	2,402	1,506
Electric power, industrial and utility (mil. kw.hrs.)	161,308	208,306	267,540
Steel ingots and steel for castings (thous. short tons)	52,798	82,837	88,836

product increased by close on 100 per cent. In four years the Americans built up on top of their old economy a new one of almost equivalent size. The same phenomenal increases in manu-facture occurred, the same stimulus was given to new methods and the use of new materials. The United States in 1946 and 1947 was without peer in the world and its economic strength was unique in the entire history of mankind. No community had ever accumulated such wealth. No people had ever enjoyed such a standard of living.

So much for the prosperity—a phenomenal, astronomical prosperity compared either with the contemporary standards of the non-American world or with the levels reached by any past age. Yet any visitor to America in the last year must have re-marked the fact that the Americans themselves seemed less impressed by their wealth than worried by the fear of losing it. It is true that the years since the end of the war have been years not only of increasing wealth, but also of stress in the national economy, expressing itself chiefly in inflation and in troubled labour-management relations. Yet it was difficult at times to see why such disturbances, which were relatively such tiny ripples on the surface of the great flood of production pouring from the fields and the factories, should have given rise to such intense preoccupation and such real foreboding. The reason is that the American economy in the past has proved itself as un-stable as it has been brilliant. Like an inexplicable genius, its best performance is breath-taking, its worst unspeakable. And as with the genius, nobody can really fathom the reason for either standard.

The record of instability in the American economy is unmis-takable. At roughly ten-year intervals, production has slackened, unemployment has increased, prices have fallen, and after a period of stagnation, sometimes brief, sometimes rather longer, the economy has drawn breath and begun again the spiral of recovery. On two occasions in the past the most violent slumps have occurred after the equally violent maladjustments of war—in 1866 and 1867, after the Civil War; in 1920 and 1921, after the first World War. But the most prolonged depression to strike the United States began in 1929, and after two or three years in the trough, the economy had only managed ten years later to regain the level prevailing before the slump. This depression did more than retard the growth of American wealth. It delivered a desperate blow at the basis of business confidence and psychology in the United States. For some time it destroyed all trace of public confidence in bankers, business men and the Republican Party. And in the business world itself, it created a nervousness about the possibility of recessions, a tendency to feel the economy's pulse which has been particularly marked in the last two years. The nervousness is enhanced by the fact that few people are agreed on the causes of the catastrophic phenomenon and even fewer on what should be done to counter it. It is as though business men were swimmers condemned to bathe in seas known to produce vast tidal waves without any sort of warning.

It is this uncertainty of diagnosis and cure that makes it particularly difficult to answer or even argue with the critics of the American system who say "But America is heading for a depression and then there will be no European Recovery Programme." However, the criticism is too relevant to be ignored. Some attempts must be made to assess the likelihood of an American slump and its effect on aid to Europe. Perhaps the safest way lies in comparing the conditions preceding the slump of 1929 with the economic position to-day. It is, after all, of the 1929 Depression that most critics are thinking, for a short recession and readjustment might not necessarily have much effect upon America's foreign relations. The question is whether a slump of the proportions of 1929 will come to reduce American production by 50 per cent. and put an end to all giving and lending.

The first difficulty in analysing the conditions of the 1929 slump is the part played by "business confidence." Was it simply a sudden scare among investors great and small that toppled over the tremendous edifice of wealth built up during the boom? If so, may not the extreme consciousness of the risk of a depression which is observable in America to-day have the same effect? No dogmatic conclusions are offered throughout this chapter, but the evidence suggests that the slump of 1929 was preceded by solid economic phenomena—such as a fall in industrial productivity and a decrease in consumption—which would have led in time to a recession whatever Wall Street had done or not done meanwhile. The fantastic speculative boom of '28 and '29[1] merely made the crash more terrifying, sudden and precipitous and probably

[1] An index of its scale may be useful. Between 1925 and 1929 the number of shares listed rose from over 433 million to over 4,757 million, and in the first nine months of 1929, 300 million more were added.

involved a deeper plunge simply because prosperity had climbed so high and lost contact to such an extent with its foundations in real earnings. It is therefore to the deeper causes of economic disturbance that one must look for an explanation, and three at least bear a heavy share of the responsibility.[1]

The first is that in a completely unregulated capitalist system the demand for producers' goods—for machines, factories, installations, for all the means which go to produce consumers' goods —is necessarily cyclical. Equipment does not wear out at once. A factory, once installed, functions for a time without replacement. And since the extensions of plant and machinery are dictated by the confidence of thousands of unconnected *entrepreneurs*, their investments will tend to increase all at the same time when business prospects seem good and fall off at the same time when a decline sets in. Their psychology therefore hastens the boom and increases the slump. So incidentally do the traditional methods of governmental finance. When times are good and industry is buoyant the Government has less need for revenue to meet unemployment and other charges and can count on a high income from both direct and indirect taxation. The instinct is therefore to lower taxation and thus increase the upward trend of business. When a depression begins, revenue falls off as consumption falls and incomes dwindle. The need is therefore for more revenue and increased taxation. Thus the State helps to press the economy farther in its downward path.

The prelude to 1929 was no exception to this rule. The first warning notes were sounded in 1927. The fall in output began, as might be expected, in the producers' goods industries. Investment in capital goods fell by some $770 million. The building trade slackened its construction both of homes and of business premises. The output of new cars was 22 per cent. below the level of 1926. For eighteen months more the speculative boom continued, but the vast increases in stocks and shares no longer represented any real increase in the community's wealth. More and more of it was simply trading in title deeds of ownership as though they were real commodities. The crash, in fact, began in September, 1929 (after the news of the Hatry affair had caused a wave of uneasiness in both London and New York). But it would have come in any case before many months had past.

[1] The examples in the next pages are drawn from the United States, but the general criticism applies to any unregulated system based on industrial capitalism and would apply to the economic union to be established in Western Europe.

The second danger signal to appear in 1927 was a fall in consumption. One of the general explanations for the instability in capitalist society has long been the failure of the system to distribute sufficient purchasing power to consume the goods which in prosperous times are poured out in ever-increasing quantities. For one reason or another, the buying power of the millions lags more and more behind the producing power of the machines. Stocks pile up. Production slackens. Men become redundant and are dismissed and with the loss of their purchasing power consumption falls again. In 1927 the beginnings of this downward trend first showed themselves. For the first time since 1921 (with the exception of 1924) the increase in wages and salaries fell below $1.5 billion. In some years, the increase had been well above this average. Now it fell to only $400 million. Taking the wage bill by categories, there was little gain in manufacturing in spite of increases in output and there was a positive fall in building, mining, and trade. Unemployment increased and a decline took place in what is normally the most stable part of the market —the purchasing of perishable goods. Superficially at least it is possible to attribute this falling away simply to a slackening of demand in the capital goods sector of the economy. In fact, the evil went deeper. A study of the American National Income between 1923 and 1929 shows that while industrial production all but doubled between 1921 and 1929 the rising share of wages and salaries marked only a 40 per cent. increase. During the same period the share of the farmers in the National Income which had stood at 16 per cent. in 1919 fell to 8.8 per cent. in 1929. But dividends over the same period increased by 100 per cent. In other words, the lion's share of the wealth created by the new productivity was going to the relatively restricted circle of industrial property owners. The point can be measured in another way by pointing out that on an average in the 'twenties and 'thirties, 90 per cent. of the liquid wealth in the United States was held by only 10 per cent. of the families.

This failure to create a purchasing power corresponding to the machines' new capacity to produce was one of the deep causes of the decline in the American economy which began to show itself in 1927. It also affected the final snowballing of the crisis. When the warning signals of an exhausted market began to appear, the huge profits earned by business were not used either to increase wages, reduce prices or undertake new capital development—all policies which might have helped to arrest the decline. On the contrary, some part of the reserves held by industry were thrown into the speculators' saturnalia on Wall Street and helped the last steep ascent of the market before its spectacular collapse.

This fact throws light on a third cause of depressions—the tendency of heavy industry to organize itself on an increasingly monopolistic basis and thus court the temptation of selling fewer goods at a high scarcity profit instead of expanding output and recovering profits by large sales of cheap products. This element of rigidity can be overestimated. We have seen the extent to which industrial production expanded in America in the 'twenties. "Monopolists" who achieved the virtual doubling of the American economy in a few years can hardly be called timid. Yet it is true that after 1927 expansion slackened and profits instead of being ploughed back into capital development were ploughed under in Wall Street.

A more striking illustration of the failings in business planning can be seen in the fact that all the 'thirties could achieve was a return to the production of 1929. Yet by 1944 another doubling of the American economy had taken place. It is generally admitted that the chief agent in this phenomenal advance was the huge investment of the Government in war plants and their ancillaries, in other words a vast capital expansion. When this expansion had taken place, it was discovered that America had sufficient economic strength to devote nearly 50 per cent. of its resources to the war effort and, with the remaining production, achieve some surprising increases in the civilian standards of its people. What was more natural than to ask what heights of prosperity might not have been scaled had the whole 100 per cent. been devoted to the civilian sector? And what more obvious than to ask whether an economy which proved to have such a tremendous slack of manpower and materials to be taken in in 1939 was being given the degree of capital expansion by its business men that it could really afford? All the plans for capital development of all the big companies put together would hardly have doubled the economy in so short a time. Could it be that a completely unregulated system was beginning to be incapable of expanding production to the real economic limit of the country's capacity?

Such questions would have seemed heresy in 1929. If business itself could not produce the necessary capital expansion, there was only one other agency capable of doing so—the Government.

But in 1929 the Government was a business man's Government. In the first place, it faced the future with the blandest confidence.[1] In the second place, even if it had had forebodings, it would have been horrified at the thought of actively intervening in industrial policy. It was the Depression growing deeper as the 'thirties opened that changed the philosophy of America and prepared for its acceptance, under President Roosevelt's New Deal, of the thesis that government can be used as a purposeful instrument of economic stability and social progress.

This, then, was the background to the 1929 slump—wild speculation on Wall Street fed in part by the undistributed profits of business, a marked falling off of production in the capital goods sector spreading to other sections, a decline in purchasing power and in employment, and a Government committed by temperament and philosophy to non-intervention. Is the position in the United States comparable to-day?

It is impossible to make absolute predictions. When, in February, 1948, a sudden break occurred in grain prices, American comment seemed to be almost exactly divided between those who thought it was and those who thought it was not the signal for a recession. Prophets would in any case be warned by the unfortunates who in 1929 attempted over and over again to make categorical forecasts of returning stability. The difficulty is that even if all the factors are different from those of 1929, it does not follow that there will be no decline. In an economy of 145 million people, guided by the choices of thousands of different business executives and conditioned by the reactions of millions of farmers and workers, the factors pressing on production, on consumption, on contraction and expansion are so various that the chain reaction of the trade cycle may be set off in a thousand different places and for as many different causes. Yet having said all this, it is possible to say, very cautiously, that the major factors which have seemed to produce major depressions in the past were not very much in evidence in the American economy in the early spring of 1948.

In the first place, war itself had acted as an economic planner on a major scale. As we have seen, it had doubled capacity and given the country an unparalleled capital expansion. During the

[1] In his message to Congress on the State of the Union in December, 1928, Mr. Coolidge, the outgoing President, declared " No Congress of the United States ever assembled . . . has met with a more pleasing prospect than that which appears at the present time."

war, much of the new product was blown up or burnt down or sunk. As soon as war ended the question of replacing civilian needs, restoring peacetime industry, taking up delayed plans of modernization were sufficient to fill the order books of heavy industry for years ahead. At the time of writing, there is no sign of any exhaustion of this demand. On the contrary, the industrialists who were called in to prepare the material for the European Recovery Programme (ERP) on the Harriman Committee reported almost without exception in the autumn of 1947 that the pressure of domestic demand was so great that surpluses for export abroad on the scale demanded could be provided only if there were some rationing of the home market.

The war also expanded in a sensational way the purchasing power of the people. As we have seen, before the war 90 per cent. of the liquid wealth was in the hands of 10 per cent. of the families. To-day the percentage has fallen to about 60 per cent. Wage increases have been won in almost every industry—average earnings were nearly doubled between 1940 and 1946—and inflation has not robbed the increase of all its value. Two branches of the economy which were chronically depressed before the war, the miners and the farm workers, have secured a remarkable rise in their standard of living. But perhaps the most startling increase in purchasing power has occurred among the farmers. Farm prices which were almost invariably below all other prices throughout the 'twenties and 'thirties and reached their nadir in 1932 (falling to 40 per cent. of the 1929 level) have increased since 1942 out of all proportion to any other prices. Between 1942 and 1947, the price of wheat rose from a dollar a bushel to 2.5 dollars. In the autumn of 1947, when drought seemed to threaten a poor harvest in 1948, and it was clear that the whole world was clamouring for grain, prices rose again, even more sharply, to reach the record figure of over $3 a bushel (in the trough of the Depression the average was about 70 cents). These prices, coupled with a great increase in output and a marked increase in mechanization, flooded the farming community with a prosperity it had not known before.

The war also modified the tendency of the more organized and cartellized sections of industry to check expansion. As we have seen, the expansion of capital to make possible America's war effort heaved the whole American community up into a new high level of production and exchange. It is true that there have been some signs of timidity in the last two years. New industrialists, such as Mr. Henry Kaiser, who are attempting to break into the sacred ring of steel, motor manufacture, and Wall Street finance, complain that every obstacle is put in their way. The hearings before the Harriman Committee led to a violent disagreement between the industrial and non-industrial members, the former asserting that a further expansion of steel production was physically impossible, the latter that at least 3 million tons more a year could be produced to meet the urgent needs of both Europe and the domestic market. It may well have been this struggle that led the powerful leader of the United Automobile Workers, Mr. Walter Reuther, early in 1948 to denounce the steel industry for practising monopolistic restriction in the interests of maintaining scarcity prices. Even so, the disagreement must seem a little fantastic to European ears. Which is the decisive figure? The 3 million extra tons that could be produced or the 76 million tons of ingots and castings that in fact flow from the mills? It may be that left to themselves the business leaders in the steel industry would fail to expand and might even contract their business. The fact remains that for the time being, the production not only of steel but of every other basic commodity is so fantastically large that it is difficult to list failures of expansion as a probable cause of recession in 1948.

Other economic differences could be noted—for instance, the almost complete absence of a Wall Street boom. On the contrary, industrial stocks are listed, on the whole, below their actual earning value. But it can be argued that the biggest contrast between 1929 and 1948 lies not in the economic but in the political sphere. The old bland confidence has vanished. Most Americans believe strongly in the free enterprise system but few of them are confident that it has found any solution for the recurring crises of depression and unemployment. In fact, for the last two years, the business world has tended to sit with its hand on its own pulse, watching anxiously for any sign of rising fever. Whereas in 1929 and 1930, statesmen, business leaders and experts of all kinds kept repeating that prosperity was just round the corner, the mood in 1946 and 1947 was the exact opposite. Every wobble in the price line, every tendency of prices to break was immediately greeted with openly expressed fears of an immediate recession.

The other political revolution is the changed American concept of what government may and may not do. Since the war, there has been, it is true, a great revolt against Government controls most of which, including price control, were flung aside in 1945. In 1946, the electors gave the Republicans, the anti-control party, a majority at the polls for the first time since 1928. But the Republicans of 1946 would have seemed reckless Socialists to the men who in 1929 held the old dogmatic belief in complete government non-intervention. In particular, the Government's overriding responsibility to take measures to check depressions and to ensure full employment have been written into the Statute Book. It can perhaps be said with a measure of confidence that if a slump started the pressures on the Government to do something to check it would be not only bigger but quite different in kind from those operating in 1929 and 1930. To give only one example, many Americans have accepted the Keynesian thesis that the planned contraction and expansion of capital investment is the best way of securing stable development in an economy; and they can argue that America's wartime experience has borne out the theory, for what is an armament programme but a programme of public works on an unbelievably ambitious scale?

This summary of the chief differences between 1929 and 1948 can perhaps answer one question. If depression comes in 1948, it will not have precisely the same immediate causes as those of 1929, nor is it likely to follow the same course or to occur on the same shattering scale. But it is not possible to answer with any certainty the two much more searching questions: is a depression already on its way? If not, is America feeling its way towards the permanent elimination of the trade cycle?

In 1948 the chief immediate reasons for believing in an early depression were, first of all, that wars have in the past been followed by depressions, secondly, that the post-war inflation has rocketed to such a height that the people's power to buy cannot keep pace with the steadily rising cost of merchandise, thirdly, that, as a result of the price-wage spiral, costs of production have been getting out of hand and discouraging new investment, fourthly, stocks and inventories are higher than they have been, fifthly, taxation is heavy and this, too, discourages further expansion. When, therefore, in February, the commodity markets, in which during the winter there had been considerable speculation, broke sharply and wheat fell 70 cents in a few days, the immediate reaction was to announce the depression. Second thoughts, however, reminded the public that in 1946 and 1947 there had been similar oscillations in the price line. Indeed, the 1947 fall had been sharper. There was, too, a reasonable localized explanation for the sag in wheat. The 1948 harvest was after all promising to be a good crop and the expectation of shortage, upon which the fantastic autumn increase had been based, vanished with the good news from Iowa and Kansas. It was therefore possible to maintain that the 70 cent fall—which left the price of wheat still above the already inflated levels of 1947—represented no more than a squeezing out of excessive inflation. In spite of all the tremors and uncertainties, the depression still seemed to be holding off. Meanwhile, the slight fall in price was of some assistance to the European Recovery Programme. It meant that the dollars voted would procure more grain. It also meant that some farmers began for the first time to cock a watchful eye at their European markets and to wonder whether after all Government buying of grain and meat might not prove a valuable bolster to farm incomes.

But if a certain tentative optimism is permissible for the immediate prospect, the further outlook is by no means so promising. Perhaps the greatest question-mark hanging over European recovery is, paradoxically, America's chance of avoiding a major depression. It is difficult to believe that with a serious fall in American production and employment, the Republicans—or the Democrats either for that matter—would be able to resist the traditional policy of retrenchment on Government expenditure, and popular feeling would need considerable education to accept the proposal that free gifts should be given to the Ruhr and not to Pittsburg. In the past, depressions have always given the signal for an American withdrawal upon itself almost automatic enough to appear a reflex action. It would need leadership even more inspired than that of Mr. Roosevelt to persuade the Americans that "international pump priming" was the road to recovery. And even if the idea of pump priming were accepted (and as we have seen, there is at least a chance that it would be) the overwhelming demand would be to see the domestic pump primed first.

Apart from the financing of recovery, the problem of the physical availability of supplies would also arise in an urgent form. Between 1929 and 1932, steel production fell from 56 million tons to just over 13 millions. Wheat and cotton were ploughed in, hogs destroyed, millions of acres withdrawn from cultivation.

Perhaps the world has escaped from that degree of insanity. In particular, the pressure of Communism which would increase fifty-fold in a period of depression might keep America off the disastrous road of total domestic deflation and drastic withdrawal from the international scene. But the fact must be faced that all past experience suggests a strengthening in the United States of the tendencies to withdrawal and isolation when times are bad.

And will they be bad? The difficulty in believing that America can avoid a depression in the long run lies in the fact that none of the basic maladjustments in capitalist industrial society has yet been overcome in the United States (or, indeed, in any other free community). The two chief corrections introduced by the war—a vast expansion of industrial capacity and a better distribution of purchasing power—are not necessarily permanent and neither the political parties nor any influential economic group are committed to seeing that the old maladjustments do not reappear. The concept of "planning" is unpopular, and the conduct of Russia and of the East European governments in the last two years has made it more so. Few people are prepared to consider whether a "high and stable level of capital investment" can be secured without grave modifications of the free enterprise system. Government intervention may not be as anathema as it was ten years ago and, if trouble started, something would be done. The point here is that no policy has been thought out in advance to prevent the trouble starting and heaven knows whether a European Recovery Programme might not slip out in the gap between the onslaught of a crisis and the Government's first moves to bring it under control.

This, clearly, is the great hope to which the Russians cling. If a capitalist community such as the United States could in the next ten years increase its own prosperity and draw up Europe in its wake, the political consequences would be incalculable. So far, however, there is no reason for the Kremlin to doubt the accuracy of its Marxist predictions. The United States has not yet had its slump—that is true; equally, it has given little enough proof so far that it knows how to avoid one.

CHAPTER VIII

IS AMERICA IMPERIALIST?

Two criticisms of American policy have still to be examined—the major criticism that behind its cloak of democratic politics and economic assistance the United States is an expanding imperialist Power bent on world domination, the second, minor criticism, that aid to Europe cannot become an issue above party and will therefore collapse with a change of government.

The lines of the major criticism are reasonably familiar. They are the stock in trade of Marxists everywhere and non-Marxists of the notoriety of Mr. Henry Wallace in America have gone far to make them their own. These men believe that the United States has embarked upon a policy of economic domination which may at any time be backed by military means. They argue that the expansion of American business in the United States during the recent war is now being followed by a new pressure to find markets elsewhere and to bring them under exclusive American influence. American business men have received initial advantages in Germany and Japan, American companies are buying up firms "on the cheap" in Italy and France, American goods are flooding into the Middle and Far East and driving out those of non-American competitors. Wherever this expansion goes, so runs the argument, reactionary regimes are bolstered up or popular democratic regimes are crushed out of existence and in their place are set up governments of bankers subservient to the interests of Wall Street. It is, therefore, obvious that the European Recovery Programme is simply one more tactic in the general strategy of American economic imperialism. Threatened with tremendous surpluses at home and by the dwindling of dollar reserves abroad, ERP is simply a device for dumping American goods in Europe and thus capturing the markets permanently for American exploitation. Behind ERP, as behind everything else, lies the cool brain and limitless ambition of "the trusts and Wall Street."

But this is not all. Not content with economic control, the United States is ready, should a depression come, to secure political and military control as well. Seen in this light, Western Europe is to be built up solely as the springboard for an attack on the only Power capable of challenging both American supremacy and its capitalist mode of production. Behind every other American move is the fundamental aim of attacking and annihilating Soviet Russia. Thus stated, the criticism of "American imperialism" appears in its extremest form. Many critics would not press it so far. They would say not that America is consciously planning an imperialist struggle, but merely drifting in that direction. But in essence, this is the picture which every organ of Communist propaganda is driving into any ear that will listen and into all the ears that must.

What is to be said of it? First, perhaps that to assume a sustained and detailed strategy for any nation governed as is the United States is to assume the impossible. By the time the great issues of American foreign policy have been submitted to the divided attentions of the White House, the State Department and Congress, its broad aim may just possibly be still unaffected. Its tactics are all over the place. It is inherently impossible for the United States to be as constant and as Machiavellian as its critics make out. If the drive to imperialism is there, it is the product of a hundred contending forces working without much conscious direction—which, of course, is what the more determinist of America's critics claim it to be. The question to be answered, therefore, is whether the inner pressures of American society are driving it towards imperialism and war.

History is not very kind to the critics. There has been in the twentieth century a big expansion of American business interests in various parts of the world, although their activities have been small compared with the tremendous levels of production achieved in the United States. But even where the concentrations of economic power have been greatest—for instance, in the Middle Eastern oilfields—no attempt has been made to follow it up with political control on the classical nineteenth century models of imperialism. The island of Bahrein, where America had all the economic assets and Britain the political liabilities, was something of a symbol of America's lack of interest in political control so long as another nation—in most cases Britain—was providing a framework of stability. Only in one case has the United States fought a definitely expansionist war—when at the end of the nineteenth century it drove Spain out of Cuba and the

Philippines and established its own rule there for a time. However, both countries have since acquired a more or less real degree of national sovereignty and the tendency in America has been to relax not tighten its imperial control.

Another imperialist blot on America's copy book can be found in its relations with Latin America in the first twenty years of this century. Many of the methods whereby the control of Panama and the pacification of the Central American republics were obtained do not bear close examination, with the result that "Yankee" or "dollar imperialism" became a byword South of the Rio Grande. Here again, however, the tendency has been not to tighten American control, but to retreat completely from the exposed imperialist position. After 1928, President Hoover began a tentative "Good Neighbour" policy, which President Roosevelt triumphantly developed into the Pan-American system of co-operation between equal partners which functions more or less successfully to-day.

But perhaps the most spectacular development in relations between the United States and Latin America occurred in 1938, when the Left Wing Government of Mexico suddenly expropriated and nationalized America's large share in the Mexican oil industry. Any imperialist aggressor worth his salt would have instantly taken violent action to meet so direct a challenge to its interests and to its way of life. In fact, the United States did even less than the British Government (which precipitately broke off diplomatic relations). There was no invasion, no military threats, no forced changes in the Mexican Government. For an imperialist Power determined to secure the triumph of the free enterprise system and the liquidation of democracy, the American Government behaved with unaccountable mildness.

It is difficult to avoid the conclusion that on the record of the United States' activities overseas hitherto the charge of imperialist expansion is hard to sustain.

And it is not only the lack of major imperialist adventures that is surprising. The timing and development of America's foreign interventions must be perplexing to the critic bent on fitting the United States into the imperialist pattern. For instance, if the tendency towards imperialist expansion increases with the development of industrialization and with the aggravation of the contradictions inherent in capitalism, why did the United States pass through a more boisterous and warlike phase in its earlier days and turn to non-intervention in its neighbours' affairs at a later date? The war against Mexico, the war against Spain, intervention in Central America took place either well before the first World War or were coincident with it. The Good Neighbour policy on the other hand was the product of the 'thirties and 'forties of this century. How, then, can this development be explained in terms of a theory which makes an advanced capitalist community increasingly prone to the temptations of imperialism?

Another curious fact to be explained is that the depressions which should have stimulated the United States (as they stimulated Germany and Japan) to imperialist adventure have led, on the contrary, to an intensification of isolationist feeling and a contraction both of external political liabilities and external economic activity. In the past, Americans have not sought to break economic deadlocks at home by conquering new markets abroad. On the contrary, they have cut foreign lending and foreign trading to the bone.[1]

At this point the critic will probably say: "But we are not referring to the past. The United States is only now advancing into its imperialist phase. We refer to the last two years during which America has extended its economic hold on foreign countries, but particularly on Europe—a process which will go further under ERP—has encouraged and supported every reactionary and anti-democratic force and has, above all, consistently plotted war against Soviet Russia."

There is no space in these few pages to give a really detailed examination of these criticisms which in fact add up to a damning indictment of everything the United States has done in Europe (or elsewhere) in the last two years, but it is at least possible to take some of the dogmatic certainty out of each statement. First, then, the question of economic control: the main American economic intervention in Europe in the last two years has been by loans and gifts, largely to Governments. The direct evidence of Americans buying up foreign undertakings (the rumours circu-

---

[1]

					Exports of U.S. merchandise.	Short-term U.S. loans.
					(millions of dollars)	
1929	..	..	..	..	..	5,157.0	2,672.7
1930	..	..	..	..	..	3,781.1	2,335.0
1931	..	..	..	..	..	2,377.9	1,303.5
1932	..	..	..	..	..	1,576.1	745.6
1933	..	..	..	..	..	1,647.2	392.0

late chiefly in France and Italy) is very slight. The largest venture appears to be the lease of prospecting rights for oil in Northern Italy. Not only are actual examples difficult to find. The general scale of such operations is rendered somewhat suspect by the fact that one of the principal complaints made by the Right against Left-wing governments in Europe is that they have "frightened American capital away"—this line is being pressed particularly vigorously by the Conservative opposition in Britain. The facts of the American situation—the booming internal market, the relatively small part traditionally played by foreign investment—also suggests that the degree of American business expansion in Europe has been exaggerated.

As for the suggestion that ERP will be used as a spearhead of control, the contrary cannot yet be proved since the Plan has still to run its course. Yet two facts suggest caution. The first is that the Plan is essentially one of industrial revival with the aim of restoring a viable and independent Europe. The idea that the United States will not in five years' time be bearing so heavy a European commitment is one of the chief attractions of the scheme. The second point is the Americans' scrupulous care taken so far to avoid demanding an economic (or political) *quid pro quo* for the gifts that are to be made. This mood of disinterested generosity may pass, but when one remembers how dire was Europe's plight in 1947, how desperate its need for help and how ready some of its more hardly pressed governments were to give away anything they were asked for, America's restraint can only mean one thing—to the unbiased eye—that imperialist control of Europe was neither the open nor the covert aim of ERP.

The second charge—that the United States has fostered reactionary forces and sought to destroy the working class—has to be clarified before it can be answered. If "reactionaries" means all non-Communists and "the working class" means the Communist Party, then certainly the United States like everybody else has found it impossible to work with Communists and has placed its reliance on the others. But they have not, of course, been liquidated in Western Europe as anti-Communists have been in the East. Only in Greece has the party been repressed. Nevertheless, nobody can accuse the Americans of encouraging Communism. At best they have only tolerated it and certainly the removal of Communists from the coalition governments of

France and Italy in the early summer of 1947 made them more acceptable to American opinion.

However, criticism of American policy goes far beyond the naïve Communist simplification quoted above. Many who are very far from Communist doubt the wisdom of American policy in Germany, for instance, where reliance on profoundly conservative elements has encouraged particularism and separatism, increased economic instability and discouraged the necessarily small group of genuine anti-Nazis who could be relied on to work against the evil legacy of Hitler and his works. If the American failure can justifiably be summed up in a single phrase, it amounts to this: on the morrow of victory, it might have been possible to make the dominant force in Western Europe—as in Western Germany—a progressive constitutional alliance of Social Democrats and the more radical Christians. One of the reasons—there are, of course, many others—why this possibility was not realized was the hostility of the local American officials to the whole idea of Social Democracy (which they found indistinguishable from Communism) and the inability of many responsible Americans to see that the business men who greeted them and talked their own language in France, in Italy, in the Low Countries, above all in Germany, had often been the first to collaborate in Hitler's New Order. The Americans, in a word, came to Europe with a certain political innocence and a lack of critical understanding of what the links between National Socialism and sections of the business world had been. The result was that in Germany in particular, American rule became identified with "reaction" and the accusation was not wholly false.

Yet it would be utterly unjust to pin on the Americans all the blame for the relative failure of Europe's non-Communist yet progressive forces. British policy was confused and fumbling. The Communists strained every nerve to break the Socialists away from the Centre and the moderate Right. The ideas linking the Christian parties and the Socialists were in many cases too nebulous to provide a basis and a policy for a new grouping. Yet even now the possibility is not entirely dead. Remnants of it are to be found in the coalitions of Holland, Belgium, France, and Italy and, under less stringent economic conditions, the ideas might flower again. And then it would be seen that although the United States intervention in Europe has been one factor in checking the growth of a genuine social democracy, there is little in the

American position inherently hostile to such an evolution. The fact that in Britain the Labour Party acquired an overwhelming majority at the polls in 1945 did not make it any more difficult for Britain to receive a large American loan a few months later— a fact hardly compatible with America's supposed war to the knife on social democracy.

Again, the absence from Interim Aid and from the first instalment of ERP of any ban on nationalization or the purposive direction of each nation's economy is again hardly the act of a government out to destroy socialism and restore complete *laisserfaire*. Even in Germany, although the American administration locally has frowned on measures of socialization, a sharp reminder came to General Clay from Washington in the middle of 1947 that socialization would be the concern of the German people and could be introduced by their popular vote. The criticism of America must therefore be reduced from an accusation of deliberately thwarting progressive developments to one of having failed to realize the real implications of post-Hitlerian Europe and thus of becoming one instrument (among many) in the resurgence of conservative and even reactionary forces.

The criticism—closely allied to that of imperialism—that America is planning a war on Russia and organizing Western Europe as a well-equipped battlefield—has to some extent been dealt with already in the chapter dealing with the development and decline of isolationism in the United States. But the charge is so grave that it must be examined rather more closely. Criticism is usually based on three different points. The first is the continued manufacture of atom bombs. The second is the action of the United States in occupying strategic islands in the Pacific and of arranging for such "warlike acts" as continued staff talks with Britain or the introduction of universal military service. The third is the amount of war talk in the United States.

The accusation of plotting atomic war cannot be sustained. There is no reason to doubt the Americans' good faith in offering to place the whole secret and the whole manufacture of atomic energy under international control provided the conditions of inspection are adequate. The American Government can hardly be blamed if Russia's tragic suspicions of the outside world led the masters of the Kremlin to suspect a trap in the inspection clause. Against the various measures of military preparations mentioned by the critics must be set the absolutely incomprehensible policy (if America has really been planning a war) of allowing every section of the Armed Forces to fall so far below strength that the maintenance of armies of occupation has become a positive embarrassment. And even if the introduction of conscription is part of the "plot," Congress fought hard against its introduction, for obviously it was not a popular measure for an election year. (It could also be pointed out in passing that if the United States' first priority were an offensive alliance with, say, Britain, its policy in Palestine makes no sense at all.)

As for war talk, in a sense it is certainly a danger signal. There are emotional depths in the American people that can be stirred to violent reaction by provocation or disaster outside their country, but in the last two decades it has taken a direct attack on their navy to exacerbate these reactions to the pitch of war. Russian policy has made every clumsy gesture conceivable to whip up a war fever in the United States and there is admittedly an awful temptation in the belief that the atom bomb would be the quick arbiter in a struggle. But in the last year, war talk has hardly increased. In fact, the announcement of the Marshall Plan steadied public opinion and, spreading out from the Department of Defence, from the State Department and from responsible opinion generally, the view has been gaining ground that "invertebrate Russia" cannot be given a knock-out blow by any bomb, atomic or otherwise, and that the last error America could make would be to invite the fate of Napoleon and Hitler. In an article widely recognized to be authoritative, written by "X" in July, 1947, in *Foreign Affairs*, the proposal was made that the United States should reconcile itself to a long period of "no-war, no-peace," during which time Russia would be contained—in other words, permitted no further advances—while the rest of the world would build up its prosperity and wait for the forces of time and history to solve the Russian problem. This policy of containment, combined with the project of positive action under the Marshall Plan to rebuild the non-Russian world, gave many Americans the sensation that here was a policy they could pursue without risk of war, and there was no doubt at all which of the two alternatives—containment or preventive war—they preferred.

The United States must be substantially cleared of the charges of imperialism and warmongering. Political mistakes have been made in Europe, it is true, but it is doubtful if they would have been so dangerous or so influential if they had not been so lavishly exploited by the Communist opposition. Americans are not the only group that have found it impossible to work with the Communists. Almost every group in Europe is now in the same case. And although America's natural instinct is sometimes to co-operate with conservative men and groups who, in the European context, may be dangerous bedfellows, conscious policy takes a wider view and in a Europe determined on its own account to work out the unsolved tension between freedom and planning, American opposition would fade—and might well change, if the experiment were successful, to enthusiastic support.

There remains the last criticism—that a change of Government will sweep ERP away. This is simply inaccurate. The most remarkable fact about the American scene since the war has been the maintenance of reasonable unity between Republican and Democrat on the broad issues of foreign policy. That this is so is due above all to the work and personality of two men. One is Mr. Marshall, whose integrity, disinterestedness and tremendous reputation acquired in other spheres place him a little above the ordinary political arena. It is rare to hear policies connected with his name denounced as Democratic or party policies. His position puts the stamp of national interest on all that he proposes. The other man is the Republican Senator from Michigan, Mr. Arthur Vandenberg. The part he has played cannot be overestimated. However impregnable Mr. Marshall's position, a Republican opposition spoiling for a fight would have succeeded in dragging his policies into the arena. The reason they have not done so is overwhelmingly the work of one man. Senator Vandenberg was a convinced isolationist up to the time of Pearl Harbour. Since then his conversion has been steady and complete. He took part in the deliberations on the United Nations Charter, and became the foremost Republican exponent of international co-operation. The extent of his conversion first became clearly visible when the debates on the Marshall Plan began. Senator Vandenberg's masterly handling of the debates in the Senate and his unchallenged leadership within the Republican Party enabled the Administration to withstand every attack and present the Plan to the country as the agreed policy of both great parties.

CHAPTER IX

MR. MARSHALL'S INITIATIVE

Many pages will be written in years to come to dispute the precise origins of Mr. Marshall's speech at Harvard. Part of the truth is that in the spring of 1947 the situation itself was pressing America in the direction of a new initiative. Two years of attempted collaboration with the Russians had convinced the leaders in the West that their desire for a working relationship was entirely one-sided and that Russia could be relied on to exploit every weakness, every grievance, every economic disturbance to extend its own power and influence. At the same time, the economic crisis, after a rally in 1946, was deepening daily. The reserves of gold and dollars at the disposal of the European nations were running out with increasing speed and the gap between the imports they needed to stave off collapse and revolt and those they could actually pay for was growing wider with each month that passed. It was against this unpromising background that, as we have seen, the unpopular Truman doctrine was announced.

At about the same time the Council of Foreign Ministers met at Moscow to discuss Germany for the first time in the presence of Mr. Marshall, who had just succeeded Mr. James Byrnes as Secretary of State. The conference ended in deadlock, but if the evidence of eye-witnesses is to be believed, the point which most impressed Mr. Marshall was not his weeks of tedious argument in the council chamber but his interview with Marshal Stalin in the course of which the Marshal remarked that Russia did not take these delays too tragically for he, Stalin, was certain that time would bring about agreement. This chance remark convinced Mr. Marshall that the Russian leaders were certain that time was on their side and the more he reflected on it the more he felt that they were probably right. If nothing was done to arrest the drift in Europe, the Continent was slipping towards a major economic upheaval with all the political consequences such an upheaval would entail. Either action would have to be taken to check the catastrophe, or time would deliver the keys of Europe into Communist hands. From that moment, Mr. Marshall cast about for the appropriate initiative.

Since it was the pressure of events themselves that were forcing the crisis on American attention, it is not surprising that other men in the State Department were coming to Mr. Marshall's conclusion at about the same time. One of the first signals of a new line of approach was a speech delivered by the retiring Under-Secretary of State, Mr. Dean Acheson, at Cleveland, Ohio, early in May in which he urged Americans to accept the responsibility of financing Europe's deficit until such time as the ravages of war would have really been repaired. Three weeks later, the same idea, clarified, developed and related to the widest issues of public policy appeared in Mr. Marshall's speech at Harvard on June 5th.

The essence of this speech can best be given in the Secretary of State's own words:—

". . . In considering the requirements for the rehabilitation of Europe, the physical loss of life, the visible destruction of cities, factories, mines, and railroads was correctly estimated, but it has become obvious during recent months that this visible destruction was probably less serious than the dislocation of the entire fabric of European economy. . . . The rehabilitation of the economic structure of Europe quite evidently will require a much longer time and greater effort than had been foreseen . . .

"The truth of the matter is that Europe's requirements for the next three or four years of foreign food and other essential products—principally from America—are so much greater than her present ability to pay that she must have substantial additional help, or face economic, social, and political deterioration of a very grave character.

". . . It is logical that the United States should do whatever it is able to do to assist in the return of normal economic health to the world, without which there can be no political stability and no assured peace. Our policy is directed, not against any country or doctrine, but against hunger, poverty, desperation, and chaos. Its purpose should be the revival of a working economy in the world so as to permit the emergence of political and social conditions in which free institutions can exist. . . . Any assistance that this Government may render in the future should provide a cure rather than a mere palliative.

". . . Before the United States Government can proceed much further in its efforts to alleviate the situation and help start the European world on its way to recovery, there must be some agreement among the countries of Europe as to the requirements of the situation and the part those countries themselves will take in order to give proper effect to whatever action might be undertaken by this Government. It would be neither fitting nor efficacious for this Government to undertake to draw up unilaterally a program designed to place Europe on its feet economically. . . . The initiative . . . must come from Europe. The role of this country should consist of friendly aid in the drafting of a European program and of later support of such a program so far as it may be practical for us to do so. The program should be a joint one agreed to by a number, if not all European nations."

There are three points to be underlined in Mr. Marshall's approach. He is concerned, not with piecemeal relief, but with "the rehabilitation of the economic structure of Europe." The programme is not to be patching here and fixing there, but an attempt to rebuild an organic functioning European economy. The second point is that the work to be done is to an overwhelming extent the responsibility of the Europeans themselves. They must take the initiative and work out the Plan. The role of the United States will be confined to giving such aid as conditions in America permit. Thirdly, it is not individual nations but Europe as a whole that must concert the plan and draw up the programme of recovery. As we have seen, the United States had already spent two years giving out assistance, nation by nation, to the tune of some 9 billion dollars. The really new element in the Marshall offer was this insistence that future aid should be fitted into a co-operative framework, that the nations of Europe should cease to jostle each other in the relief queue and come together as a single co-operative team to make the best use of whatever supplies could be made available.

Another matter which historians will debate is the degree of response Mr. Marshall expected his speech to arouse in Europe. In the past, it has not been usual for major developments in foreign policy to be announced at an academic function and it may be that the Harvard speech, like the Cleveland speech, was a *ballon d'essai*. If so, the speed and scale of the reply from Europe

must have surprised even Mr. Marshall and his advisers.[1] Within
a few days of receiving the text of the speech, Mr. Bevin had flown
to Paris, made certain of France's willingness to become joint
sponsor of a conference on European recovery, issued an invitation to Russia to concert an agenda and fixed the preliminary
Three Power talks for the next week-end. The opportunity offered
at Harvard had been decisively seized and Mr. Bevin's chief claim
to greatness in his career as Foreign Secretary may well prove to
be the fact that without his instant response the curtain might
never have gone up on the great drama of European recovery.

European recovery in the full sense, however, it was not to be.
The attempt to draw Russia into the talks failed. Neither Mr.
Bevin nor M. Bidault could convince Mr. Molotov that the
whole initiative was not an attempt to trap Russia and to pene-
trate its East European "security zone" under the pretext of
economic revival. No agreement could be reached on a programme for the proposed conference. Mr. Molotov said that the
proposals of Britain and France infringed the national sovereignty
of the European nations and had in any case been "framed" by
them. After two days' fruitless effort, the Soviet delegation withdrew and its withdrawal entailed the refusal of the Czechs and
Poles to attend, even though the Polish Government had given a
favourable preliminary response and the Czech Government had
formally accepted the Anglo-French invitation. Thus the hope of
a new effort at recovery which would cover the whole of Europe
faded. The division would remain and the recovery programme
would be confined to the lands outside the Russian sphere of
influence, all of them with the exception of Greece and Turkey
lying in Western Europe. The Representatives of Sixteen Nations
assembled in Paris early in July,[2] they formed a Committee of
European Economic Co-operation (the CEEC) under the chairmanship of the chief British delegate, Sir Oliver Franks, and set
to work to draw up estimates of what they could do to help
themselves in the next four years and of how big a deficit would
still have to be made good by American assistance.

[1] One American newspaper thus irreverently summed up America's surprise at
the moves in Europe : " We expected them to jump 2 inches and they've jumped
6 feet."

[2] They were : Austria, Belgium, Denmark, Eire, France, Greece, Iceland, Italy,
Luxemburg, the Netherlands, Norway, Portugal, Sweden, Switzerland, Turkey, and
the United Kingdom. The role of Western Germany in the programme was also
taken into account. Spain was excluded on obvious political grounds.

The preparation of their report—which came to be known as the Paris Report—was carried on by a number of technical sub-committees under the guidance of a central committee. In those days of stifling sub-tropical heat when the thermometer obstinately refused to fall all night and temperatures exceeded those of Dakar, the goad spurring on the toiling delegates was the need for speed. Not only were they driven forward by a further deterioration of the economic situation caused by the failure of eleven different harvests in various parts of the world. Every message from Washington spoke of the American Administration's insistence on speed and its desire to have the finished Report in time to call, if necessary, a special session of Congress to consider it before Christmas.

Early in September the Report was virtually completed. Then occurred an incident which, relatively unimportant in itself, deserves some attention, for it was a reminder of the kind of difficulty which might arise throughout the four years of the Marshall Plan and it gave the European nations at the very outset a hint of the type of criticism to which their efforts were and would continue to be most vulnerable. It became known that the American administration were very dissatisfied with various aspects of the Report in its draft form and Mr. Clayton, at that time Under-Secretary for State, arrived in Paris to secure certain modifications. The intervention was carried out in a somewhat abrupt manner and some of the European delegations took offence. The Communist press expanded on the theme delightedly, reminding the Western nations that this was precisely the kind of invasion of their national sovereignty against which Mr. Molotov had warned them. "Plan as carefully as you like," they said in effect, "and the Americans will come in and trample all over your work." The irritations raised by the American method of giving advice soon subsided, but they were the first sharp reminder of a political fact of cardinal importance—that between the United States on the one hand, and the Sixteen Nations on the other, a working relationship could be established over the years only if both sides exercised the utmost forbearance and remembered that nothing is so sore as national dignity and nothing so easy to outrage as national pride.

The criticisms themselves had more substance and they deserve to be set out at length, for they had an immediate influence on the shaping of the Plan and are likely to recur throughout its implementation. The most urgent criticism concerned the scale of the deficit which the European nations were proposing to ask the United States to cover. The figure has not been officially published but it is believed to have been in the neighbourhood of $30 billion over the four years. This, Mr. Clayton said, was absurd and would ensure from the start that no American Congressman would be persuaded to look at the programme. But his criticism was not simply concerned with what Americans would swallow. He was convinced that the sum itself was excessive and that the methods by which it had been computed were unsound. He pointed out that the different national delegations had simply put in their claims and that the central committee had made virtually no attempt to screen the estimates in order to determine whether or not they were exaggerated. The committee could reply that the time-table to which, at America's request, they had worked made any such scrutiny impossible. Not only was the statistical apparatus in most countries extremely faulty. The attempt to scrutinize their figures at that stage might have split the conference from stem to stern on the reef of outraged nationalism. The committee had not been able in two short months, working under extreme pressure, to exorcise the jealous nationalism of centuries. The defence was reasonable, but it left a trace of suspicion at the back of some American minds.

Mr. Clayton's other criticisms were more specific. Two concerned the nation's domestic policies. He complained that they had not given sufficient guarantees or explicit proof that they would put an end to inflation, stabilize their currencies and balance their budgets. Nor had they given any formal undertaking to reach the targets for domestic production which they had been ready to write into the Report. Another criticism concerned the financing of the deficit. Mr. Clayton asked why the whole load had been placed on the United States Treasury and no attempt made to explore alternative methods of financing, such as the International Bank. The rest of the criticisms were really different aspects of the same thing—the alleged failure of the Sixteen Nations to achieve a genuine measure of co-operation. The whisper had been going round Paris that the Report would be little more than Western Europe's "shopping list" and Mr. Clayton voiced a similar fear when he attacked the various Governments for lacking "guiding principles of common action." There was every sign, he complained, of pressure for individual national needs but little sign of a co-operative or European approach. Similarly almost no data had been given on concrete plans for freer trade, for the lowering of tariffs, for an increased exchange of goods in Europe. And, perhaps most serious of all in American eyes, no concrete work had been done on the vital issue of a Continuing Organization to act for Western Europe as a whole. The delegates in Paris were told of the particular importance the United States attached to such an organization in which it saw an effective weapon against national particularism and perhaps at some point the germ of that "more perfect union" which lay at the back of so much American thinking about Europe.

There was one answer to Mr. Clayton's criticisms that the representatives of the Sixteen could perhaps have made. It lay in pointing out a certain inconsistency between Mr. Clayton's demands at Paris for joint action on the part of the European nations and the campaign he was conducting at about the same time at Geneva. All through the summer of 1947 the nations of the world—with the exception of the Soviet bloc—had been toiling at Geneva to produce the constitution of an International Trade Organization which would act as guardian and policeman of world trade. Its constitution sought to lay down the practices which nations would abjure in the practice of foreign commerce and, given the weight of American influence, it was not surprising that, on the whole, the draft bore the imprint of American thought. And as we have had occasion to notice in an earlier chapter, America, as the most powerful economic system in the world, tended to have views much resembling those held by Britain when, a century earlier, it had been the economic centre of the universe.

The essence of these ideas is that tariffs are the great obstacle to expanding trade, and that the best means of increasing the exchanges between nations is to reduce tariffs in such a way as to benefit all traders by the reduction. The attraction of such a theory to nineteenth-century Britain and twentieth-century America is obvious. As the largest and most successful manufacturing nations of their time, they could, generally speaking, produce and sell more cheaply than other nations. They objected to tariffs because they prevented them underselling the domestic producer in his own market. But at least under the rules of non-discrimination, tariffs were at the same level for all foreign competitors and, other things being equal, the British and the Americans could still hope to sell their goods. But the kind of obstruction to trade which they found completely unacceptable was the imposing of restrictions which gave one foreign competitor an advantage over another—as is the case, for instance, if a government imposes import restrictions and only allows a certain volume of, say, American produce to enter the country, or when one nation lowers its tariffs to another nation or group of nations but not to all nations indiscriminately. To the Americans, the classic example of such discrimination was the agreement reached between Britain and the Dominions at Ottawa in 1932 whereby the Dominions received certain exclusive advantages in the British market and in return gave Britain certain exclusive concessions in their own. As we have seen, the only type of "discrimination" admissible in American thinking is the total discrimination of a customs union. Any intermediate stage, any partial lowering of tariffs, any creation of what is called a "low tariff area" remained anathema.

Nor was discrimination the only method of regulating foreign trade frowned on at Geneva. The Americans showed some hostility to the idea of any direct intervention by governments in foreign trade, either by the conclusion of long-term contracts to buy the commodities of other nations—bulk purchase—or by the direct regulation of foreign trade by a system of exchange control under which all foreign currency or a part of the foreign currency earned by foreign trade is handed back to the government exchequer and is reissued for trade only through a series of import and export permits.

The American point of view, although dominant at Geneva, was in fact considerably modified in the actual drafting of the Trade Charter. The success of American influence can be measured by what the nations accepted as the ideal of commercial relations —full free non-discriminatory multilateral trade. But the success of the other nations in modifying American thinking can be seen in all the exceptions and permissions granted for an "interim period" before normal conditions could be restored. These exceptions amounted to very wide rights of discrimination, intervention and regulation and any other measures necessary for maintaining a nation's trading position in times of exceptional stress.

Events were on the side of those who pleaded the abnormal nature of the times. Even as the delegates sat and argued at Geneva, the dollars of the world drained away and the governments found themselves asked to pledge themselves to "non-discrimination" with one hand, while with the other they signed bilateral pact after bilateral pact, ensuring in the utmost detail that the goods they bought from a country would be balanced exactly by the goods that country bought in return—a regulation which, by excluding other nations from the bargain, was about as discriminatory as any arrangement could be. The American delegation was compelled to see the force of the argument. In a world in which the currency most in need was at the same time the scarcest, ordinary economic rules could not apply. Escape clauses were introduced, giving nations in economic difficulties of various kinds the right to discriminate, to trade bilaterally (in other words, to barter) to impose restrictions on imports, to practise exchange control. At the same time the ultimate aim was made quite clear—that in five years, by which time abnormal conditions would no longer prevail, the full doctrine of non-discriminatory free trade would be adopted.

Mr. Clayton came straight from these discussions to Paris to make his criticism of the lack of organic unity and co-operative planning in the Paris Report. Yet all the more obvious forms of co-operative planning would have almost certainly fallen under the ban on discrimination. As a first step towards a full customs union, for instance, it might have been practicable to suggest the lowering of some tariffs to create in Western Europe a "low tariff area" in which the Sixteen would give each other advantages denied to other nations. But such a plan would have been discriminatory. Another possible first step would have been to propose a central pool for the dollar earnings of the Sixteen (on the lines of the sterling area) and a joint plan for restricting their expenditure to the most essential imports. But such a policy would have again involved discrimination, since to reserve dollars for essential imports only would mean refusing dollars for inessential imports. Thus, behind Mr. Clayton's intervention, there appeared for the first time, very unexplicitly and in a vague and ambiguous manner, the risk that to create the kind of unity the Americans hoped for and to secure the balance in Europe's dollar account (which was the fundamental aim behind the Marshall Plan) the Sixteen Nations might be obliged to pursue policies which the United States, theoretically at least, would find unacceptable.

Nor was the risk confined simply to the field of foreign trade. The adopting of "organic policies" might come into conflict with another of America's strongest economic beliefs—the belief that cartels, particularly international cartels, are dangerous and even immoral. Cartels may take a number of forms, for instance, an agreement between various branches of an industry to concentrate on different products so as to avoid "wasteful competition" and thus maintain the price level. Another method is to divide up possible markets, each firm securing its own exclusive share. In this way again, competition is eliminated. The Americans, from their experience with their own mammoth trusts, distrust profoundly these structures, on the grounds that their chief aim is to keep prices up, if necessary by keeping production down. By a series of legislative acts, of which the most famous is the Sherman anti-trust act, attempts have been made in the United States (with limited success) to eliminate cartels, and they have always been one of the foremost targets of liberal American thought. During the second World War this emotional reaction was reinforced by the discovery that some of the biggest American corporations, such as Dupont de Nemours, had cartel agreements with German companies and had, so the accusation went, kept back processes and patents which might have helped the American war effort. One of the first acts of the American occupation forces in the American Zone of Germany was to dissolve all cartels and the policy was later extended to the whole Anglo-American Zone.

Yet some of the "organic policies of integration" advocated by Mr. Clayton could look perilously like the formation of cartels. If, for instance, the French and British automobile industry were to agree to cease competing directly with each other and instead to divide up production between them, the one concentrating on light and medium cars, the other on large cars and lorries, the result would be a big step forward—from the point of view of economic integration in Europe. But to the outside world, might it not seem that an Anglo-French cartel had been established in the motor-car industry?

These issues did not come into the open at Paris. They were indeed still very far from clear in people's minds. The delegates had not set about the task of evolving methods of close European co-operation. Sub-committees had been set up to study some aspects of it—there was one on Customs Unions, another on a balance of payments agreement—but no delegate could have said in September, 1947, "The only way in which we can conquer our appalling dollar deficit and stand again on our own feet is by methods of planning so vigorous and so discriminatory that they will shock American opinion." Nor had Mr. Clayton a very clear idea of what "organic co-operation" could mean beyond the formation of a full customs union, the only radical solution permissible in nineteenth-century dogma and practice. Thus at the first hint of the difficulty, it was still too imprecise to become a real issue. It remained, however, unsolved yet urgent, waiting to reappear the moment a first genuine attempt would be made to discover what European economic integration really meant.

Meanwhile, Mr. Clayton's visit to Paris was a timely reminder of two facts—that the United States laid great emphasis on the need for vigorous European self-help and that equal importance was attached to the idea of full European co-operation. In so far as it was possible in so short a time, the Committee modified its findings to meet the American case, and on September 22nd the Paris Report appeared.

PART III

THE MARSHALL PLAN

CHAPTER X

THE PARIS REPORT

The basic aim outlined in the Paris Report is to free Western Europe by 1951 of its dependence upon outside loans and credits. By that time the Sixteen Nations should be able to obtain the supplies they need from the outside world in general and from the Western Hemisphere in particular, by exporting to them goods and services in return. In other words, their foreign trade would once again be in some sort of equilibrium. This aim naturally includes another—that of maintaining or rather recreating a reasonable standard of living for the peoples of Europe. If the town dwellers of Western Europe were ready to survive on boiled fish, greens, one suit every seven years and no domestic heating, a balance in Europe's foreign trade could be struck straight away without American aid—simply by reducing consumption to the amounts exports would in fact buy. The chief difficulty of such a policy is the political and social upheaval it would entail. The statesmen of Western Europe rightly believe that the degree of misery involved in cutting consumption to what can be bought with exports would evoke a sufficiently violent political reaction to destroy democracy. American aid is offered in the same belief. The aim of the Marshall Plan is therefore to balance Europe's budget at a level of consumption—in other words, a standard of living—high enough to give political stability.

Given this aim, what methods do the nations propose for achieving it? They can be summed up under two headings—great increases in production and a really striking rise in exports. The combination of the two methods will, it is hoped, create a position of equilibrium by 1952. The first point is, obviously, the expansion of production, for without it there will be no increase in exports and, to a great extent, this part of the programme depends upon European effort alone. The goal which the Sixteen Nations propose to achieve before 1952 can best be summed up by saying that they seek an industrial and agricultural expansion equal to the tremendous increase in the American economy between

125

1940 and 1944.[1] More specifically the nations set themselves the following targets:—

(1) Restoration of pre-war bread-grain production and of an intensive livestock economy.

(2) Increase of coal production to 584 million tons yearly, an increase of 32 million tons above the 1938 level.

(3) Expansion of electricity output by nearly 70 billion kilowatt-hours and an increase of generating capacity by 25 million kilowatts, which is two-thirds above pre-war.

(4) Development of oil-refining capacity to two and one-half times pre-war.

(5) Increase in crude-steel production to 55 million tons yearly or 20 per cent. above pre-war.

(6) Expansion of inland transport to carry 25 per cent. more than pre-war.

(7) Rehabilitation and restoration of the merchant fleets of the participating countries.

(8) Supply from European production of most of the capital equipment needed for these expansions.

The claims that such a programme will make on the productive effort of individual nations can be judged by studying the figures of a few key products—coal, steel, grain, fertilizers, and certain manufactures. In 1938, the figures of output for the three chief coal producers in Western Europe were as follows: France, 48 million tons, Great Britain, 231 million tons, and Western Germany, 221 million tons. In 1947, output had fallen to 199 million tons in Britain and to 144 million tons in Germany. Only France registered a small increase of 2 million tons. Yet by 1951, Britain has guaranteed to raise output by 50 million tons a year to 249 million tons, France to 62 million tons, and Germany to 210 million tons. The target may be possible, but no one should underestimate the great and sustained effort which alone will make it possible.

The steel figures demand a comparable effort. Belgium and Luxemburg are to more than double their pre-war output of finished steel, Norwegian output is to rise from 82,000 metric tons (the 1938 figure) to 120,000 tons, even though output in 1947

---

[1] The relevant percentages are the following : coal output increased by 34 per cent., steel output by 31 per cent., electric power by 61 per cent. The proposed percentages for Europe are : coal output 33 per cent., steel output 60 per cent., and electricity by 39 per cent.

was no more than 53,000 tons. Western German output of crude steel is to rise from below 4 million tons in 1947 to 10 million by 1951. Sweden is to double its pre-war output of crude and finished steel, Italy its 1938 level of finished steel and pig-iron. The biggest increases are planned in France and Great Britain. French production was running at a low level between 1929 and 1938 and at an even lower level in 1946-47, when much of the steel-making capacity was lying idle. The figures for these two periods are thus abnormally restricted. Yet it will take a stupendous effort to treble the figures for finished steel and double the output of crude steel—which is the scale of expansion called for by the Paris Report.[1] The largest volume of steel will come from Britain. Before the war, its average production was at an annual level of 8.2 million tons of finished steel, 10.6 million tons of crude steel and 6.8 million tons of pig iron. For 1951, the planned figures are 12.4 millions, 15 millions and 9.9 millions respectively.

The figures for grain, bread grains and coarse grains, tend to follow, country by country, a similar sharp rise in the first years of the Plan and later a slight fall with a corresponding increase in the figures for meat. This trend represents the European hope that towards the end of the four-year period the mass markets for grain in the New World, in the Commonwealth, in Eastern Europe, and in Asia, will not be as overtaxed as they are to-day, and that Europe will again be able to practise the more advantageous husbandry of importing fodder and raising livestock. As we shall see, the Americans find this forecast over-optimistic and have recommended a more sustained effort to increase the production of cereals. The important point here is the scale of increase which must be secured even on the basis of the lower figures of the Paris Report. Belgium has undertaken to increase its output of bread-grains from 225,000 tons in 1947, to 580,000 in 1950, Luxemburg from 16,000 to 42,000. Western Germany will increase its output of both bread and coarse grains by about one million tons; so will the Italians. The French have to rise from the drought figure of 1947-48 of 3,783,000 tons of bread-grains to 8,750,000 tons by 1951. (In both the French and the

[1] French steel production :—

('000 metric tons)

					1934–38	1946–47	1951–52
Finished steel	..	..	..	..	4,115	4,090	12,690
Crude steel ..	..	..	..	..	6,221	4,812	12,106
Pig iron	..	..	..	..	5,967	3,299	4,612

Italian case this roughly represents the pre-war level of production.) In the case of Great Britain it is a question not of increasing output, but of more or less maintaining the very high
levels reached during the war.

The most striking increases scheduled for the agricultural
sector are, however, those planned for the production of fertilizers.
Almost without exception, each of the Sixteen Nations has
planned for higher output, in some cases for a total output three
times higher than either pre-war production or production in
1947. It is on these figures that the nations base their hope for
revived agricultural productivity and for the opening up of new
possibilities in the export market.[1]

The rise in production scheduled for industry is no less impressive. It is impossible here to do more than quote one or two
examples which are important not only as symbols of the effort
that is required, but also as cardinal factors in the success of the
whole programme. The European output of ships, freight cars, and
locomotives is the key to removing all the present stultifying bottlenecks in transport. Output of mining machinery is essential to
achieving the targets for coal. The whole programme of agricultural output is dependent upon securing sufficient agricultural
machinery. Here, then, are some of the figures for transport,
mining machinery, and agricultural machinery. Since a large percentage of the shipping of the Sixteen Nations was lost during
the war—the figure is 22 million gross registered tons—their
target of restoring their merchant fleets to their pre-war level
involves a building programme of some 7 million deadweight
tons of dry cargo shipping and 3 million tons of tankers between
1948 and 1951. About one-third of this might be bought in the
United States, although the unwillingness of the American mari-
time unions to countenance the transaction may upset this plan.

[1]Output of fertilizers :—

					('000 tons)	1934–38 (average)	1946–47	1951
Italy	..	..	nitrates ..	..	..	..	83	85	305
			phosphates	..	..	..	190	120	350
France	..	..	nitrates ..	..	..	..	150	150	350
			phosphates	..	..	..	405	340	800
			potash ..	..	..	..	470	570	1,000
Great Britain	..	..	nitrates ..	..	..	..	137	240	252
			phosphates	..	..	..	150	311	370

In any case, with or without American assistance the shipping programme calls for a large and concentrated effort in the European shipyards. In inland transport, freight cars continue to be one of Europe's most serious bottlenecks. The Paris Report proposes to meet this by an increase in French production from 3,000 a year in 1947-48 to 25,000 in 1951, in Belgian production from 18,000 in 1947 to 24,000 from 1948 onwards, in Britain from 59,000 in 1947-48 to 76,000 in 1951, and in Italy from just over 5,000 in 1946 to 15,200 in 1951.

The production of mining machinery is roughly equal to the requirements of the different coal-producing countries and out of a total requirement of $3,563 million, about 90 per cent. (or $3,078 million) will be produced in Europe by the mining countries themselves. Agricultural machinery will be produced in Italy, France, Great Britain, and Western Germany, Italy increasing its output of tractors from 2,300 units in 1946 to 12,000 in 1951, France from 3,500 to 63,000, and Great Britain from 33,000 to 275,000.

These figures do not give the whole picture, but they do suggest its order of magnitude. Nothing could be more mistaken than to think of the Marshall Plan as a scheme for turning over to America the problem of supplying Europe. If all the supplies asked for under the Marshall Plan were added together for the four years of its operation, they would still not equal 5 per cent. of the national product of the Sixteen Nations over the same period. A completely wrong emphasis has already tended to fall on the programme, stressing the amounts Congress will give, not the amounts Europe will produce. American aid is like the last cog in a complicated machine. Its absence may bring the wheels to a standstill, but its presence does not guarantee that they will grind on. For that they need their own lubrication and their own power.[1]

[1] The following table illustrates the extent to which in various vital categories Europe will provide its own supplies :—

Item.					(percentages of total programme)		
					1948–49	1949–50	1950–51
Bread grains	..	..	..	..	63	66	68
Nitrogen ..	..	..	..	..	90	99	109
Coal	..	..	..	..	92	94	96
Timber	..	..	..	..	71	70	69
Agricultural machinery*		..	..	..	63	74	80

*Excluding tractors.

But this "cog" is vital, for it represents the American share of the commodities which the European nations cannot produce themselves, which they must buy abroad and without which they cannot reach the targets they have set themselves. It is not necessary to give the full details of the estimated requirements of imports—for one thing, the American experts queried many of them and lowered quite a few—but the major items should perhaps be mentioned as a reminder that, since in each category European production is much larger than the supplementary imports, it is the scale of output in Europe that is crucial, not the size of outside help. The total Paris estimate for the import of bread-grains amounted to some 56 million metric tons, coarse grains to 31.7 million. Fertilizers amounted to 310,000 tons for nitrogen, 646,000 for phosphates and 1,891,000 tons for potash. Among needed imports of agricultural machinery were 1,400 light and 51,000 heavy tractors.

Coal imports, put at 58 million tons for 1948, are to fall to 37 million by 1951, and by that time 30 millions will come from Poland and only seven from the United States. (Before the war, there were no American coal exports to Europe and American exports in 1948—40 million tons—represent a flagrant example of Europe's uneconomic dependence upon the United States. Heavy transatlantic freight rates make American coal extremely expensive, yet lack of European, particularly of British, production had compelled Europe to spend its few dollars on American coal.)

The Sixteen Nations' desire to supplement their coal supplies by producing more electricity[1] and by converting some machines and certain forms of transport to oil is expressed in demands for special electrical generating equipment valued at $500 million, for 156 million metric tons of refined oil products and 87.5 millions of crude oil (an increase in the case of crude oil imports of 179 per cent. between 1947 and 1951).

Steel is the key to the entire manufacturing programme forecast at Paris and although the figures for steel imports may not appear very large compared with Europe's own production, they

---

[1] The planned rate of expansion for both electricity and oil is yet another reminder of the scale of the effort the European nations have undertaken. Electrical power is to increase from 178 billion k.w.h. in 1947 to 243 billion k.w.h. in 1951 and practically the entire equipment necessary for this expansion will be provided by Europe. Expenditure on new refineries to deal with the enormous increase in crude oil imports is to be of the order of $1,848 million. Of this, $1,260 million, or 68 per cent., will be provided by the Sixteen Nations.

represent materials of great strategic importance in the flow of European production. The full figures appear in a table on page 142; here it is only necessary to mention the chief items— over 2 million metric tons of finished steel, nearly 12 million tons of crude and semi-finished steel, just over 8 million tons of scrap and $400 million worth of steel-making equipment.[1]

When the question arose in Paris of estimating the total cost of all these imports over the Four Years of the Plan, it was obvious that the calculation would be almost impossible to make, since nobody had any idea what the prices of the various commodities were likely to be one year hence, two years hence, three years hence, and the further removed the year, the greater the difficulty of making any estimate at all. The Paris experts had therefore to make some arbitrary decisions. They decided to base their estimates on the understanding that in 1948 the prices would remain the same as at July, 1947, that in 1949 they would fall $7\frac{1}{2}$ per cent., in 1950 10 per cent., and in 1951 $12\frac{1}{2}$ per cent. This they felt was a fair guess at the extent to which, with more normal harvests and greater world supplies, the price of basic commodities would decline. On this basis, they estimated that the total bill for the imports of the Sixteen over the next four years would amount to $57.4 billion.[2] The next step was to estimate the rate of exports upon which the Sixteen could fairly count. The following table gives the estimate in the Paris Report:

(Millions of United States dollars)				
	1948	1949	1950	1951
Exports to :—				
United States	848	1,109	1,229	1,484
Rest of American Continent ..	1,715	1,715	2,139	2,461
Other non-participating countries	4,297	4,981	5,963	6,816
Deficit (−) or surplus (+) on invisible account, i.e., earnings from shipping, interest, etc., with :—				
United States	− 558	−450	− 250	− 325
Rest of American Continent ..	− 16	—	+ 25	—
Other non-participating countries	+384	+500	+550	+625

[1] This equipment is part of a general import programme for all kinds of equipment, amounting to some $4 billion for the four years ; one other particular figure in this programme perhaps deserves mention—$367 million on the import of freight cars.

[2] American imports would account for $20.4 billion, imports from other countries in the Western Hemisphere for $14.8 billion, and from all other non-participating countries, $22.2 billion.

This table puts the earnings the Sixteen Nations could expect to make from exports at a total of some $34.6 billion (including any balance from "invisible" items such as tourism or insurance or earnings on shipping). Subtract this from the figure for total imports and the European deficit for the four years amounts to just over $22 billion. This figure was reduced to $19.3 billion by transferring to the International Bank the cost of importing $3 billion of capital equipment. Thus $19.3 billion was the final figure put forward as the sum required under the Marshall Plan to tide Europe over to full recovery.

Before we go on to consider the American reactions, there are two points of great importance to be established. A glance at the table of exports forecast for the next four years will show how enormous are the proposed increases. The Sixteen Nations are to double their exports to the United States and to the rest of the American Hemisphere (and already the difficulty of finding markets there is one of the factors inhibiting European recovery) and they are to increase their exports to the rest of the world, which are already high, by another third. It may be possible to achieve these targets, but it must be clearly realized that they place another tremendous burden on the productive effort of the Western fringe.

The second point is even more important. It is quite simply that in 1951, the European trading account will still be unbalanced[1] to the extent of over a billion dollars, even if every optimistic forecast in the Paris Report is fulfilled—if production is as high as it is planned to be, if prices fall in the way forecast, if exports can be expanded to the extent laid down.

This conclusion could mean only one thing—that the action proposed in the Paris Report, while it would enormously increase production in each country, while it would boost the whole level of imports and exports throughout Western Europe and would make possible a return to something a little closer to the standard of living prevailing in 1938, would not do what the Report set out to do in the first place—to balance the trading accounts of Western Europe and abolish completely the need for outside assistance.

[1] The Paris Report's estimate of the balance of payments is as follows :—

(Millions of United States dollars)

	1948	1949	1950	1951
With American Continent	- 8,035	- 6,350	- 4,650	- 3,400
With other non-participating countries	- 240	+ 250	+1,000	+1,800

CHAPTER XI

AMERICAN REACTIONS

After the publication of the Paris Report, the scene moved speedily to Washington. The Report appeared on September 22nd. By the first week in October, Sir Oliver Franks, the Chairman of the Paris Committee and a group of delegates and experts, were on their way to Washington to explain the Report to the various agencies already at work on the problem of foreign aid. The need was urgent, for France, Italy, and Austria were down to their last reserves and it was clear that it would be necessary to pass a smaller Interim Aid Bill in order both to save them and at the same time allow Congress sufficient time to study the wider measure. The President had also decided that since the neediest nations could not wait until January, 1948, a special Session of Congress would have to be summoned in November.

While the Sixteen Nations had been toiling at their figures in Paris, considerable activity was beginning on the other side of the Atlantic. On June 22nd, President Truman set up three groups to advise him on different aspects of the Plan. The first of these, a body of distinguished citizens drawn from both parties and from business and labour and the world of education, met under the chairmanship of Mr. Averell Harriman, the Secretary of Commerce, to discuss the resources that America could afford to make available for foreign aid, to determine on what scale they might safely be given and what the impact on the domestic economy of such a programme would be. The two other groups were drawn from official circles. Mr. Krug's committee studied the effect of a foreign aid programme on American resources in the broadest sense and Dr. Nourse's committee its impact on the American economy. All three bodies had issued their Reports by the time the special Session of Congress assembled early in November.

The President was not the only one to initiate action. Under the leadership of a Republican Congressman, Mr. Christian Herter, a Committee of Congressmen of both parties visited Europe in the course of the summer and worked in a sustained and studious manner to master the facts of the situation. Similar visits were paid by members of the Senate. In all, over 200 Congressmen crossed the Atlantic—a greater number bent on a more serious mission than at any time in American history. Their experience had a remarkable effect upon their thinking. The easy American criticism of the spring—that Europe was eating too much and working too little—weakened before the evidence of daily European life—the hungry faces of the Ruhr, the unremitting labour of Italian peasants, the patience and good humour of the British man in the street.

Even unofficial groups bestirred themselves and booked passages for Europe. From the Middle West, for instance, the traditionally isolationist, anti-internationalist heart of America, came a self-financed group of farmers to learn the facts at first hand. All this interest and experience, coupled with the continuous reporting and explaining of the Press which, on the whole, adopted a positive and constructive attitude towards the need for European aid, began to seep down into the public mind. When Congress reassembled, its members knew that even if the high cost of living and the scale of taxation continued to hold first place in their constituents' political preoccupations, European aid had, nevertheless, become a reasonable and acceptable subject which could be supported without exposing the supporter to the opposite charges of "warmonger" or "fellow-traveller."

The atmosphere in Washington was thus not unfavourable to the idea of a European recovery programme when the delegates from the Paris Conference arrived, but the atmosphere was not necessarily very favourable to them, for the criticisms made of the Report had travelled ahead of them. In fact, however, the excellence of the leadership provided by Sir Oliver Franks and the increasingly obvious fact that in the time allowed the Paris estimates were the most serious and solid that any group of experts were likely to collect, stilled the criticism and the State Department very largely based their own calculations and the Bill they were drafting on the Paris Report. The whole point would hardly be worth mentioning were it not a reminder of a factor which will play a part throughout the years of the Plan. It is the need to maintain in Washington men of sufficient calibre to understand and counter the inevitable undercurrent of criticism which will continue in Washington and, particularly, in Congress, so long as free American gifts are being spent in other countries.

In this context, the appointment of Sir Oliver Franks as British Ambassador to the United States may have the most far-reaching results.

While the State Department worked on its preparations, the Harriman Committee, consulting freely with the European representatives, prepared its Report. It is not necessary to describe it in any detail for its most important recommendations appeared in the President's final European Co-operation Bill. Its general conclusion was to support the proposal for aid, and to reaffirm the conviction of both the Krug and the Nourse Committees that the resources for such a programme were available and that although the inflationary effect of taking goods out of such an eager market as that of the United States would need to be carefully watched, the programme could be undertaken without endangering the domestic economy. But one aspect of the Harriman Committee does deserve more attention—not its conclusions so much as the manner in which it reached them, not so much the final results as the struggle within the Committee to reach them.

One of the criticisms which the project of a joint European Recovery programme will have to counter throughout its course is that it is a plot on the part of American capital to infiltrate the European market and to reduce it to colonial status by capital investment on the one hand, and on the other by safeguarding its markets as a dumping ground for American goods. The Communists took up the theme from the morrow of Mr. Molotov's withdrawal, which had given the key-note to the campaign—that of national sovereign independence struggling for freedom from capitalist and imperialist control. "America," said the Communists, "is on the verge of a slump. It is already suffering from those crises of over-production which precipitate the crash. In a last desperate effort, its capitalists are trying in the old imperialist fashion to seize markets overseas as a safety valve for the goods they cannot sell to an impoverished working-class at home. The European Recovery Programme is only American imperialism writ small for foreign consumption."

The Harriman Committee—the first thoroughly representative American body to consider ERP—throws considerable light on the Communist criticism. It included representatives of big business. Its chairman, Mr. Harriman, came from a family with a long tradition of wealth and industrial power. Even among the educational leaders, there were a number of men whose sympathies would tend to lie with business. The effective representation of Labour was reduced to one. since the delegate from the American Federation of Labour only attended a couple of meetings. Here, then, if anywhere, the beginnings of the capitalist plot should have been observable.

The history of the Committee's deliberations is an almost comic rebuttal of the "capitalist, imperialist," line of criticism. From the first day, it was quite clear that the chief support for the idea of ERP came from the Chairman, from the non-business representatives and from the delegate of the Congress of Industrial Organizations. The business men were inclined to believe that America could not afford so big a programme of assistance. They did not see where the extra supplies of raw materials and manufactures were to come from. Apart from coal, cotton, tobacco, and possibly grain, the United States had no surpluses at all. Diversion of precious goods from the home market would increase inflationary pressures. For imperialists searching desperately for an outlet for their glutted goods, the business leaders on the Harriman Committee certainly behaved in a very curious fashion. It was almost as though they did not want to export to Europe at all, and if there were gluts on the American market they apparently had not noticed them. They simply looked at their order books, crammed with safe domestic orders for the next four years and European markets looked to them more dubious than ever. On one point, in particular, they remained adamant. They could not and would not export more crude steel or scrap. Such a step would be endangering America's domestic production. All the dissenting members of the Committee could write into the Report was a grudging admission that the steel companies might reconsider the question of expanding steel capacity in the United States.

The keenest supporter of the Plan, with the possible exception of its able and persuasive chairman, was the representative of the CIO. He made no secret of his belief that the aid should be much larger and that only "the selfishness of the vested interests" was keeping it between the $12 billion and $17 billion which the Committee decided were reasonable upper and lower limits to set. Thus the chief exponent of the "imperialist plot" at this, its first crucial discussion, was the secretary of the more radical of

America's two major unions. The working-class representative backed most strongly the "plot to enslave the working class."

When Congress assembled in special Session on November 13th, its principal task was to consider and pass a Bill for Interim Aid for France, Italy, and Austria—three countries which were already in the throes of a dollar crisis. Any reservations Congressmen might have had on the urgency of the measure were dispelled by the choice of November by the French Communists for the first of their obviously political strikes, designed to undo the plan for European recovery by ensuring that the participating nations should be ruined before outside relief could come to their assistance. The events in Paris and Washington reacted upon each other. The French crisis speeded the passage of Interim Aid, the prospect of rapid assistance strengthened the hands of the Centre Government in France and gave trade union leaders such as Léon Jouhaux the opportunity to denounce the Communists for striking against their country's material recovery. Without the certainty of further help, neither Government nor independent trade unionist could have mastered the situation without capitulation on the one hand, or violence on the other. If the men in Congress and in the American street wished for concrete proof of the effectiveness of the Marshall Plan as a peaceful counter-offensive against Communism, the petering out of the November strikes in France and the resulting split of the powerful *Confédération Générale du Travail* into a Communist and a non-Communist wing provided it at a crucial moment. The Bill for Interim Aid was passed and a few days later the President published the draft of a Bill for European Recovery—the "Economic Co-operation Act of 1948."

It is not necessary to recall in detail the debate whereby both Houses of Congress between January and early April convinced themselves that it was necessary to pass the Economic Co-operation Act. Their final version did not differ much in structure from the proposals put forward by the President and the main provisions will be discussed in later pages. Here two points only need be considered. The first is the impact on the debate in Congress of the Communist *coup* in Czechoslovakia. With the brutal suppression of free government in Prague, the Russians proved to all whom fanaticism does not blind that in their present mood not only can they not co-operate with other nations, but that they will suppress all save Communist influence in any area they can control. In Czechoslovakia no mitigating excuse of strategic fear or of anxiety for Russian security could be brought forward. Every party in Czechoslovakia, from Right to Left, blindly supported the Russian alliance. So convinced were all Czechs that Germany, a revived, militarist Germany, was the real danger, that virtually no one questioned the completely essential nature of securing and maintaining Russian friendship and support. The *coup d'état* showed with melancholy force that for the time being at least, Russia is capable of treating other nations only as enemies or slaves.

In Western Europe, the Communist *coup* reinforced a hundredfold the need for the remaining democracies to concert their strength and reinforce their co-operation. In Washington, the Communist aggression once again underlined the need for the quick passing of the Marshall Plan at a turning point in the Congressional debate and the fact that the Bill was law by the first days of April, without substantial modifications or inconvenient annexes, must be laid in the first place at the Communist door.

Welcome as was this speedy legislation to the hard-pressed nations in Western Europe, the more alert among them were conscious of a danger. The Bill had been passed by a large, an unnaturally large majority, isolationists, Pacific-firsters, British baiters and anti-Europeans all voting on the same side, hypnotized by the Communist threat. The motive behind their voting was thus predominantly negative—their fear of Communism, not their positive support for the idea of European reconstruction. Clearly negative support tends to be the most ephemeral and uncertain. What, then, would be the consequence if the Russians were to realize that their intransigence was only stimulating America to action and were to try instead a quiet and conciliatory policy? Would Congressional support for the whole idea of European recovery abruptly decline? The Czech *coup*, by stampeding everyone into the anti-Communist camp, helped to mask the degree of genuine, convinced and positive support for the Recovery Programme. The first large majority for its passage in April, 1948, gave no hint how the same or similar Congressmen would vote for a continuance of the measure in a later year.

The second point to be made is the scale of assistance promised by the Bill. President Truman had originally thought of asking for $17 billion for the four years. (This compares with the Paris figure of $19.3 billion.) On the advice of the Congressional leaders, he deleted the four-year figure before submitting the Bill to Congress. Instead he asked for $6.8 billion for the first year. In the course of the debate, Congress decided not to legislate for the full year from June, 1948, to June, 1949, but to leave the financing of the second 1949 quarter to the Congress which would be elected in November, 1948. The figure was therefore reduced to $5.3 billion and it was laid down that one billion should be provided in the shape of loans. This was the final figure authorized by Congress.

This figure, however, is too indeterminate to be used as a basis of comparison between the Paris estimates of what ERP would entail and the American estimates upon which the President based his original Bill. The surest basis of comparison is to use the report which the President presented to Congress when the Bill was first introduced and which represents the most detailed American examination made of the Plan, not only for the first year, but the full four years of its working.

In analysing this report, three points must first of all be established. The first is the question whether the United States can fulfil the estimates of need established at Paris; the second is whether the United States considers the Paris estimates of Europe's own production are reasonable and possible; the third is whether the Paris and the Washington proposals agree on the scale of the deficit which may remain at the end of the four years. The three questions are obviously closely interconnected. If the supplies available to Europe are, in fact, less than the Paris estimates, it may follow that the targets for European production will have to be lowered and less European production might result in a decline in exports greater than any decline in imports brought about by the unavailability of certain supplies—in which case the risk of a deficit would be greater. But before any detailed comparison between Paris figures and Washington figures is made, it should be quite clear that the only reason for noting whether American supplies fall short of European demands is to assess squarely the extra burden of effort and planning which these short-falls place upon the Sixteen Nations. It is emphatically not in any way to belittle the scale of American assistance. It cannot be repeated too often that American aid, a large part of which is to be transferred as a free gift, represents a gesture of international solidarity un-

paralleled in peacetime.[1] If the allocations do not at every point
reach the amounts hoped for, the almost invariable reason is a
shortage of the particular commodity in the United States—and
everywhere else. As we have already seen, there are, for the time
being, few surpluses of any commodity waiting to be disposed of
in America.

In a world in which the habitual exports between nations seem
to be animosity, slander, suspicion, and ill will, the American
programme of assistance represents a redeeming act of solidarity,
and this fact should be steadily borne in mind when any comparisons between European hopes and American availabilities
are being considered.

[1] The following table represents an estimate of the total supplies to be transferred
over the four years:—

(In millions of dollars)

Commodity.	April-June, 1948	1948–49	1949–50	1950–51	1951–52	Total.
1. Bread grains	218.3	535.5	509.7	411.6	411.6	2,086.7
2. Coarse grains ..	5.8	82.9	120.0	133.0	133.0	474.7
3. Fats and oils ..	20.0	80.4	88.0	97.4	97.4	383.2
4. Oilcake and meal ..	4.4	17.7	22.6	22.6	27.1	94.4
5. Sugar	6.5	21.4	17.3	10.5	11.0	66.7
6. Meat	1.7	6.0	12.1	17.9	23.8	61.5
7. Dairy products ..	75.2	160.0	105.7	101.5	90.3	532.7
8. Eggs	12.0	24.0	12.0	12.0	12.0	72.0
9. Dried fruits	6.9	26.6	25.2	17.6	20.0	96.3
10. Rice	1.1	6.1	6.1	6.1	11.9	31.3
11. Coffee	—	—	—	—	—	—
12. Other foods	9.2	64.6	61.2	80.4	80.4	295.8
13. Tobacco	52.5	210.0	217.4	215.6	215.6	911.1
14. Cotton	142.5	438.3	437.6	458.7	480.5	1,957.6
15. Nitrogen	2.4	14.0	7.8	—	—	24.2
16. Phosphates	0.6	2.5	2.5	2.5	2.5	10.6
17. Potash	—	—	—	—	—	—
18. Agricultural machinery	—	136.3	161.5	131.8	115.5	545.1
19. Coal	92.3	297.0	135.1	49.6	24.9	598.9
20. Coal-mining machinery	—	81.9	52.7	37.6	34.5	206.7
21. Petroleum	121.3	530.6	546.2	570.5	537.0	2,305.6
22. Timber	24.0	96.3	93.1	88.0	76.4	377.8
23. Iron and steel—						
23a. Finished steel ..	44.6	182.1	186.9	179.3	126.6	719.5
23b. Crude and semi-finished	11.9	47.2	47.2	47.2	43.5	197.0
23c. Pig iron	0.3	1.3	1.3	—	—	2.9
23d. Scrap	0.4	1.6	—	—	—	2.0
23e. Rich iron ore ..	—	—	—	—	—	—
24. Trucks	19.7	80.9	40.1	33.9	33.6	208.2
25. Freight cars	—	60.0	18.0	—	—	78.0
26. Steel equipment ..	—	48.1	48.2	48.2	48.2	192.7
27. Timber equipment ..	—	16.9	22.2	11.7	11.7	62.5
28. Electrical equipment	—	95.0	100.7	85.0	65.0	345.7
Total	873.6	3,365.2	3,098.4	2,870.2	2,734.0	12,941.3

The clearest method of comparison is to take the chief categories already examined in relation to the Paris Report. In all save two commodities—cotton and tobacco, of which genuine export surpluses exist—the United States' figures for agricultural supplies are below the estimated needs of the Sixteen Nations. Between 1948 and 1951 bread grains will be less by over 7 million tons, coarse grains by over 10 million, fats and oils by 3 million, meat by nearly 2 million.[1] The Americans' reasons for these reductions are certainly prudent. They point out that the United States has now had seven or eight bumper harvests in succession and that such a sequence cannot be relied upon to continue, especially since the world demand for grain has had the effect of bringing marginal land into cultivation in the United States with all the risks it entails of recreating the Dust Bowl of the 'thirties when four or five droughts in succession dried up and blew away the thin top soil already loosened by excessive ploughing.

The Americans are in a position to meet the estimates for coal put forward by the Sixteen Nations. The scale of need after 1948 is difficult to estimate, for it is the intention of the Sixteen to rely more and more on Polish coal for their small deficit (which is no more than a few per cent. of their own high annual production —435 million tons by early 1949). American coal has never been part of the pattern of European imports, for the shipping of it is entirely uneconomic. The Americans have guaranteed the needed figure of 41 million tons for 1948. Thereafter, their contribution will be determined by the available exports of Polish coal.

[1] The full figures for three years of the Plan are as follows:—

ESTIMATED IMPORTS OF SELECTED AGRICULTURAL COMMODITIES*

(In millions of metric tons)

	1948–49 Paris Report	1948–49 United States	1949–50 Paris Report	1949–50 United States	1950–51 Paris Report	1950–51 United States
Bread grains†	19.6	16.0	18.7	16.7	17.9	15.9
Coarse grains†	9.9	6.0	11.1	8.0	11.7	8.8
Fats and oils	1.9	1.1	2.2	0.9	2.3	1.1
Meat	2.3	1.8	2.4	1.8	2.5	1.8
Sugar	2.2	2.3	2.3	2.1	2.3	2.0
Canned and dried milk	0.21	0.32	0.21	0.21	0.21	0.17
Dried fruit ..	0.23	0.22	0.21	0.21	0.14	0.24
Tobacco	0.17	0.27	0.17	0.28	0.17	0.28
Cotton	—	1.1	—	1.2	—	1.3
Nitrogen	0.23	0.18	0.08	0.12	—	0.04

* Imports from non-participating countries only, except where otherwise specified.
†Total imports from all sources, including participating countries.

Petroleum products cannot, on the other hand, be provided on the scale required by the Sixteen Nations. The Paris estimates have therefore been cut by 10 per cent. Only domestic petrol rationing in the United States could provide a sufficient surplus and it is not possible to reintroduce rationing in peacetime. As it is, the Americans feel some anxiety about their own domestic reserves and a large part of the petrol for the Sixteen will be exported from American (and British) sources in the Middle East.

The gravest shortfall—the one which affects the widest area of the Recovery Programme—is the shortfall in steel.[1] The figure for finished steel has been increased to offset the very serious shortages of crude steel and scrap and even this concession will entail some rationing in the United States and some diversion of steel from urgent domestic production. The Americans suggest that some of the deficit in scrap can be made good by scrap collections in Germany and that some of the steel-making plant may be obtainable by way of reparations. But these sources are quite inadequate to fill in the gap and the effect on the Recovery Programme will be to create a serious maladjustment in all its industrial estimates which only careful and co-ordinated planning can overcome. It is over the allocation of universally needed steel that the Sixteen's capacity for joint agreement and action may first be seriously tested.

The shortage is made more difficult by the fact that the United States can provide only a part of the industrial equipment for which the Sixteen Nations put in a bid. The shortfall in steel equipment has already been given (in note[1] below). Freight cars are not available to the required amount.[2] Agricultural equipment is to be cut from an estimated need valued at $1.2 billion to $637 million, the Americans doubting whether small-scale European farms can absorb all the heavy tractors and harvesters for which they have asked. On the other hand, the estimates for

[1] The actual figures are as follows:—

Item	Unit	1948-49 Paris Report	1948-49 United States	1949-50 Paris Report	1949-50 United States	1950-51 Paris Report	1950-51 United States	1951-52 Paris Report	1951-52 United States
Steel—	Thousand								
Finished	metric tons	1,272	1,802	534	1,769	300	1,630	250	1,152
Crude and semi-finished	do.	2,863	1,266	2,921	1,266	3,105	1,266	3,013	1,208
Scrap iron and steel ..	do.	1,514	146	1,878	125	2,206	115	2,346	115
Steel-making equipment	Million dollars	100	48	100	48	100	48	100	48

[2] Between 1948 and 1951 the Sixteen asked for 101,000 freight cars and are to receive 26,000.

supplies of all types of mining machinery are only slightly below the estimate in the Paris Report, and the United States also hopes to supply the specialized extra equipment needed to expand the production of electricity.

These cuts, some of them severe, must clearly lead to a number of drastic readjustments in the national programmes of the Sixteen. The shortages in grain suggest that more European production will have to be devoted to cereals and the general intention to turn, as the Programme advances, from grain to the raising of livestock will have to be postponed. American experts believe that the Sixteen Nations can do better than restore their pre-war levels in the production of cereals with the help of more fertilizers and more mechanization, but part of the increase must necessarily be at the cost of producing more meat, fats, and dairy products.[1]

But more mechanization of agriculture and a greater output of fertilizers depend upon the general level of industrial activity, yet, as we have seen, less iron and steel and less capital equipment are to be made available than was originally hoped. Thus, without new plans and new effort, it follows that industrial activity will be lower than was forecast at Paris and this in turn will affect the prospects for agriculture. Is the prospect, therefore, a declining spiral in Western Europe in both industry and agriculture?

The only way to counter this danger is to raise the sights in European production, and since coal is the basis of the industrial pyramid, the key to increased productivity lies to some extent in Europe's own hands. Can coal production be increased?

The present position is that even after the substitution of some electricity and petrol as sources of energy, three-quarters of the power needed to turn the wheels of the West European economy will be derived from coal. American experts believe that Europe can reach its targets—the coal, the manpower, the equipment,

---

[1] This table contrasts European and American forecasts of agricultural production in Europe:—

(Average 1934–38 = 100)

				1948–49			1950–51	
				Paris Report	United States		Paris Report	United States
Bread grains	..	..	..	90	92	..	101	105
Coarse grains	..	..	..	97	104	..	108	117
All cereals	..	..	..	94	98	..	104	110
Fats and oils	..	..	..	81	80	..	98	91
Raw sugar ..	..	..	..	104	98	..	114	108
Meats	..	..	..	71	72	..	88	80

will be available. But they underline the extent to which sustained effort from the workers and skilful management from the technicians can make or mar the attainment of the targets. If the present coal target is fulfilled by increasing output to 45 million tons a year more than the 1938 figure, most of the general European Recovery Programme can be fulfilled. But a greater increase would help to make good the inevitable gaps in American assistance. For instance, petroleum consumption is likely to be cut by the equivalent (in calorific value) of some 55 million tons of coal over the four years. The addition of all or part of this figure from the coal mines would maintain a higher level of industrial activity and at the same time avoid the cost of transferring sections of industry and transport on to an oil-burning basis. Again, the production of fertilizers and of steel could probably be increased still further if more coal, and in particular more coking coal, could be provided. Any addition to coal is an addition to Europe's chance of prosperity and it is hardly necessary to underline at this point how heavy is the British responsibility to see that targets are reached and even raised.

Not only may imports of steel fall short, but without an extra effort, domestic production may not reach the levels forecast in the Paris Report. The present American estimate is that the European steel programme may lag as much as one year behind the estimates in the Report.[1] This possibility, combined with the shortfall in American supplies, may reduce the consumption of finished steel forecast in the Paris estimates by 4 million tons in 1948-49, and 2 million tons in 1950-51. This possibility in turn affects the American estimate of the amount of capital development which can be achieved in the four years of the Plan. In each category, the American forecasts are rather more pessimistic than those of the Paris Report—inevitably so, since they are based on lower availabilities of basic supplies. It follows that the capital development proposed in the Paris Report is to some

[1]FINISHED STEEL OUTPUT OF PARTICIPATING COUNTRIES

(In millions of metric tons)

	Paris Report	United States estimates
1938	34.1	34.1
1947	23.7	23.7
1948–49	34.0	28.6
1949–50	36.9	33.7
1950–51	40.4	37.6
1951–52	43.9	40.6

extent over-ambitious. It can be achieved in time, but certainly not in the four years of the Plan. The Sixteen Nations cannot mechanize agriculture, restore their merchant fleets to the pre-war level, more than double their oil-refining capacity, increase their inland transport by 25 per cent. above pre-war, expand the production of coal and steel well above the pre-war averages and provide most of the capital equipment necessary to do so and nearly double their exports—or at least they cannot achieve all this in four years. The materials are not likely to be available (even with a phenomenal increase in the output of coal and steel) and their economies probably cannot stand without grave risk of continued and increased inflation the diversion of so much manpower and so many supplies to the production of capital and not of consumer goods.

These conclusions do not mean that the European Recovery Programme cannot succeed. Even if these reductions and reservations are made, both the possibilities of European production and the scale of American aid are tremendous, but the fact that they may not be as great as was first expected entails two consequences—that the need of each nation to fulfil its own quota of production is doubly urgent and this is particularly true of Britain where the bulk of the coal, steel, and industrial equipment is to be produced. If British production falters, the whole European programme is in jeopardy. The second consequence will be discussed at greater length on a later page. Here it need only be mentioned once more. The greater the shortages, the greater the need for joint planning and joint allocation of the scarce supplies.

CHAPTER XII

THE DOLLAR DEFICIT

There remains the problem of the cost of the programme and the vital question whether, on American estimates, the aim of creating a balance between imports and exports can be attained within the framework of the Marshall Plan. It is a tribute to the seriousness with which the experts at Paris went to work that the final figures of financial aid proposed by the President did not differ very greatly from those suggested at Paris. The President dealt with the problem of the probable level of prices by assuming an upper and a lower limit. If prices failed to fall and remained above the July, 1947 level, then the deficit to be financed by the United States would be in the neighbourhood of $22 billion —almost the exact deficit calculated at Paris. Prices might, however, fall and the President fixed the lower limit at $19.4 billion. From these two figures, he subtracted about $4 billion, which would be drawn from other sources, such as the International Bank, and about $800 million representing the War Department's appropriation for supplies for Germany. These deductions gave an upper limit of $17.8 billion and a lower limit of $15.1 billion. The President therefore assumed that a $17 billion appropriation might reasonably be expected to cover the deficit. The figure of $17 billion is, however, important only as showing the possible order of magnitude of American help. It was, as we have seen, dropped before the proposals went to Congress, with the excuse that Congress cannot in any case appropriate money for more than one year at a time. A more significant figure was therefore the figure for the first year of the Plan. The Paris figure was about $7 billion. The President proposed instead $6.8 billion and finally a figure of $5.3 for the first nine months. This latter figure was finally adopted.

In general, it can be seen that the American estimates of the size of the four-year deficit to be financed by the United States are not very different from those made in Paris. However, on the question whether, at the end of the four years of the Programme, a balance would have been restored between imports and exports and whether the aim of restoring economic independence to Western Europe would have been achieved, the American conclusions were, if anything, more pessimistic than those of the Paris Report. If the figures for the whole period are studied,[1] one fact emerges with startling force. The Americans expect the balance between European imports and European exports in 1951-52 to be out of balance with each of Europe's three groups of trading partners—the United States, the other nations in the Western Hemisphere, and the other non-participating countries. In spite of a favourable balance on certain invisible items, the deficit in 1951-52 is expected to be not much short of $3 billion (the actual figure is $2,847 million)—in other words, the 1951 deficit would still be 50 per cent. of the deficit for 1948. This possibility appears all the more disturbing in the light of the fact that the United States estimates put European exports to the Western Hemisphere at a consistently higher figure than does the Paris Report, while the import figures in both documents are

[1]BALANCE OF PAYMENTS ON CURRENT ACCOUNT OF THE PARTICIPATING COUNTRIES WITH THE REST OF THE WORLD, APRIL 1, 1948, TO JUNE 30, 1952

Millions of dollars—July 1, 1947, prices

	1949–50	1950–51	1951–52
Imports from—			
United States	5,209	4,858	4,598
Other Western Hemisphere	4,114	4,255	4,273
Other non-participants	5,777	6,203	6,327
Exports to—			
United States	2,134	2,462	2,759
Other Western Hemisphere	1,892	2,298	2,589
Other non-participants	5,070	5,635	6,075
Merchandise balance—			
United States	−3,075	−2,396	−1,839
Other Western Hemisphere	−2,222	−1,957	−1,684
Other non-participants	−707	−568	−252
Net invisibles—			
United States	+244	+403	+299
Other Western Hemisphere	−147	−90	−69
Other non-participants	+605	+656	+698
Balance on Current Account—			
United States	−2,831	−1,993	−1,540
Other Western Hemisphere	−2,369	−2,047	−1,753
Other non-participants	−102	+88	+446

not strikingly divergent.[1] From this fact only one conclusion can be drawn. If, as seems all too likely, the Sixteen Nations do not achieve such a high level of exports to the Americas, the deficit in 1951 will be bigger still.

This possibility is borne out by other reports prepared by American experts, in particular by various studies on the Sixteen Nations published separately, country by country. According to these studies only three nations will have covered their dollar deficits by 1951—Sweden, Switzerland, and Turkey. Norway and Portugal will be in a position to meet 80 to 85 per cent. of it, Britain and France 70 per cent., Belgium 60 per cent., Holland 45 per cent., Germany 40 per cent., and Italy, Greece, and Denmark only 30 per cent. Admittedly all these figures are only estimates. Yet they all point in the same direction—to the fact that however valuable the Marshall Plan may be in the raising of European productivity and in maintaining a standard of living in Western Europe and in giving the necessary impetus to revived European effort, it does not automatically, without further thought or effort, solve the basic problem of Western Europe— that it is permanently short of dollars and permanently tending to fall into debt.

If the solution to this problem is not to be found automatically in the unfolding of the Marshall Plan, it must be inserted into it by positive action. It cannot be found by bilateral planning, each nation attempting in isolation to contract its imports and expand its exports particularly to dollar countries. This line has been pursued over the last eighteen months and the results were the dislocation and deadlock of 1947. As each nation reduces its imports, others can sell less and therefore buy less, so the vicious spiral of falling markets circles downwards. And each nation urgently seeking to sell in the same dollar markets, by duplication and wasteful competition, reduces the effectiveness of Europe's efforts to export. There is only one way out of the deadlock and it is a drastic one—to concert between the Sixteen Nations, with all the sacrifices of separate sovereignty it would entail, a total

[1]COMPARATIVE ESTIMATES OF EUROPEAN TRADE WITH THE WESTERN HEMISPHERE

(Millions of dollars at July, 1947, prices)

	1949		1950		1951	
	Imports	Exports	Imports	Exports	Imports	Exports
United States Estimates ..	9,323	4,026	9,113	4,760	8,871	5,348
Paris Report Estimates ..	9,149	2,824	8,576	3,368	8,182	3,945

dollar saving strategy in which every move would be related to the principal end—the expansion of domestic production, the expansion of sales to hard currency areas, and the elimination of all unessential dollar purchases.

Something will be said of such a programme in a later chapter. Here it is only necessary to mention some of its features—expansion of grain production, for instance, to reduce dependence upon cereals from the New World, substitution of wool and rayon, which can be bought in Europe and in Australia, for cotton which must mainly be purchased in America's Deep South, replacement of American tobacco by tobacco from Europe and the Commonwealth, integration of the European steel industry to rationalize production and make possible a unified marketing policy, complete pooling of dollar earnings to ensure that they are spent only on essential articles—these are only a few of the policies which would be necessary in any serious attempt to put an end to the disequilibrium in the Western European balance of payments and restore the area as an independent economic community. But these policies in their turn demand a degree of economic co-operation and central planning at least as great as those achieved by the chief belligerents during the war through their Combined Boards and Combined Chiefs of Staff. Indeed, since the legitimate objectives of policy in peacetime are so much more complex than the overriding wartime aim to defeat the enemy, effective co-operation to-day probably demands stronger central direction and more far-reaching co-ordination of policy than anything achieved between 1941 and 1945. It follows that the Sixteen Nations cannot hope to work out a common strategy unless their Continuing Organization has the powers and scope of an Economic General Staff, entrusted with the task of "winning the battle for the dollar" with every means and every strategy at its disposal.

It is for this reason that measures such as the formation of a Customs Union and even an agreement on a system of balancing inter-European payments are subsidiary to the policies necessary to solve the overriding problem of the dollar shortage. They have, naturally, their own importance and they will be discussed on a later page, but they are not to be thought of as substitutes for genuine economic co-ordination and planning. They merely make easier and bigger an existing flow of trade. They do not alter its direction. A European Customs Union, conceived without any co-ordination of European steel or coal or grain policy, would not affect the problem of the dollar shortage. A united Europe could, just as does a disunited Europe, buy too many goods in the Western Hemisphere and provide too few in exchange. On a smaller scale, the first round of negotiations between the nations of the Benelux Union has shown the force of this difficulty. On January 1st, 1948, a common tariff for all three countries came into operation and all tariffs between them were abolished. Yet this step has done nothing and can do nothing to counteract the greatest obstacle to economic unity—the lack of balance between impoverished and war-torn Holland and the prosperous productive Belgian economy. Removals of tariffs will not automatically provide Holland with more goods to sell to Belgium nor give the Dutch guilder the same strength as the Belgian franc. For that, much more drastic plans for economic unification are necessary.

The chief conclusion to be drawn from this examination of the European Recovery Programme confirms the warning with which the examination started. The Programme itself in its first form neither creates nor prevents Western Association. The Sixteen Nations can either use it as a project for piecemeal assistance, or they can make it the foundation of a new co-operative venture, designed to bring about something which nations have only once or twice in the history of man achieved in peacetime, and by voluntary consent—the union of different States into a single economic and political community. But the estimates contained in the various proposals take the warning a step further, for they show that the way of bilateral uncoordinated economic assistance leads back to where the Plan begins—to a Western Europe still unable to pay its way, still seeking to spend a billion dollars more each year than it can earn. In other words, the lesson of the estimates sharply reinforces the larger lesson of history—that Western Europe must unite in order to survive.

Here surely is a remarkable coincidence of interests. History's lesson is that the old nineteenth-century dispensation of separate national sovereignties has passed away, leaving behind it the urgent problem of reordering Western society. The growing political threat of Communism in Soviet-controlled Eastern Europe underlines the need for the union of Western Europe's resources. The European Recovery Plan's success depends upon a full co-ordination of economic policy between the Sixteen, and

America, the sponsor of the scheme, demands "more perfect union" as one of the Plan's first objectives. Nobody can deny the impressive completeness of the needs and hopes all pressing Europe along the road towards association. Yet at the risk of disturbing this harmony, it must be pointed out that, in the unfolding of the Plan, some features of the steps the Sixteen Nations should take in pursuit of unity may not prove as acceptable to America as the idea of unity itself.

The Americans' conception of European Union is based upon their own experience of creating in 1787 an economic union between the thirteen States of the Confederation. None of the problems facing a possible Western European Customs Union was at issue in those days. The economic bait offered by the party supporting union—the Federalists—was a high uniform protection for America's new industries. The common interest which both gave scope for future development and at the same time provided an economic safety valve, was the existence of vast new territories lying to the West, and the crucial decision of the new economic union was to hold these territories in trust for the whole republic, not for individual states. In Europe to-day, protection is no bait since it has been universally adopted. The African Continent, large stretches of which are under various European sovereignties, is the closest analogy to a fund of land waiting to be developed—and it is not very close. But these are not the chief reasons why the economic union of 1787, which is the model to which most Americans look, consciously or subconsciously, in order to judge the European experiment, is irrelevant to Europe's present plight. The crucial reason has already been described. It is that a Customs Union, however useful as a subsidiary instrument of co-operation, does not touch the core of Europe's economic problem—the dollar shortage.

The dollar shortage can only be dealt with by drastic measures of regulation, co-ordination, and planning, which have no part in the American experience. On the contrary, some of them will resemble measures for which, traditionally, Americans have felt considerable disapproval. We are back again at the difficulties which made their first appearance when Mr. Clayton came to Paris in September, 1947, to ask for modifications in the first draft of the Paris Report. Many of the policies necessary to conserve dollars, to use them on essential purposes only, to plan dollar imports and to work out a co-ordinated sales policy for

Europe's various products fall under the heading of "discrimination," and as such, are unacceptable to the United States. It is discrimination to take steps to exclude Virginian tobacco—even although it does also save dollars. It can be discrimination to buy rayon in preference to cotton—although less dollars are spent thereby. There is no evading the issue that the types of organic co-operation necessary to balance Western Europe's budget by 1952 are not necessarily the types of economic co-operation permissible according to nineteenth-century conceptions of trade, or enshrined in American memory as the methods used by the Founding Fathers to create America's economic unity.

This American confidence that methods which may broadly be called of the nineteenth century will be enough to unite Western Europe in a single prosperous, stable community is, in fact, one aspect of a general state of mind we have already observed—the natural American tendency to believe that with a few more loans, a few more gifts, a little more economic assistance lasting over a few more years, the old world will return. There is, inevitably, in the United States a belief that somewhere, lurking behind the torn and shabby façade of the post-war years, lie the open streets and solid monuments of the old familiar and stable world. It is a measure of the emotional gulf between the Old and New Worlds that Europe no longer shares that faith. Indeed, the roles are reversed. In a sense, America is now the old world and Europe must learn to be a new world or perish.

There are possibilities of misunderstanding and friction in these new realities. Neither men nor nations are anxious to relinquish a familiar past. But it is to a tremendous venture in pioneering that Western Europe is committed with American assistance and as in all pioneering, the methods used will be challenging, unfamiliar, and sometimes crude. Will the relationship between the American and the European communities stand the strain? Will the American assistance needed to make the Western experiment possible at all survive the spectacle of Europe practising policies at variance with America's deepest convictions? To give a practical instance, will the interests damaged by the planned reduction of Europe's purchases in America—the cotton lobby, the tobacco lobby, even the potential coal lobby—lessen the chances of Congress making not only the first appropriation for European aid, but the third and fourth as well?

The answer lies with Europe. A Western Europe working to meet and pass its targets of production, a Western Europe matching economic co-ordination with ever-closer political unity, a Western Europe showing an upsurge of faith and vitality and a new confidence in democratic society, need have no fear that the Americans, after putting their hand to the European plough, will draw it back. These pages have already described America's readiness to change, its quick reaction to new situations, its sensitiveness to a genuine lead, its idealism. If Western Europe can rise to its new opportunity, it is not simply a four-year bounty between benefactor and dependents that will be achieved. The foundations will be laid for a lasting partnership between equals and friends.

PART IV

WESTERN ASSOCIATION

CHAPTER XIII

WESTERN DEFENCE

Now, after what may have seemed a long digression, we are back at our starting point—the problem of Western Europe's next step. The vanishing of the old nineteenth-century world has left a vacuum which time alone will not fill acceptably. We have seen how, in 1947, the Western nations had not even the minimum economic elbow-room to act. We have seen the readiness of America—against all expectation—to provide that elbow-room. And on examining the proposals of aid in some detail, we have discovered, not so much that their realization might make a Western association possible, as that they cannot be realized without forging closer links between the Western States. The urgencies of history thus unite with the urgencies of immediate economic survival—and both press towards union in the West. That is the first lesson of 1948. But how? That is the year's first riddle.

This point in time—early March, 1948—is in many ways an unfortunate moment at which to write of the prospects of Western association. In the seven months that must elapse before this book can appear, many of the steps which to-day seem all too remote may have been taken. Difficulties which seem insurmountable may have vanished. Co-operation may have been advanced to points which now seem visionary. No one can have lived through the months between the issue of the Paris Report and the Communist *coup d'état* in Prague without having the sense that the great stream of history is suddenly gathering speed. In setting up a signpost now, a writer takes the risk that, when the time comes to read its directions, they will not be pointing forwards to new stretches of human endeavour, but foolishly backwards to results already achieved. Yet the risk has to be taken and there is consolation in this fact at least—the Marshall Plan is to last four years and the full articulation of a Western Union is likely to take even longer. It was not after all on the first day of the wartime alliance between Britain and America that SHAEF was established, with its complete pooling of the men and the resources of each country. The possibilities of integration grew in the daily experience of common operations. Some such process will take place in Europe, provided the will to co-operate is consistent and strong. Western association will not spring, fully formed, from its creators' minds. They can only lay the foundations. It is the process of working together and acquiring joint experience that over the years will build the edifice.

Another difficulty in writing on Western association does not, however, spring simply from the necessity of writing in advance. It is the dreadful ease with which one can draw up paper plans and federal structures and conjectural constitutions and the equal difficulty of discussing the future in terms of concrete facts and possibilities. The literature of current politics is strewn with excellently composed schemes for union between regional groups and Continental groups, and even world groups. But the reader puts down each new plan with the feeling of having studied one more chart of Never-Never Land. To say this is not to underrate the necessity of politics and of constitutional procedures. On the contrary, it cannot be too strongly asserted that the decision to establish a Western association is a political decision for which no amount of juggling with economic co-operation is a substitute. But the formal writing of constitutions is certainly not the first step, for sovereignty can take so many forms, from the completely centralized government of a formal federation such as Soviet Russia, to the total lack of central government characterizing the British Commonwealth. The validity of the political decision to pool sovereignty—for that is what in essence a Western Union implies—can only be tested by the nation's readiness to make the sacrifices that a pooling of sovereignty demands in such vital fields as defence, economic planning, capital development, or foreign trade. These pages will be primarily concerned with the concrete questions of strategic and economic co-operation, not because they are substitutes for political decision, but because they are the difficult tests by which the genuineness of the nations' political will is to be judged.

The changed strategic position in Western Europe was described on an earlier page. Its essence is that the elimination of Germany, the weakening of France and of Britain, and the consolidation from the Elbe to the Urals of Soviet power, have totally destroyed the old balance of power in Europe. Whether or not Russian policy is fundamentally aggressive, the fact remains that a divided and disorganized Europe lies completely exposed to a military threat from the East. The obvious step for the nations of the Western fringe is to strengthen their defences by a regional defence pact, and the first step was taken when on March 17th Britain, France, and the Benelux Union signed a Treaty of Western Union, with military commitments to provide each other with automatic assistance in the event of aggression. To be effective this basic agreement needs to be completed by the kind of pooling which united British and American forces during the war—by a combined Chiefs of Staff committee at the top of the pyramid of command and by the integration of all three services on the genuinely international basis achieved inside SHAEF. This integration of command and armies would need to be backed by the complete standardization of weapons and equipment and by the division of production according to national capacity.[1] Such developments will, naturally, be made easier by the extent to which completely integrated defence was realized in the closing stages of the recent war. In the Allied air forces, armies, and navy, Belgian, Dutch, and French units served under the same jurisdiction as their British allies. In a Western Defence Union the commands would not be exclusively British, but the experience of the war could still be drawn upon. National prestige and national pride would, of course, be skilfully exploited by Communist opposition. To-day, the French Communists actively denounce as "Anglo-Saxon imperialism" any suggestions that the French air force should remedy its catastrophic lack of modern planes by co-operating more closely with the British. It is also certain that some of the members of a Western Union—the Swiss, for instance, and some of the Scandinavian countries—would remain outside any defensive arrangements. But these obstacles are hardly grave enough to prevent the development of the strong regional defence system based upon Britain, France, and the Low Countries, and open to all nations willing to accept its conditions.

The chief obstacle to the effectiveness of the defence pact is economic, not political. It is quite simply the doubt whether, given the destruction and exhaustion of war, the Western allies can afford to divert to military preparations the manpower and

[1] It would probably be wise to modify a complete division of function by planning for a strategic reserve of industrial production in Britain behind the tank trap of the Channel.

the industrial capacity they need desperately for their economic reconstruction. Is it any use giving a man with a weak heart a mailed fist? Of what use would a regional defence pact prove if, in the process of arming themselves, the nations concerned collapsed in economic ruin? The estimates for British defence in 1948 show how real is the risk. The sum of nearly £700 million to be spent on an armed force of a million men is a crippling load on a nation short of manpower and losing its reserves to the tune of £600 million a year. In the long run, a pooling of Western European defence will lead to a reduction of the load on each nation individually. But in economic survival, it is the short term that counts.

The only genuine and lasting solution is to place the conception of Western European defence in its proper setting. As we have seen, the balance of power is not simply the concern of Europe. It runs round the whole world, and Western Europe is one part of a chain of defence which includes the British Commonwealth and the United States. Western Europe is not simply the non-Russian part of the Continent. It is the vital frontier of the Atlantic world and as such should be defended in concert with the United States and Canada. More, it is the front line of free government for the whole world and as such is the concern of areas as distant as the British Dominions in the Southern Hemisphere. In the short run, while the nations of Western Union restore their economic life, a relatively greater burden should fall on other members of the Atlantic community who emerged from the war, not only less damaged, but with enlarged resources. The American role can be exercised relatively easily, since there are American garrisons in Germany, Austria, and Trieste, but two further possibilities need consideration—the offer to Western Europe of a formal military guarantee by the United States and possibly by Canada, together with a limited restoration of Lend-Lease to relieve the strain on Western Europe's industrial production.

These steps will lead undoubtedly to Communist cries of "encirclement" and military aggression, and to the accusation that Germany is being revived as the military core of an imperialist alliance against Russia. To this, there are two answers, the first that nobody in the West thinks of rearming the Germans. The one factor likely to spring any defensive association in the West wide open would be the discovery that any of the Allies thought of using German troops. But the wider answer is not so simple. Is it not a fact that competitive alliance building has led in the past to war? That alliances, non-aggressive in theory, have been, nevertheless, as aggressive as any in practice? Certainly, no sane man or woman in the West contemplates with pleasure the gradual edging of the defence problem into first place. In America the first glad relief of peace emptied the armed forces and left American armed might a hollow titan. Similarly in Britain, all the pressure of public opinion has been towards demobilization and a return to the nation's profoundly civilian conception of normal life. But whatever the inclination of the Western world, it has been compelled by the follies and paranoias of Russian policy to return to the posture of defence. It is not in Western Europe that the building of a network of defence pacts began. It was not in Western Europe that the first step was taken to substitute the general category of "warmongers" for the old definition of "Germany" as the potential enemy. The position had been reached early in 1948 that there existed a more or less fully organized military *bloc* in Eastern Europe and nothing at all in the West. However profoundly pacific the instincts of the Western world might be, the desire for reassurance and self-defence had to reassert itself. If the Communists go back to 1938 to criticize these moves and cry "encirclement," the Western Powers must also go back to 1938 and remember another word—"appeasement."

Even though such Russian moves as the Communist coup in Prague have forced the issue of Western defence to the fore, it is not necessary to believe in the inescapable imminence of war. The Communists have shown that they cannot co-operate with any other group, since they are not prepared to accept the fundamental issue of parliamentary government—that parties must be ready for their political fortunes to wax and wane and that the people may decide and must be allowed to change their government. The Czech Communists seized power because they feared the verdict of the polls. But it does not necessarily follow that the Russians are prepared to use force to establish Communist regimes outside the sphere of influence unhappily allotted to them at Teheran and Yalta. The Czech move may well have been in reality a defensive move—a move to stem the ebbing of Communist popularity, as a result, in part, of the new hopes raised in Western Europe by the Marshall Plan. In fact it can be argued that the Czech crisis was an indirect tribute to the force and attractiveness of the ideas latent in Western recovery, rather than the first step in a calculated plan of aggression against the West. If this interpretation is correct, the building of a defensive system in Western Europe, although urgent, is in the long run less important than pursuing with every resource at the various nations' disposal the recovery and integration of the Western fringe.

CHAPTER XIV

INSTRUMENTS FOR A WESTERN PLAN

The general aim of Western Europe's economic strategy has already been laid down—to achieve by 1951 a balance in its foreign accounts at a level of consumption not lower than that of 1946 and in some countries, considerably higher. This aim has two aspects—a negative aspect which is, in general, to make Marshall dollars go as far as they can, to cut down all unnecessary dollar imports, to allocate between the Sixteen Nations the available supplies in such a way as to make the most use of them, to check and prevent any diversion of precious materials to less essential purposes. The other aspect is positive—to encourage by every means the expansion of European production, to seek for alternative sources of materials ordinarily bought with dollars, to secure long-term markets, to open up new areas of production in hitherto unexploited territories. All these far-reaching powers have to be exercised on behalf of Sixteen Governments (or the number, whatever it may be, of Governments ready to co-operate) and they have to be co-ordinated day by day with American policies. The undertaking is formidable.

These functions are essentially central functions of planning and over-all direction, and the need for a central "Continuing Organization" has already been recognized by the Sixteen Nations. Before discussing its duties—negative and positive—in more detail, a word has to be said about its relationship with the American administration of the European Recovery Programme. The Economic Co-operation Act in its final form attempts to take the running of the Marshall Plan—both in Washington and in Europe—as much as possible away from the Government's direct administration. The head of the whole structure will be an Economic Administrator of Cabinet rank who will consult with the State Department, but will not be subordinate to the Secretary of State. He will have a free hand to choose his own staff and to work out methods of operation, but it is laid down in the Bill that his headquarters will be in Washington, that he will be represented by an Ambassador-at-Large in Europe, and by missions attached to each participating country and working in the Embassies under the loose supervision of the local American Ambassador. The pressure of Republican opinion has been enough to separate the functions of the Economic Co-operation Administration from the control of the State Department, and to see to it that a business man of independent status with a high standing in the business and financial world has been appointed. Before discussing the relationship of this Administration with the Sixteen Governments and with their Continuing Organization, it is perhaps relevant to point out that one cause of confusion in the development of the Plan may spring from the uneasy division of function between the State Department and the new Administration. During the war, the attempt to set up a Board of Economic Warfare, separate from the State Department, and under the jurisdiction of Mr. Wallace, the Vice-President, led to incredible confusion in the field of operations where attempts were made to play one agency off against the other; and this disorder was resolved only by a pitched battle which the State Department finally won. The President's original proposals for the new Economic Administration placed it under the Secretary of State. It might have been less confusing for Europe if such a course had been pursued.

But the chief difficulties in the relationship between the Economic Administration and the Sixteen Nations will spring from the unavoidable problem of reconciling the Sixteen's independence with the need for enough American control to satisfy Congress. The whole Recovery Programme will be under constant fire in Europe from the extreme Left, on the grounds that it is the cloak for imperialist capitalist intervention. Molotov set the key for this chorus when he left the Paris Conference "sooner than betray Europe's right to national self-determination." The theme has been plugged incessantly ever since. The American Administration, as well as such independent representative bodies as the Harriman Committee, are completely aware of this danger and have done their utmost to exclude from the programme any conditions or "strings" damaging to national prestige which might become the occasion of effective Communist propaganda. Mr. Stassen's plea that the European nations should guarantee not to nationalize any more industry has gone very little further than Mr. Stassen, and the few commitments demanded in the Economic Co-operation Act are no menace to a reasonable national self-respect.

The first commitment, which also figured in the Interim Aid Bill, requires that the Governments receiving free American assistance and selling it to their own people should put the proceeds of these sales aside in special "Local Currency Funds." These funds are to be spent only by mutual agreement between the local government and Washington and at one time there seemed a danger that the earmarking of some of these funds for later expenditure on capital developments might leave the Americans in a position to veto or at least influence the local Government's decision on so vital a subject as the scale and timing of a capital works programme. The possibilities of interference and of friction in such a project were, however, realized and the aims to which the Funds may be put have been scaled down to measures both useful and innocuous—for instance, the reduction of inflationary tendencies by actually destroying the money carried by the sale of dollar goods or by using the sums to retire public debt. One other suggestion is that the funds should provide the local currency necessary to build up stock piles of vital raw materials for American use.

This brings us to another condition—that after a certain period, the European Governments should be ready to make available raw materials to the United States to compensate the Americans for the raw materials used up in providing goods for the Recovery Programme. This condition, which is in many ways perfectly safe and reasonable, nevertheless demands rather closer attention, for it can lead back to Western Europe's central difficulty—the dollar shortage. If these stock piles of strategic raw materials are later to be purchased in dollars, no difficulties arise. On the contrary, if the United States, after a century of providing most of its own needs in raw materials, at last begins to search for those materials extensively abroad, there will be an automatic easing of the dollar problem. American practice will begin to come a little more into line with that of nineteenth-century Britain, and as dollars go out in search of iron ore and tungsten and copper and manganese, other nations will be able to buy the American goods, of which, at present, they must go short. The strategic stock piles would become one part of the general solution, which in the long run offers the only hope of a satisfactory relationship between America and the rest of the world—the solution resting on a policy of increased American imports, of massive American purchases abroad which would enable the dollar to play the stabilizing role played by sterling in the last century.

But if when the question of strategic stock piles arose, it were to become clear that America expected to obtain these materials either in return for the local currency funds, or as a reverse lend-lease for to-day's free goods, then it cannot be stated too soon that such an expectation would recreate in the 'fifties precisely the same problems as those which bedevil the world of 1948. If Europe cannot earn dollars on its raw materials but must transfer them to America free, the problem of securing enough dollars to buy goods in America will be as acute as ever. It will even be more acute, for free transfers would mean that a whole range of raw materials that might have been worked up into dollar exports would have to be handed over without return in their cheapest state. The result would be a serious loss to the Western European economy and one more factor in a continued inability to balance its foreign trade account.

To return to the question of the relationship between the Sixteen Nations in Europe and the American Economic Administration, we have seen that the Americans have gone out of their way to avoid conditions wounding to European national pride; the difficulty is that the actual relationship between Europe and America can of itself produce the wounds unless intense care is taken on both sides to reduce friction and misunderstanding to an absolute minimum. It is impossible in a book of this scope to discuss the intricate and detailed interrelations between American and European administrators, but certain general rules can perhaps be laid down.

The first is that the more the Americans can deal, not with each Government separately, but with a collective organization representing the collective will of the Sixteen, the less are the chances of opening the door to Communist charges of "imperialist intervention," "economic penetration," and so forth. The more, too, will the Americans serve the end they have made their own—that of using the Recovery Plan as an instrument of European integration. The other rule is closely connected with this first principle. It is that the greater number of issues the Europeans can agree upon among themselves, the easier will be their relationship with the American economic administration and with each other.

The only way to illustrate these rules is to apply them to a hypothetical case. Let us take the question of crude steel—a vital commodity for most of the Sixteen. The first stage is for the Americans to determine the amounts that are available. This, as we have seen, they have already done and the figure is something like 4 million tons less for 1949 than the amount the Sixteen had hoped to obtain. At this point, the methods of allocating the reduced amounts of steel between the claimants can diverge sharply. One method would be for the Americans to do the whole job of allocation themselves, saying to the British, "Here is your share," to the French, "Here is yours"—and so on. There are some signs that this approach has been considered, for in the papers published by the President in January, 1948, some lists of national allocations were given, in which the shares of the Sixteen in the key products were worked out for as far in advance as 1951. This method would involve the American Administrator in sixteen different bilateral negotiations in which it would be his task to test the accuracy of the national figures put before him, weigh them against the urgency of other claims from other nations and decide whether, in the light of the general programme, it would be more valuable for a steel priority to go to France, say, or to Luxemburg. In the course of such investigations, the Americans would find themselves very heavily and very directly involved in every aspect of each nation's domestic economy and they would incidentally be obliged to rely very greatly on the assistance of local experts, since an American body of investigators does not exist on a scale to deal with sixteen separate national economies in Europe. This method of allocation may perhaps best be described as treating Europe as a queue, the Americans moving the nations up and down the queue according to their own judgment of the urgency of the various needs.

Although the President's Bill speaks of a series of bilateral negotiations between America and the Governments of the Sixteen, there is a possibility that other methods are envisaged. In the papers accompanying the President's first draft of a Bill on European Co-operation, it is stated that:

"Although the ultimate determination of all allocations of United States supplies must remain with the United States, it is desirable to base these decisions on the multilaterally agreed recommendations of the European Continuing Organization of the participating countries or of other international recommendatory bodies."

This statement points to a very different method of allocation. If we return to the case of crude steel, the first step is the same in both methods[1]—the American Economic Administration determines the availability and this figure is given to the Continuing Organization. As we have seen, in the case of crude steel it would be very much lower than the figure of need estimated in the Paris Report, which had in its turn been reached by adding up the individual demands of the Sixteen Nations. The question would now be: Who is to take the cuts? And a decision should be reached on one basis only: Which cuts interfere least with the maximum production and development of European steel? The most obvious procedure would be to hand the problem over to a technical sub-committee of experts who would produce a provisional estimate of the best way to use the available steel and the cuts such a use would imply. It would then be the task of the Continuing Organization to persuade each member government to agree to the reasons put forward for the different cuts and to accept them in its own case. The more obviously the decision was based on public interest and broad economic advantage, the more easily would the member governments accept the sacrifices involved. Only when private agreement had been reached would the time come to discuss the allocations in public committee and to produce an agreed list of allocations for the American Administration. The idea, current in some circles, that the Sixteen Nations could not ration themselves because, in any final disagreement, Iceland would have the same voting power on the Continuing Organization as the United Kingdom, not only overlooks the practical experience of a number of international allocating agencies. It ignores the fact that the Organization would be a private negotiating body before it was a public allocating body. Such a distinction naturally requires that only men of the highest quality and of unquestioned integrity should be appointed to the Organization, but without such men the administration will in any case fail.

It has already been pointed out that the allocation of resources

[1] A different first step would be necessary where the commodity is controlled by some "international recommendatory body." Wheat, for instance, is allocated by the International Emergency Food Committee which now functions as part of the Food and Agriculture Organization. European coal is allocated by the European Coal Organization which is now a part of the United Nations Economic Commission for Europe. Where such bodies exist, the general availability of the commodity would presumably first be decided by consultation between the United States and the appropriate international body.

between the Sixteen is only one of the possible functions of an effective central planning staff. Others include the drawing up of programmes for the reduction of dollar imports, schemes for the expansion of sales in America, for the development of new non-dollar sources of raw materials. Such a body would also be responsible for the drafting of progress reports to keep each Government informed of the general state of recovery, and it would have to devise and persuade governments to accept measures to speed up production here or to divert it there in order to keep the overall plan in harmony. One particularly important function, in view of America's attitude to the Marshall Plan, would be to pursue the goods provided by dollar aid down to their "end-uses" to make certain that they were in fact being used to the maximum advantage. A regular auditing of this kind worked out in the closest co-operation with the American Ambassador at Large would be of immense value when, year by year, the question of the next Congressional appropriation came round again. At one point during the testimony on ERP before the Senate Committee on Foreign Relations, Mr. McCloy, the President of the International Bank, said that he thought the British would have been in a better position if they had kept and offered an exact account of the way in which the British Loan had been spent. Senator Vandenberg took up the hint enthusiastically and said that the existence of some such auditing system would make all the difference to the smooth working of ERP.

No doubt most people's instinct will be at this point to protest that no agency can be expected to accomplish so much and that the degree of integrated effort implied is far beyond the will or capacity of the Sixteen Nations. If, however, one studies the work accomplished by various international bodies during the war, it will be seen that very far-reaching results were achieved by joint planning. At the base of the pyramid of the Anglo-American war effort were the Combined Boards for Food and for Raw Materials and the Combined Shipping Board, through which passed most of the major decisions on the use and allocation of vital war resources. The problems these bodies had to face involved the most intricate balancing of one advantage against another—for instance, between the allocation of a scarce metal to a naval or to a military programme; or again, between the general advantage of securing a contented population by the distribution of imported civilian goods behind the front line and the immediate military

M

advantage of using scarce shipping for war supplies only. It is true that only two nations were involved in most of the decisions, but the Allied Shipping Administration had to secure the co-operation of Norwegians and Dutch and Greeks under the most difficult of circumstances—the almost certain loss of the ships involved.

Another relevant example of international planning during the war is to be found in the work of the Middle East Supply Centre, some of whose functions bear a strange resemblance to the prob-lems facing the Western Association. The Supply Centre was established in Cairo in April, 1941, as a British organization to which the Americans adhered a year later so that, like the Com-bined Boards, it became a joint Anglo-American concern. The reason for its establishment was the necessity of preserving order and economic stability in the hinterland of the Libyan battles at a time when the acute shortage of shipping made it necessary to cut back imports to the area and exports from it. This hinterland was conceived in the broadest manner and came to include Egypt, the Sudan, Tripolitania, Cyrenaica, Eritrea, Ethiopia, British and French Somaliland, Aden, Palestine, Syria, the Lebanon, Transjordan, Saudi Arabia, the Arab sheikhdoms, Iraq, Persia, and Cyprus. Malta was within its jurisdiction for a time, and Turkey was included for certain purposes.

The first task of the Centre was to cut the imports and exports of this vast area to the minimum. The aim was the saving of priceless shipping space. For absolutely essential articles—wheat and other foodstuffs, oilseeds, hides, fertilizers, coal, motor vehicles, and tinplate, the governments drew up programmes of their minimum requirements and after these had been carefully scrutinized at the Centre's headquarters in Cairo and matched with available supplies of goods and of shipping by the Combined Boards, the goods were purchased in bulk and distributed by the Centre. Less essential imports were covered by other methods, but all involved the securing of import licences before shipping was made available.

Since neither the supplies nor the shipping needed to maintain a reasonable level of subsistence in the Middle East were in fact available, the next task of the Centre was to advise governments on methods of increasing local supplies and to provide them with the means of doing so. In a couple of years, for instance, 2 million extra acres were brought under cereal cultivation by such expedients as turning over Egyptian cotton fields to wheat and cultivating new land in Syria with the aid of tractors. Another aspect of the work of increasing local resources to supplement lost imports lay in such programmes as a very rapid conversion of locomotives from coal to oil burning, and in the boosting of local industrial production in such vital necessities as fertilizers and the canning and preserving of foodstuffs. As an accompaniment to all these activities, Middle Eastern governments were encouraged to come together to exchange technical information and experience, work out methods of economic collaboration, and generally to take a timid step out of the cloistered seclusion in which they had pursued their national policies in the past.

Lastly, the Centre had considerable influence in ensuring that the imports were, in fact, devoted to the purposes for which they had been asked, and in an area disorganized, unruly, and unused to the complicated administrative methods of Western States, the Centre managed to secure a fairly orderly distribution of wheat, and even in Syria and Lebanon to organize an effective body for the collection of grain.

Thus on a small scale—for although the geographical area in the Middle East was vast, the density of population was low—the Middle East Supply Centre dealt with problems not altogether dissimilar from those which will face Western Europe. The basic problem of unavailable imports is common to both; the fact that the chief limiting factor in the Middle East was shipping, while in Western Europe it is dollars, does not entirely alter the principles upon which any programme of conservation, allocation and alternative supply should be based. The Middle East faced, in its modest way, the problem of increasing local production to replace supplies no longer available from overseas, and this is a problem which the central body of Western Europe must tackle on a vastly enlarged scale if some 2 billion dollars are to be cut out of its import programmes by 1951. The Supply Centre showed that governments as relatively backward and as technically ill-equipped as those, say, of Saudi Arabia or Iraq, could be coaxed and cajoled into using their allotted supplies to good advantage and improving local distribution in an area in which, even in peacetime, the blackest of markets found their natural habitat. In an area as much more developed, civilized, and sophisticated as Western Europe, a similar achievement should not be impossible. For the chief lesson of the Middle East Supply Centre is both a

simple and a very encouraging one. The organization worked. It
fulfilled its aims, it maintained reasonable prosperity and considerable stability behind the Allied lines and, had it been
developed on the basis of genuine Anglo-American understanding, it might still be an instrument of co-operation in the Middle
East. And if under such relatively unpromising conditions,
rationing, allocating, cutting back, developing local resources,
relating needs to availabilities could be achieved, there is surely
hope for a similar success with an infinitely stronger, better
backed and better equipped organization in Western Europe.

The criticism will no doubt be made—"Yes, but the backbone
of the Middle East Supply Centre was not the dozen governments
concerned. It was the Anglo-American staff at the centre and the
absolute control over all outside supplies exercised by the Anglo-
American Combined Boards. Conditions in Western Europe will
be very different. A single American authority will control most
of the supplies while Sixteen different sovereign States will sit
at the receiving end. Can such a structure be expected to work
as did the Supply Centre?"

Then let us take another example. Between 1945 and 1947,
during which time its main work was done, the United Nations
Relief and Rehabilitation Administration represented all the
Allies in its formal constitution. All sat at the supplying end, since
the basis of UNRRA'S finances was a contribution of one per
cent. from each national income. At the receiving end were the
nations of Eastern Europe, Austria, Italy, the White Russian
and Ukrainian Soviet Republics, and China. The argument that
since America and the British Commonwealth had the largest
national incomes and thus gave the bulk of the money (America's
share was about 70 per cent.), British-American control was, in
fact, complete, is not really valid, for UNRRA was set up as an
agency of the United Nations where the equality of the Great
Powers is a cardinal principle and where each member State is
jealously aware of its own rights and sovereignty. Those who
believe that UNRRA was dominated by the British and the
Americans (save in its demise) are ignorant of its internal working.
Far from being subservient to the dominant Powers, it was one
of the forces instrumental in securing in 1946 the transfer of the
allocation of the world's scarce food supplies from a body open
to the criticism of Anglo-American control—the Combined Food
Board—to a new international body, the International Emergency

Food Committee, and the procedures whereby UNRRA first received the programmes of the needy countries, scrutinized them for reliability, related them in the IEFC (or in its own commodity committees) to available supplies and then drew up programmes for each separate claimant might well be adopted as a working model of how such a process can be carried on in Western Europe's Continuing Organization.

It is particularly relevant to point out that the committee of UNRRA concerned with allocations at no time used the technique of voting to determine the various national shares. The proposed allotment was thoroughly discussed and explained to each government and their acquiescence secured. Lest the success of this method should be thought easy or obvious, it is only necessary to recall that among the receiving nations were Greece on the one hand, and the Ukraine on the other, while at the end of 1945 an ex-enemy, Italy, was added to the number of needy nations. The achievement may seem all the more remarkable if the actual programmes with their different scales are compared. The Ukraine received only some $188 million, whereas the share of Greece was $350.5 million, and that of Italy $420.7 million. Yet the Russian delegates accepted the figure and there were no cries of outraged national dignity or angry comparisons of war sacrifice and achievement.

It is impossible in face of this evidence to say that a system of allocations and priorities cannot be run on an international basis. The political good will of the Sixteen participating nations must, of course, be secured, but presumably that good will may be taken to be proved by their decision to come together in the first place. It is also necessary to establish cordial and confident relations with the supplying body in Washington—the Economic Administration—but again, the desire for such relations may be presumed to exist. Above all, the successful working of such a system requires administrators whose ability and independence of mind are beyond question—but it cannot be repeated too often that the Continuing Organization in any case depends upon securing the services of such men.

An instrument for international planning can be forged. But how much should it plan? Is the elaboration of a "dollar strategy" for Western Europe to involve every aspect of its economic life in a web of control? Is the attempt to be made to evolve a method of centralized planning even more elaborate than the total control exercised by such countries as Great Britain during the war? It is only necessary to state the question to see how impossible it is to envisage anything so far-reaching. It is after all sixteen different economies—seventeen with Western Germany—that come under consideration, and none of them before has attempted any genuine integration; and the limited efforts that have been made—for instance, the negotiations between the Benelux nations—have shown what formidable obstacles stand in the way. If joint planning is to be effective, it must determine its own limits and abide by them. And the limits should be set by confining planned control strictly to the essentials.

The lesson from national life is surely the same. The number of activities which can be genuinely and effectively planned and controlled are relatively few. The more detailed and all-pervasive physical controls become—the controls which depend upon forms and licences and permits—the more difficult it is to work them efficiently and to prevent them from clogging the wheels of effort. And if this is true inside the national community, in the undifferentiated economic climate between, say, London and Glasgow, how much more is it true of an area which until yesterday was criss-crossed with a score of national frontiers, a hundred separate authorities and a thousand active, vigorous, and entirely un-co-operative economic interests? So formidable, indeed, is the prospect of conducting economic collaboration over an area that includes the fishermen of Norway and Naples, the iron miners of Narvik and Lorraine, the farmers of Denmark and Donegal, and the bankers and brokers of sixteen different financial systems that, if it were not for some of the Allies' wartime experience of co-operation, the course of common sense might seem to abandon the attempt at planning altogether.

But if a warning is necessary on the possible extent of effective planning, an equally strong word is necessary in opposition to those who, looking at the difficulties and confusions of the last two years, announce their reconversion to *laisser-faire*, forgetting that it is precisely because *laisser-faire* in the old nineteenth-century sense will not work that the world has reached its present economic *impasse*. The techniques, the instruments of planning in a modern industrial society are admittedly new. They resemble the first efforts of men to build up a dam to canalize and harness a mighty rush of water. The first efforts will no doubt sweep away the dam—and the men with it—and the floods beyond will con-

vince a number of realists looking on that all these newfangled
ideas about control and purposive direction for water power are
not only nonsense, but dangerous nonsense. "Look what happens
when you interfere," they say. "More floods, more disasters.
It would have been much better to leave the whole thing alone."

But if that voice had been the voice of all mankind, abandoning
at the first check the effort to control and tame man's physical
environment, the men of Western Europe would no doubt still
be running about in wolfskins and woad. The challenge of man's
economic environment is no less. Admittedly, we have not yet
mastered the technique of controlling the rising flood of prosperity as it sweeps up towards a boom. Nor do we yet know how
to stay its fall. The tides we deal with are still unruly tides, but to
abandon the effort to discover the secret of reasonable control is
sheer abdication. And it offers no way out. For if these unregulated
tides are left to sweep this way and that across the lives of men,
the vast body of the dispossessed—the unemployed, the bankrupt,
the *déclassés*—will in their blind misery seize the instruments of
control which the totalitarians offer. They will be ready to accept
stability at the cost of the concentration camp and pay the price
of forced labour for the ending of unemployment. The abandonment of the idea of possible control is one more form of esca-
pist nostalgia for the dead golden world of nineteenth-century
enterprise and free trade and uncontrolled economic initiative.
But that world cannot be resurrected in its old shape because the
price it exacted for its liberties was, as we have seen, too high.
The dislocations introduced by too much control, such as sup-
pressed inflation, or the deadening of initiative, or the uneconomic
running of nationalized industries, are no worse than, only
different from, the dislocations introduced by too little—the dislocations of mass unemployment, low wages, or extreme economic
instability, and to argue that the policy of no planning and no
control produces its own automatic checks and balances is to
forget the point at which, instead of evolving a self-regulating
economic system, the community finds itself as it did in Germany
after the Great Depression, in the supremely regulated system of
some Hitlerian police state. No, the search for the appropriate
and effective methods of control has to continue; it is only the
added burden of our distracted world that the search has now to
be conducted, not only at the national level, but at the international as well.

CHAPTER XV

THE PLANNED SECTOR

The key to the planned sector of a Western European economy lies in the first place in the chief raw materials to be imported under ERP. Their use will in any case have to be controlled in order to satisfy the yearly investigation of Congress.that they are being devoted to the ends for which they were given, and the most appropriate instrument of planning in the first instance would seem to be the setting up, under the Central Planning staff, of sub-committees of experts dealing with each commodity. Such sub-committees did the preparatory work for the Paris Report and although each national Government faces severe difficulties in parting with its really capable officials to an international staff, a Western European union cannot be evolved without them.

The chief supplies provided under the Plan are, as we have seen, grain, fertilizers, fuel, steel, and materials for transport. Here, then, is the field in which the chief effort must be made to plan and integrate the resources of Western Europe. Before examining the various possibilities in detail, there are one or two general points to be considered. The first is clearly that no uniform pattern of integration should be attempted. The methods which are appropriate in dealing with a scattered and individualistic community, such as the farmers, are quite out of place when examining schemes, say, for a Western European electricity grid. From the start, the conception of tidy patterns has to be abandoned. If a genuine economic community is to be built in Western Europe, it must have some organic growth, in which case it must be allowed to be as rich and diverse and unsymmetrical as a natural organism usually is.

The second point is that planning and integration are not static policies, but imply development and change. To give one example, the first stage in a policy for steel might consist in the allocating of scarce steel supplies from abroad—they will be very scarce—and in the stimulating of local steel production in those mills likely to give the speediest result. The planning body could be the sub-committee on steel, the executive agents, the various steel companies in the different countries. The next stage would be to substitute for the sub-committee on steel the board of management of a Western European Iron and Steel federation which would begin the task of substituting regional and functional groupings for the purely national divisions prevailing now. The last stage could be the establishment of a West European Steel Corporation, with branches in different regions all ultimately under the same management. Such a corporation would be very large, but not so large as the United States Steel Corporation, and it could copy from some of the biggest of the American concerns the experiments in decentralization and devolution upon which they have been engaged for some time past.

A similar pattern might be followed with regard to coal—first, allocation and stimulus of production by a coal sub-committee, then the establishment of a coal federation based on the various national industries, most of which are already nationalized, and, lastly, a coal corporation operating freely across frontiers and planning its policy to meet the economic needs and to forward the interests of Western Europe as a whole.

The establishment of such corporations would go some of the way to meet two difficulties—one economic and one political— both of which can be severe obstacles to the development of closer integration. The first is the difference in standards of living and in wage levels between different groups of Western European workers. A quick solution of the problem is not possible, nor need it ever be complete, for within a national economy there are great differences in the well-being of the same class of worker in different parts of the country or in the general standard of wealth between different regions. The Black Country is wealthier than Tyneside, and the Londoner better off than the average citizen of Glasgow. But if some of the major industries were organized as international corporations there would be considerable pressure from within, forcing them to adopt roughly equivalent wage and salary rates and to approximate the benefits available to different national groups within the concern as a whole. In this way an important step would have been taken towards the equalization of Western European living standards.

The political difficulty is more grave and more immediate. For the last two years all attempts to reach agreement between

Britain, America, and France on the future of Germany have broken down on the refusal of the French to consider either the integration of their zone of occupation with the fused Anglo-American Zones—Bizonia—or the establishment of a government with effective powers for all non-Russian Germany so long as their demands for international control of the economic power house of the Ruhr have not been conceded. At first the French argued that the Ruhr and the Rhineland should be completely separated from the rest of Germany and set up as a separate sovereign state. They also demanded a reversal of the old economic division of activity between the German Ruhr and French Lorraine according to which the iron ore mined in Lorraine was despatched to the coking coal produced in the Ruhr to be worked up into steel. The French argued that greater security would be achieved if in future this division were reversed and the bulk of the steel making concentrated in France. In the last year the French have abandoned their extreme political demands, but are as insistent as ever that economic control of the Ruhr shall be made an inter-allied responsibility, that later, at some suitable time, it should become international by the addition to the board of management of responsible Germans. In this objective, they are supported by the nations of the Benelux Union whose attitude towards Germany is exactly compounded of an economic need for it to recover and a political fear of the consequences if it did.

Hitherto, the British and the Americans have made no move. They have hoped against hope to get agreement with Russia for policies covering Germany as a whole. They have also preferred the Ruhr to be under their own exclusive jurisdiction. But it is now clear that the only way in which economic integration in Western Europe can be made to prosper is by including the Ruhr with its rich resources within the framework. If its coal mines and its steel industry were subordinate branches of Western European Coal and Steel Corporations, a form of international integration as close as anything the French could desire would be achieved, and the question of how many steel mills should actually be located upon German or French or Luxemburg territory could be decided on the only finally valid basis—the technical criterion of securing efficiency and the lowest possible costs of production.

Coal, iron and steel are the dominant factors in heavy industry. Their "internationalization" would go far to create a genuine

Western European economy, but the links binding the new community together would be strengthened if a similar approach were applied to electricity, petroleum and to transport. The establishment of a central distributing system or grid for Western European electricity is not a task of the same complexity as that of unifying the production of coal and steel. The experience of the grid in Great Britain or the Tennessee Valley Authority in the United States are working models of its technical possibilities, and already electricity runs across frontiers in many areas—for instance, on the Rhine and in the Alps. The question of petroleum is rather more complicated. Three different processes are involved. First, the actual production of crude oil, of which there is virtually none in Western Europe,[1] but in which large British, French and Dutch interests are engaged abroad, mainly in the Middle East. Then comes the processing of crude oil into different products such as petrol, paraffin, kerosene and lubricants. Lastly, there is the question of distribution. Each of these phases is, as far as Europe is concerned, already organized on super-national lines and there are very considerable American interests in the field. It is difficult to be dogmatic about methods of integration, but it can perhaps be tentatively suggested that the different European oil producing interests could be joined together in a still closer federation, or even a single corporation with branches in Iraq, Persia and Arabia, and that joint subsidiaries should manage the refineries of Western Europe and be responsible for the large pro- gramme of expansion in refining capacity outlined in the Paris Report. In distribution, the wartime experience of the advantages to be derived from the extensive laying of oil pipelines—of which "Operation Pluto" was the most spectacular—might encourage the subsidiary established for distribution to contemplate a petrol grid on the lines of the electricity grid. A basic service of this sort, controlled by a single Western European distributive agency, would naturally be no bar to American companies working in the same field but, after the initial capital expenditure, a petrol grid might develop considerable economy of operation.

The railways, the roads, the canals, the rivers and the air lines of Western Europe are potentially the arteries of a single economic organism, and national divisions and frontiers do not necessarily

[1] The Zistersdorf oilfields in Austria are capable of producing about one million tons of crude oil a year, but at the time of writing it is uncertain if or when they can be recovered from the Russians.

correspond to the functional, technical and geographical arrangements necessary to secure the most efficient methods of transport.
Anyone who in the last two years has sat at a European airport,
watching half-empty machines of almost every European nationality taking off at half-hour intervals on almost identically the same
routes, must have wondered whether a pooling of air lines might
not bring with it more effective service. In land transport, a system
of trunk railways and trunk roads running from one end of the
Continent to another, served by regional systems of "feeder" roads
and railways, could give traffic greatly increased mobility, and
the standardization of railway equipment and of commercial road
transport should make possible the most efficient use of wagons
and lorries. And the same advantages could be derived from a
system of trunk canals and waterways, with standardized barges
and standardized methods of building and operating the locks.
It is, of course, obvious that side by side with the trunk systems
there would need to be vigorous regional development, but the
regions could be drawn not on the basis of national frontiers, but
of natural geographical areas, for instance, an Alpine region
from Basle to Linz and Bavaria to Milan or an extension of the
French "Nord" railway system to include the whole industrial area
of Northern France and Southern Belgium.

One of the vital categories of the Marshall Plan remains to be
considered—foodstuffs, the grain and fodder and fats and meat
which Europe hopes to secure with dollar gifts in the next four
years. It is clearly impracticable to contemplate the establishment
of international corporations or integrated organisms in the field
of agriculture. It is more a question of overall direction, of securing
the acceptance of balanced agricultural programmes and of
initiating the schemes for increased production and for cutting
back any wasteful or secondary employment of scarce resources.
In the next four years the sub-committees of the central body
dealing with cereals will have to find means of persuading most of
the participating nations to devote more land to bread grains and
fodder and to cut down less essential crops such as vegetables and
fruit and flowers. In particular, the plan already commented on in
the Paris Report—that of allowing grain production to fall towards
the end of the four-year period and of transferring the land set free
to stock raising—must be postponed until the world supplies of
grain are more plentiful and less confined to countries with hard
currencies.

At the same time the appropriate sub-committees for such items as meat and fats will be vigorously pursuing the policy of developing alternative supplies of these commodities. Both Britain and France have started programmes for increased supplies of fats from ground-nut plantations in Africa, and other examples of the expansion that can be secured in return for the offer of stable markets are to be found in the agreements reached between various Australian states and Great Britain for an increase in dairy farming and pig farming to serve British needs.

The functions of a planning staff for basic European foodstuffs need not cease with the end of the period of shortage. If there is one thing above all else to which the farmer and the peasant are attached it is a reasonable stability of price, and most governments in Western Europe have had at various times to guarantee the price of various agricultural products, particularly of wheat. There is no real reason why the staff entrusted during the Plan with the task of rationing and allocating might not remain as a permanent body to advise the Western European farming community on the amounts of various products consumption is likely to warrant, on the types of production most suited to particular areas, on the new possibilities of production opened up by new methods. Now that most of the major importing and exporting nations have reached a Wheat Agreement to stabilize prices and production for the next five years, a European regional council would find its task simplified by the possibility of carrying it out within an orderly international framework. To such a council could be attached a scientific advisory body with regional offices, charged with such tasks as the improving of stock and the organizing and running of experimental farms and seed stations. In this aspect of its work it would naturally seek affiliation with the Food and Agriculture Organization.

Ought a central agency responsible for interests and activities as vital as the steady and plentiful supply of foodstuffs to have no more than advisory powers? The difficulty lies in the impossibility of creating anything like an international organization to bring together millions of farmers, peasants and smallholders. Yet a measure of discipline might be developed through a more centralized production and distribution of fertilizers. Loose regional farming federations or co-operatives could be entrusted with the distribution of fertilizer—which will in any case figure on ERP's list of scarce commodities for some years to come—and the sanction on regions failing to fulfil their quota of any crop vitally needed might be a reduction in their supplies of phosphates and nitrogen.

This inevitably sketchy and incomplete outline of what might appear in the integrated sector of a Western European economy needs to be completed by two general points. The first is that the fundamental aim of any central planning staff should be to move away as soon as possible from the physical controls made necessary to-day by the severe shortages in so many vital raw materials. Systems of licensing, of forms and permits are inevitably clumsy and cumbrous. They are necessary to planning in a time of shortage but they are not an essential part of the machinery of integration. The international corporations, the transport system, the farming community of Western Europe ought to be able in more normal times of plenty to pay their own way, and to be guided broadly speaking by the price mechanism. It is no derogation from the idea of planning to say that financial controls are smoother, more efficacious and administratively more satisfactory than detailed physical controls. Taxation, minimum wage legislation, control over capital expansion—these are in the long run better instruments of central control than physical rationing, which, however necessary in time of dire shortage, is not an end in itself, but an instrument to be discarded the day its usefulness has passed.

The second general point is closely connected with this choice between financial and physical controls. It will be nowhere doubted that once the first crisis of shortage and under-production has passed, the real challenge to the economic stability of Western Europe will lie in the possible recurrence of the traditional cycles of depression and boom with all their attendant risks of instability, dislocation and mass unemployment. The control of the trade cycle remains the most momentous economic test of the Western conception of free society, and there is no more urgent question than to ask what are the prospects of mastering it in an organized economy covering all Western Europe. On an earlier page, mention was made of the theory of the trade cycle associated with the name of Lord Keynes. Its broad outline is relevant here. The theory suggests that the chief reason for the trade cycle is the essentially cyclical character of the demand for capital goods—for factories, for power stations, for railway transport; when demand begins to slacken in this vital sector, profits fall and workers are laid off and lose their wages; as a result, the demand for consumer goods slackens as well and the spiral of declining demand runs disastrously from top to bottom of the economy, until the exhaustion of stocks begins to create new demand which then spirals its way up again. Hitherto in capitalist economies both the upward and the downward spiral have been aggravated by the alternate waves of confidence and depression in business psychology, and by the unhappy incidence of the Government's financial policy which remits taxation in times of prosperity and increases it when times are bad, thus encouraging inflation when a boom threatens and increasing deflation in time of depression.

How can this deplorable economic phenomenon be countered? There is one possibility upon which schools of opinion as diverse as the economic experts of a vast private monopoly such as Lever Brothers on the one hand, and the theorists of the Labour Party on the other, are agreed, and that is the claim that if the expenditure of the community on capital goods can be spread evenly over the years and be maintained at a reasonably high level—say ten to fifteen per cent. of the national income—there is at least a very good chance that the major oscillations in the nation's line of economic development can be evened out.

The difficulty of applying this theory to individual countries in Western Europe is the degree of their dependence upon outside markets. For instance, the fact that Britain to-day has to pay three and four times as much as before the war for its food has brought the country face to face with national bankruptcy and no amount of sane and well-spaced internal capital development will remedy that fact. All the other trading nations of Western Europe are in the same case. In fact, there are virtually only two communities in the world to-day sufficiently independent of outside influences to make the experiment. One is Soviet Russia, and, indeed, one of its claims is to have banished the trade cycle, but this achievement has been carried through by measures of control so total, and in economic conditions so backward, as to offer no very sure conclusions to the Western World. On the other hand, the United States, an economy at once free and immensely wealthy, is most unlikely to make the first experiment in planned capital development, so strong is its present reaction against the very idea of regulation. But in a West European economy in which the chief sectors of heavy industry were under central control, both the scope and the means for such an experiment would exist. Western

Europe as a whole should in five years' time be wealthy enough and independent enough to have its economic destiny predominantly in its own hands. At the same time, the planning and phasing of the capital programmes of the coal, steel and electricity industries together with the industries connected with transport would provide a solid instrument for evening out the flow of fresh capital into the community.

The task of a central planning board would be to determine year by year, with all the relevant facts of the economy before it and in close consultation with the major industries—internationalized and private—whether or not the degree of proposed capital expenditure was sufficient to preserve stability and whether increases in productivity or the discovery of new materials or new techniques might not make possible an increase in the rate of capital investment without a counteracting danger of inflation. Such a mechanism would not be perfect. There would be endless loopholes still for instability, and it might take many years to train the type of expert able to undertake this new function of capital controller. Yet it offers hope at least of mastering the trade cycle without resorting to totalitarian control. And at the same time, year by year, it would knit more closely together the interests and the ventures capable of underwriting a genuine European economy.

It is possible that these last pages have been read with increasing impatience. "Why," the critic will complain, "Why abjure any attempt to write paper constitutions and blue prints for political union when all the time the extent of economic planning proposed is so wildly, so farcically exaggerated? Even if this is not the Never-Never Land of federation without tears, it is a Cloud Cuckoo Land of imaginary economics. If these are the measures proposed for a functioning Western Europe, let us reconcile ourselves at once to the idea of it not functioning, for all these international controls and monopolies and cartels and planning agencies demand sacrifices of sovereignty which no statesman in his senses can even consider."

The criticism is to this extent valid that the measures outlined in these pages are not easy and all involve some sacrifice of sovereignty. They demand a break with a past which clings to each national community with all the tenacity that memories and traditions and history and interest can lend it. Yet there are two possible lines of defence. The first is to return to the old question: "What then is the alternative? Let us admit that this course is difficult and often painful, but at least at the end of it lies hope. Will the alternatives of slow decline or sudden collapse prove less difficult or less painful, especially since they are of their very nature hopeless as well?"

CHAPTER XVI

EXPERIMENTS IN INTEGRATION

The second line of defence is more concrete. The assumption behind the criticism is that the degree of unification and control proposed for the various industries in Western Europe is so exaggerated as to be entirely unobtainable. But is it generally known how much co-operation and consolidation has already gone on in the various industries under discussion, both before and since the war? Before dismissing as nonsense the whole conception of a planned sector in a Western European economy, it would be as well to see how much, in however uncoordinated a way, has already been accomplished in these fields.

Of all the commodities in short supply after the war, coal should have proved the most difficult to allocate. Coal is the principal foundation of most of Europe's industrial activity and no nation could hope to achieve economic recovery without securing at least a minimum coal supply. The pressure of demand was therefore tremendous. At the same time, the direct political power which could potentially be exercised by a producer with a coal surplus was equally great. The stage thus seemed to be set for an unholy scramble. In fact, in no field has the machinery of international allocation worked more smoothly or given more unsensational and profoundly valuable results. The instrument of planning was, until January, 1948, the European Coal Organization which, after an initial period under the wing of SHAEF, came into independent life in January, 1946. Its work has not ceased. It has merely been transferred to the ægis of the United Nations Economic Commission for Europe, and since the Commission covers Eastern as well as Western Europe, and one of the factors in the Marshall estimates is the securing of coal exports from Poland, the coal committee is likely to continue to play an influential part and to be closely consulted and supported by whatever sub-committee on coal is set up under the central agency of the Sixteen. Indeed, this principle applies to all the activities of the Sixteen. They have everything to gain and little to lose by maintaining economic relations with Eastern Europe which, especially in the vital fields of coal, timber and foodstuffs, may provide them before long with valuable dollar-saving surpluses. And if these contacts are to be maintained no better instrument exists than the Economic Commission for Europe which is already in being.

The way in which the European Coal Organization has conducted its operations can best be described in the words of one who had the opportunity of seeing it work at close quarters:—

" The purpose of ECO, as set out in its Agreement, was to 'promote the supply and equitable distribution of coal and scarce items of coal-mining supplies and equipment,' as well as to 'safeguard, as far as possible, the interests of both producers and consumers.' Its principal instruments were a General Purposes Committee which acted, in most respects, as the steering body, and an Allocation Purposes Committee which kept the supply and demand relationship under constant review and made the appropriate recommendations to the governments concerned. Full members of ECO were: Belgium, Czechoslovakia, Denmark, France, Greece, Luxemburg, Netherlands, Norway, Poland, Turkey, the United Kingdom, and the United States. Finland, Italy, Portugal, Sweden, and Switzerland participated as associate members. Austria was neither a member nor an associate, its coal requirements having in the past been met by a direct allocation from the Bizone of Germany.

"In the field of allocations, the first objective was to secure for each country a minimum amount of coal. Coal committed by bilateral agreements (mainly Polish coal) was naturally taken into account in assessing each country's quota. This left Ruhr, Saar, and American coal for direct allocation. The yardstick employed was a complicated allocations formula which made allowance for each country's internal production, its bilateral exports and imports, its war damage, its reconstruction plans, its development of hydro-electric and other sources of power and a number of lesser factors. On the basis of this formula—which was itself subject to frequent revision— governments consented each quarter to confine their purchases of Ruhr, Saar, and American coal to within agreed percentages of the total quarterly supplies."[1]

Allocations have not been its only task. It has had to take a part in solving the difficult problem-within-a-problem of allocating to

[1] *The Economist*, January 10, 1948, p. 61.

the best advantage not only coal, but coking coal as well. The Sixteen Nations originally sought to secure supplies of coking coal abroad, but these proved to be unavailable. Their sub-committees on Iron and Steel and the Mixed Sub-Committee on Coke then explored ways and means of making better use of the coking coal supplies in Europe, and as a result, were able to produce a programme whereby, with careful allocation, enough could be made available to meet the principal requirements of the Sixteen.

Another vital topic taken up by the ECO was the study of the measures necessary to introduce the standardization of many types of mining equipment and to encourage different countries to specialize on different branches of mining machinery so as to get the best results from mass production. Yet another topic, studied in collaboration with another international body set up after the war, the European Central Inland Transport Commission (ECITO), was the method of improving coal deliveries by making the best use of existing rolling stock and by avoiding expensive crosshauls and detours.

Enough surely has been said to show the extent to which the kind of question which would come within the competence of a board of management of a Western European Coal Corporation has already been discussed and considered at an international level. The Coal Sub-Committee of the Sixteen, together with the ECO, would be in possession of both the information and the authority necessary to control an integrated coal industry. The step to be made from the present type of international consultation and agreement over to the creation of a single coal federation or corporation is still a big one, admittedly, but it is nowhere near so big as those who have not followed the development of international co-operation in the last two years probably imagine.

Mention has been made of the ECITO. Its work in connexion with transport in Western Europe again bears out the belief that international integration in certain fields of Western European activity is not as distant as is sometimes supposed. Transport is in any case a field in which a measure of international co-operation has long been the rule. Before the war, companies such as *Compagnie Internationale des Wagons Lits* attached their coaches to trains running from one end of Europe to the other. International bodies regulated shipping on the great inland waterways of the Rhine and the Danube. In 1921, an International Wagon Union was established to lay down rules for the common use of freight cars in international traffic. Since the war, the ECITO has been giving a more general oversight to the problems of European transport. In 1945 it set up a Freight Car Exchange Committee to prevent any empty running of wagons and to use to the fullest advantage the greatly reduced stock of freight cars. It is now proposed, with its assistance, to go further and set up a permanent International Pool of freight cars to which governments and industries can turn, particularly to help them to deal with seasonal variations in the amount of traffic they require. The Sixteen hope to supplement the creation of this pool by another step. The International Technical Standards Conference has been asked to advise on methods of producing standardized designs for the 453,000[1] new wagons which have to be built in the next years. In this way the new stock should be perfectly interchangeable. Another interesting experiment is the decision of the Sixteen to attempt to distribute the production of this vast building programme in such a way as to avoid the creation of an excessive expansion of capacity in any one country. On the contrary, the attempt will be made to distribute the orders in the best long-term interests of European coach-building in general.

This brief account has said nothing of the ECITO'S efforts to secure the best routing of traffic to make the fullest use of existing capacity and its effort to guide commerce back into the main arteries of traffic from which the dislocation of war has diverted them. But again, enough has been said to suggest that it is not too fantastic to conceive of a central body for European transport and for the integration of its different branches on an international basis.

Another telling example of international co-operation is that of electricity. In the first place, the Sixteen Nations, which, as we have seen, are planning a very great increase in their generating capacity, have agreed to give each other all possible information and assistance in producing the maximum amount of electricity from their own systems and in making it available to others in the best interests of Western recovery as a whole. A Public Utilities Panel was set up for this purpose and the Power Committee established by the Economic Commission for Europe will also be used. The Sixteen have, however, gone further. So pressing is the need

---

[1] The total need for new wagons is 724,000, but those of Britain and Eire (271,000) are not included, for they are not of Continental design.

for more electricity that they have agreed to build nine new power stations at the cost of $315 million. These stations have been chosen simply on their economic merits without regard to national frontiers or interests, and the task of building them will be a joint undertaking, the Sixteen making themselves responsible for the extra materials needed. When the programme is complete, an annual output of 6,645 million k.w.h. will have been added to West Europe's supply.[1]

At this point the criticism may be put forward that most of these examples of co-operation belong to the days of acute dislocation which have followed the war. In quite exceptional circumstances, it may be necessary to take exceptional steps, but what reason is there to suppose that the measures of co-operation would be sustained, once more normal times had returned? But this objection overlooks the extent to which, in times of peace, without any of the pressures or disturbances produced by the aftermath of war, the industries of Europe have in the past succeeded in co-ordinating their policies. Perhaps the most striking example is also the most influential and decisive, since it concerns a process essential to the carrying on of almost every industry— the production of steel.

The first step in establishing closer collaboration between Europe's steel interests after the first World War was taken in October, 1926, when the German steel interests, organized in a close domestic cartel, persuaded the Belgian, French, and Luxem-

[1] INTERNATIONAL PROGRAMME FOR ADDITIONAL HYDRO-ELECTRIC, BROWN COAL AND GEOTHERMIC ELECTRICITY GENERATING PLANT PROJECTS

Name of plant (H=Hydro) (B=Brown Coal) (G=Geothermic)	Country in which situated	Country to which supply would be given	Installed capacity (thousand kw.)	Cost (million) $
Adige Noce (H)	Italy	Italy	140	22
Bouthier (H)	,,	,,	972	46
Fessenheim (H)	France	France	120	67
Goldenberg (B)	Germany	,, Benelux	190	18
Larderello (G)	Italy	Italy	75	6
Piave (H)	,,	,,	130	16
Sarca Molveno (H)	,,	,,	180	30
Upper Inn (H)	Austria Switzerland Italy	,, Austria	349*	80*
Weisweiler (B)	Germany	France Benelux	—	—

* These figures relate only to the Austrian part of the project.

burg steel interests to enter into the *Entente Internationale de l'Acier*. Between them they accounted for about 30 per cent. of the world's production of steel, but close on 70 per cent. of its steel exports. This agreement fixed quotas for domestic production and for export, and nations exceeding their quotas paid fines which went in part to those who had failed to reach their allotted output. A Chairman and a Management Committee controlled the whole *Entente*, each with voting rights related to the size of its quota. Normally the chairmanship was to rotate each year, but the political neutrality of Luxemburg made it the most acceptable choice and its representative retained the chair during the three years of the *Entente's* life. The whole business of quotas, fines and reimbursements were under the external audit of a Swiss firm.

The purpose of the *Entente*, it need hardly be pointed out, was restrictive. It was an attempt to stabilize and organize production and to prevent "wasteful competition" which, in effect, meant almost any form of competition. Its control extended to the closest details of domestic production and it placed great pressure on the different steel interests within each nation to combine in a single domestic cartel by making those groups which had entered the international cartel responsible for the production of all producers, those who were affiliated and those who were not. In other words, if firm X which was not a member of the domestic cartel increased its output of steel and pushed the figure of national steel production above the permitted national quota, the firms Y and Z, which were part of the domestic cartel and affiliated to the international *Entente*, would find themselves paying fines for X's behaviour. Their interest in bringing X into the cartel was thus obvious.

This structure and organization is not cited in order to recommend the aim of the old *Entente*. It is merely given as an example of how close international organization and control of the steel industry has been in the past—without any governmental intervention, or any effort of public planning. The companies themselves simply decided they had better plan and proceeded to do so.

The first *Entente* did not survive the crash of 1929. The catastrophic fall in foreign markets destroyed the *Entente's* discipline and the fierce competition for the shrinking export trade encouraged every fissiparous tendency both internationally and within the domestic cartels. Equally, however, the disastrous losses suffered, the closing of plants, the laying off of men, the stoppage in production encouraged the industry after the first shock had passed to take stock of the position and to revert to the process of organizing itself and planning itself out of the depression. As we have seen, in the first phase the emphasis had been on national quotas for steel production. The second phase began with the control of individual end products. Agreements were drawn up between the four founders of the old *Entente* to regulate the price of such materials as structural steel, semi-finished materials, merchant bars, hoops, and strips, and through "export sales comptoirs," one for each product, to allot to each nation its quota for export. This attempt, however, again failed in face of the continuing depression and between 1931 and 1933 there was no general steel agreement.

In 1933 a new attempt was made to regulate steel policy on the basis of fixed quotas for export. For a time there was a general quota for crude steel, but this was gradually replaced by the organization of export sales comptoirs for almost every form of steel product. The new agreements were on a firmer basis than had been the pre-depression *Entente*, for the internal organization of the steel industries in France, Belgium, and Luxemburg was now almost as far-reaching as that of Germany, and the number of products covered was also much more complete. Its strength received new recognition when Poland and Czechoslovakia, both with practically nationalized steel industries, joined the *Entente* in 1935 and 1936. In 1935 the British steel industry, now organized in a loose cartel or federation, reached an agreement with the *Entente* and the combination of the *Entente* on the one hand, and the British Federation on the other, formed the European Steel Cartel. In 1938 the whole process of cartelization was crowned by the entry of the United States steel producers (through their Steel Export Association) into the agreement which set up the International Steel Cartel.

A word may be said of the organization of this vast structure. Originally the four member nations of the *Entente Internationale de l'Acier* set up two bodies, a management committee and a comptoir committee, each with a chairman (a Luxemburg representative retained both offices) and a board drawn from the participating national steel cartels. The management committee discussed general policy and met only about once a quarter. The comptoir committee met very often, whenever necessary, without fixed intervals and dealt with practical problems of prices and quotas. When first the British and then the Americans joined the cartel, new committees of management were set up, but the two agencies of the *Entente* remained as the general staff and secretariat of the wider bodies.

The essence of the work accomplished by the Cartel was to fix export prices and quotas on the one hand, and on the other to protect the domestic markets of the participants from competition from outside. But although these two functions represented the core of the undertaking, the management committee in fact ranged over a much wider field. Problems of production, exchange of information, protection of the interests of the steel industry as a whole, were regularly considered, and the central body went far towards becoming the central direction of a single co-ordinated steel industry covering Europe and, though in a less effective way, crossing the Atlantic to include the United States. The only question which the Cartel did not ask itself—and in the nature of its organization could not ask itself—was the question whether its activities, by their restrictionism, their price main-tenance schemes, and their protection of domestic markets, were not harmful and wasteful to the economy at large.

But the point here is not to defend the policy and the aims of the steel cartel. They were frankly restrictive or, if not restrictive, stabilizing. The aim was, given industries of different sizes and demand of a certain size, to ensure that a steady share of that demand was divided between the different participating nations. They did not ask themselves whether the companies were as efficient as they might be, whether, in each nation, the optimum production had been reached; they offered no solution to the problem of the inefficient producer. Nor on the side of the market was it any responsibility of theirs to find out whether real demand might not in fact be much larger than actual demand could be at the monopoly prices fixed by the comptoirs. There was no principle of growth and expansion within the organization itself and by eliminating competition and fixing prices it eliminated the capacity for growth represented by the individual *entre-preneur's* desire to go after bigger profits. In fact, it took a world war to demonstrate to the American Steel companies that they could double their output and still leave the American economy hungry for steel.

The importance of the steel cartel in the context of Western European association is not therefore its aims and economic policies, but the extent to which, by spontaneous collaboration, the separate units of the cartel came together in what was virtually a single controlled industrial structure, embracing in the closest unity the inner core of France, Germany, and what we would now call the Benelux Union and integrating into that association the steel producers of Great Britain. It is nonsense to say, in face of this demonstration, that the establishment of a single United European Steel Corporation is utterly impossible. The problem of organization has to a very large extent already been solved. The chief question is whether such a corporation could be made to pursue expansive and enterprising policies and meet the tremendous demand for steel which will endure in Europe until the last blitzed city has been rebuilt and the last development scheme in Africa (or India or China for that matter) has been completed.

An organized West European steel industry can exist, for it has already done so. But can Western Europe create a steel industry fit to be the mainspring of an expanding Western economy, an industry which might resemble the old cartel in structure, but by coming under the control of a positive programme for European reconstruction might break once and for all with the cartel's restrictive past? A public steel corporation geared to meet a demand for steel second only to that of the United States—such should be the aim of Western Europe, and although past history does not offer complete proof that it can be accomplished, it does at least lay down beyond the possibility of doubt the fact that the closest co-operation and integration are possible, even without any intervention by governments or any kind of pressure from without. And if private interests, unaided, can build the machinery, it should not be beyond the wit of public policy to provide the proper aim.

CHAPTER XVII

AN ORGANIC WESTERN ECONOMY

It is important to remember that this, the planned sector of a possible Western European economy, is only a part, even a small part, of the great web of industrial activity and commercial exchange which would, in a genuine Western Union, hold the countries together in a single economic community. The economic interests falling outside the control of governments and planning authorities would be large and important, and it is not enough simply to ensure that fuel and iron and steel and basic foodstuffs are organized and directed on an international basis. It is equally important to see that every activity, every venture, serves the same purpose of widening the basis of a Western European economy. The aim should be to emulate the prosperity of the United States by reproducing its lack of inhibiting internal conditions—the absence of trade barriers, the absence of competing currencies, the freedom of men and capital to move more or less freely from one end of the Union to the other. This is the aim, but before we study the means to attain it, two warnings must be made. The first is that just because the factors now under discussion belong to the unplanned sector of a Western Union, to the uncontrolled and unorganized area of economic endeavour, blue prints are out of place. The programme is bound to consist more of removing obstacles than of creating policies, and it may appear negative simply because the positive part has to be filled in by the great army of traders and workers and managers and business men whose actions and decisions—the mainspring of unregulated economic life—cannot be predicted or described in advance.

The second warning is more serious, for it is concerned not only with the problem of Western Union, but with one of the fundamental obstacles to the achievement of greater freedom in the world economy. The starting point is the inescapable fact that communities cannot stand more than a certain degree of economic freedom. Perhaps the point can best be illustrated by a practical example. On the eastern seaboard of the United States, in a rugged countryside where only hard work could coax a living from the soil and where the raw materials for industry were scanty and scattered, the first settlers in America built up with toil and thrift the New England states, and it was there that in a community of farmers and traders and fishermen the first foundations of American industrialism were laid—in textile mills beside the quick-running streams, in small iron foundries, in the sawmills standing in the woods and run by water power. To-day the visitor to New England may stop beside some old stone bridge and see at the river's edge a pile of crumbling masonry. It was once a mill. Or at a crossroads, he may find some old mound of earth and rubble and be told that there, once upon a time, stood the first iron foundry to be set up in the United States. And if his walks take him through the wooded hills of Massachusetts and New Hampshire, he will find, scattered here and there, grown over with bramble and brushwood, the barns and the outbuildings and the once solid frame houses of long deserted farms. The ghost of an old economy lies beneath the surface of these states which now turn more and more to tourism and winter sports and hunting to earn a living for the depopulated countryside.

Why did this change come about? Simply because the march of the westward settlers opened up more fertile and productive lands. The farmers of Iowa, the fruit growers of California, the new steel masters of Pittsburg destroyed in one competitive wave the old New England industries which, since they belonged to the same economic union, had neither tariffs nor protection to ward off the invasion. But if the men and women of New England were exposed to the rigours of free trade, they also enjoyed the advantages of free movement. As the economy crumbled, the people moved on to the West. The grandchildren of those deserted farmhouses may now be farmers themselves in Kansas or Imperial Valley. An adjustment could be made and the community at large gained the advantage of cheaper and more plentiful goods, while the New England states were not asked to pay an intolerable local penalty for the general good. But there is a double lesson in the abandoned farms and broken mill wheels of New England— a lesson for the United States and a lesson for Europe.

The first lesson is of the limits of completely free trade as the final determinant of economic policy, unless it can be accompanied by the freedom of movement for men and goods which is possible within the continental economy of the United States. Let us suppose for instance that in free competition with Old England, the United States in the field of heavy industry could repeat the feat of the late nineteenth century when, under completely free trade, British agriculture all but disappeared under the competition of grain from the New World. The result would be the decline of the Black Country and the North and the appearance of mass unemployment there—resembling the stagnation and depopulation of the English countryside after the 1870's. If the workers of Birmingham and Manchester could, however, like the iron masters and steel workers of Massachusetts some eighty years before, move on to the new centres of industry in Pennsylvania and Ohio and Illinois, England could be in a position to make the adjustment made by New England—to abandon heavy industry and to turn to other activities. But no such movement is possible. Strict immigration laws prevent the free movements of peoples to the American continent, and far from discovering a natural adjustment, Old England would be compelled to lose its wealth and keep its population. This example is perhaps extreme, but it is a warning that free trade, limited to the right of American goods to go anywhere, can create economic maladjustments with social consequences so disastrous that no other nation can accept them.

The second warning is to Europe. The removing of tariff barriers and other obstacles to free trade, desirable though it undoubtedly is, will prove more complex and more troublesome than is admitted by some who advocate a "customs union at the stroke of a pen" as the best and quickest solution of Europe's ills. To say so much is not to deny that the ultimate objective is the creation of a single, free, continental economy in Europe with a single financial system. It is simply to stress the amount of hard work and preparation such a solution entails and how many and how various are the obstacles which have to be removed before it can be achieved.

All the practical work accomplished so far on the subject of customs unions bears out this fact. The most advanced stage of negotiations has been reached by Holland, Belgium, and Luxemburg. After eighteen months' discussion they reached on January 1, 1948, the point of establishing a common tariff wall round their three countries and of removing tariffs internally. At this point they realized that economic union—in the sense in which any three states within the United States are unified—was still very far to seek and the obstacles which they found to be impeding them most are instructive for the rest of Europe. One was technical —the extent to which excise duties differed between the two countries and the different importance of such taxes in the countries' budgets. The second was more fundamental. In spite of a reasonably high degree of differentiation between the two economies—the Belgians being highly industrialized, the Dutch mainly an agricultural people—this naturally complementary character of their two economies was becoming endangered by the impoverishment of Holland (as a result of the war) and by the country's belief that it must industrialize itself to make good its losses. It was therefore found necessary to set up a joint council to advise on industrial development in the two countries and to attempt to prevent overlapping and competitive industrial development. But the crucial obstacle to the fusing of the two economies was found to lie in the weakness of the Dutch guilder in relation to the Belgian franc and the low productivity of the war-shattered Dutch economy. A system of exchange control, of import and export licences, of frontier controls, of work permits is still necessary to prevent the Belgian economy from being flooded by Dutch demand, reserves, and man power. The Benelux countries have decided to move on to deal with these problems, but the lesson is clear—a customs union is only one step in a full economic union or it is almost nothing at all.

Very much the same conclusion can be drawn from the preliminary stages of the discussions between France and Italy on the customs union which their two governments have decided to undertake. A mixed Commission explored the possibilities of integration, industry by industry, surveyed the vital field of agricultural production, and studied transport, the export market and problems of finance. The conclusions throw light on the whole question of methods of closer union. In general, the members of the Commission came to the conclusion that a customs union was possible and necessary. An enlarged domestic market and a specialization and rationalization of industry and agriculture in both countries would enable them to produce goods more efficiently and more cheaply, to compete more effectively abroad and thus to raise their own standards. But the Report made it clear that a mere removing of tariff barriers would not in itself produce the desired effect and other more positive policies would need to be pursued. For instance, in certain fields, in wine growing and in the production of fruit and vegetables, the two economies are so competitive that a joint production and sales organization would be necessary to prevent "destructive competition." Similar agreements would be needed in textile manufacture and in various engineering trades, even though the pressure of present demand did not make these measures of cartelization immediately necessary.

The Report also expressed the belief that a Union would be a great benefit in helping to solve the two countries' problems of population. France's population is static with a strong tendency to decline, while Italy's increases steadily and is already several millions beyond the economic capacity of the country to carry. Yet the Commission did not suggest that a customs union as such would solve this problem. It would only provide a framework within which the two governments could work out practical schemes for the transfer of labour, schemes in which standards of work and the conditions of employment, of settlement, and of possible repatriation would be carefully established.

The most significant comment in the Report, however, referred to the practical difficulties in the way of implementing a customs union so long as the currencies of both countries had a fluctuating value and one which was not related to their real purchasing power. The Commission suggested that until a minimum degree of stability had been achieved in this field, it would be useless to expect much from a mere reduction of tariffs. Thus the Franco-Italian experience comes to the same conclusion as the Benelux experiments—that there are certain economic conditions which are more vital to the achievement of economic union than the abolition of internal tariffs and the establishment of a single tariff wall round the economy. In other words, a customs union can be an immensely important factor in the creation of an economic union, but it will not, as it did in simpler conditions a hundred years ago, of itself create economic unity. For such an achievement other methods are more necessary and more urgent.

Before going on to discuss the nature of some of these other more immediate instruments of economic integration, we ought to consider, however briefly, one other difficulty raised by the project of a Western Customs Union. This is not a general difficulty inherent in the nature of a customs union as such, but a particular difficulty lying in the path of the Western Union's most powerful potential member—the United Kingdom. Ever since the Ottawa agreements of 1932, Britain has, together with the other Dominions of the Commonwealth, been a partner in a system of preferential tariffs. The essence of the arrangement, as we have seen, is the granting to each other of preferences in the domestic market not open to non-members of the group. Great Britain's chief concessions lay in the sphere of agricultural commodities. In return, British manufactures enjoyed certain privileges in the Dominions markets. As a discriminatory arrangement, this system of Imperial preference established at Ottawa has always been particularly unpalatable to the Americans, who have exerted considerable pressure at the various post-war conferences on international trade—at Geneva and Havana—to get the system modified. But the new difficulty facing the system is not American dislike, but the problem of reconciling the entry of the most powerful unit in the Ottawa system, Great Britain, into an entirely new economic system in Europe. If Britain entered a complete customs union, New Zealand, far from enjoying exclusive privileges in the British market, would find itself at a disadvantage in competing with the dairy produce of Denmark and Holland. At the same time, the manufactures of Britain could hardly enjoy privileges in Dominion markets denied to its other European partners.

Various solutions have been discussed. The entry of the Dominions into a European customs union together with Britain can probably be ruled out. The Canadian economy is too closely linked with that of the United States to enter a union one of whose aims must be to establish a certain independence of dollar imports. The Southern Dominions could perhaps be coaxed into closer association in return for the guarantee of vastly extended markets for their meat, wool and dairy products in a union which would not be self-sufficient in any of these. But the difficulty is that Australia in particular has embarked on a considerable local expansion of industry and although the entry of British manufactures on a preferential basis can just be absorbed, the local industry—an "infant industry" classically in need of protection —could not withstand the competition of duty-free manufactures from the whole of Western Europe. The likelihood of the Commonwealth entering a Western economic union is thus not very great.

There might be a possible solution if the nations of Western Europe determined to establish, not a complete customs union (in which tariffs are reduced to zero), but instead a "low tariff area" in which all tariffs are uniformly reduced to some low figure—say 5 to 10 per cent. *ad valorem*—for all members of the group, while remaining at their former level for non-members. Under such a system the British, by permitting some Commonwealth products to enter duty free into Britain, could still combine membership in one trading system—that of Europe—with membership in another—the Commonwealth. Such a device might also be adopted by the French and the Dutch and the Belgians if they were unwilling to bring their colonial dependencies into the European Union on a completely equal footing.

The real obstacle to such an arrangement would, of course, lie with the keen objection felt by the Americans for any discriminatory measure which does not go so far as the total discrimination of a complete customs union. If, however, the creation of a "low tariff area" in Western Europe could be shown to be the almost essential precursor of a later customs union and meanwhile to permit of a really valuable expansion in European trade, it is probable that American agreement could be secured.

Political difficulties such as Britain's equivocal position inside two potentially competing economic systems and America's somewhat dogmatic approach to what is and what is not permissible in the sphere of economic integration are not, however, likely to be the most difficult or the most immediate obstacles to an economic union. To judge by the experience of the Benelux countries and of France and Italy in discussing their customs unions, a single economic difficulty underlies all present attempts to produce closer economic integration—whether it is ambitiously conceived as a total economic union or confined more modestly to what the French call "a tariff community." This difficulty is the lack of stability in some local European currencies, which in its turn springs from a lack of production in the local economy. Low levels of production produce the phenomenon of inflation in which consumers' demands outstrip the supply of goods available, prices are forced up and the value of money falls—sometimes uncontrollably; and this in turn undermines the value of a currency in international terms, for foreign customers are as sensitive as domestic purchasers to a currency's capacity or incapacity to buy sufficient goods.

In a sense we meet here, in the microcosm of each European nation, the difficulty which has thrown the whole economic relationship between the Old and the New World out of gear. The general problem of Europe's lack of production is the sum of the failure of each nation in Europe to produce and their local failures not only destroy the general balance. They make it exceptionally difficult within Europe itself to restore a functioning trading system based on a more intensive exchange of goods—an exchange which could have the effect of somewhat mitigating the general economic dislocation. We have seen the obstacle to the Benelux Union presented by Holland's difficulties in restoring its production. The collapse of the German economy is one of the factors in Holland's embarrassment and lack of German production has had the result of cutting off the German exports which might have bought in the Low Countries and Scandinavia the foodstuffs which were formerly produced there, leaving them with an unsaleable surplus while Germans starve. Italy, with production barely at 80 per cent. of pre-war, and France crippled by the droughts and strikes of 1947, have been unable to regain their old exporting position. Britain, compelled in 1947 to buy coal from America, whereas before its annual export figure was in the neighbourhood of 50 million tons a year, is in some ways the most dramatic example of all. All these local dislocations added together have had the effect of undermining a trading area which, before the war, was one of the most prosperous and active in the world.

This is not to say that these nations have not been exporting. Britain in particular has raised its exports 20 to 30 per cent. above the level of 1938 and many of the European countries have attempted to restore the old flow. The difficulty is that the need for imports has grown even faster than any increase in exports. We have already noticed some of the reasons for this disequilibrium, for instance, the loss of all income from overseas investments, which have been sacrificed to the war, and from shipping, sunk in the same cause. (Before the war, nearly all nations in Europe balanced their trading accounts by such invisible items.) To this has been added the need for a greatly increased volume of imports to make up war loss and war damage, and at the same time phenomenal increases have occurred in the price of all these needed goods. In face of these conditions it has not been enough for Europe to restore its production to the 1938 level—many countries, including Britain, have achieved so much. The challenge and the tragedy is that production needs to be very much above the 1938 level, and that until such an expansion is achieved the obstacles to trade already mentioned will continue to bedevil Europe's efforts to restore its foreign trade, both with the New

World and within the area of a possible Western association.

It is important to understand just how shortages of production affect both currencies and commercial exchanges. If a nation, let us say Britain, cannot pay for all it requires by its own production and is constantly buying more than it sells, its currency—sterling— will become a glut on the market, for while Britain is paying other nations in sterling, their traders, being unable to buy what they need in Britain (owing to the shortages in British production) will not require sterling, and little by little Britain's trading partners will find themselves holding more and more sterling which cannot be transformed into goods. Nor under these conditions is sterling readily convertible into other currencies, for other nations are also not ready to accept a currency which does not procure them what they want to buy. It could be accepted in lieu of other currencies only if the British were ready themselves to turn it on demand into gold or into one of the currencies (hard currencies, with the dollar at their head) which do buy the goods—the wheat, the steel, the machinery—that traders most urgently require. But if the British Treasury were to make sterling convertible in this way—as it did briefly in 1947—it would simply find its own reserves of gold and dollars melting away. And this is in fact what has happened, and to-day (in March, 1948) Britain is losing its reserves at the rate of about £1 million a day. Under these conditions, international trade can go on just so long as nations such as Britain, whose currency has fallen into disequilibrium and is no longer generally acceptable as a means of payment, have gold (or dollars or Swiss francs) to pay for their imports. When they run out of these reserves, trade slackens and can even reach a full-stop. This is the process which has, in fact, been spreading in Europe in the last nine months.

Commercial exchanges can be kept alive to a limited extent by a series of bilateral treaties which avoid the necessity of transferring gold in settlement of debt by resorting to barter. Britain has signed a score of such agreements in the last year, in which British goods up to a certain value are exchanged for about the same amount of, say, Swiss or Portuguese goods. The cumbrousness of this method can easily be grasped by thinking of the barter which would need to go on in a city if it had no money and each transaction in the shops had to be carried out in kind, the butcher bringing along a chop to buy a packet of soap, the grocer taking candles to the Post Office.

These barter agreements are sometimes amplified a little by the inclusion of an agreement under which one or other of the trading partners agrees to hold a certain amount of the other's currency before asking for gold to settle the debt. Belgium, for instance, has agreed to hold £27 million before demanding hard currency. This device is really the equivalent to the granting of a small credit to the debtor country.

Another attempt to modify and render less rigid the bilateral system was proposed and developed after the Paris Conference. Belgium took the initiative in suggesting that some restoration of multilateral trade could be achieved by the drawing up of a "compensation agreement." The idea behind a compensation agreement is roughly similar to the practice of banks when they balance their clients' accounts; credits and debits are set against each other and cancelled out and transfers of credit actually take place only to meet the remaining outstanding debts. The advantage of such a system is that it reduces the actual transfer of gold or dollars to settle debts to a minimum, and as a result gives a little more elbow room to trade. The governments of Benelux, Italy, and France entered into such an agreement at the beginning of 1948, balancing their accounts every month and making no gold payments until the possibilities of balancing off their accumulations of local currencies had been exhausted.

These policies—pure bilateralism or bilateralism modified by compensation agreements—are, however, palliatives, and compensation agreements cannot work at all if one of the partners begins to fall into constant debt to the others. There are only two possible approaches to a genuine solution of the problem of restoring European trade and recreating confidence in European currencies. The first is temporary and limited. The second is a fundamental cure. A temporary expedient could be found if the United States were ready, for the first years of the Recovery Programme, to use some of the dollars voted for Marshall Aid not to procure particular commodities but to underpin a general European multilateral trading agreement. The dollars thus provided could be held in reserve to remedy any serious disequilibrium between the participants and could act as lubricants to a revived circulation of trade in Europe. For instance, if the Belgians knew that any debit in inter-European trade would, for the time being, be made good in dollars, they might be prepared to sell steel to France in return for francs or machinery to Britain in return for sterling. This method of meeting the immediate needs of both countries would prove less cumbrous than the alternative of the United States providing the needed commodities by its own purchases in the overstrained steel and machinery markets of the United States. Congress has shown some distrust of loans of this sort. The feeling that "floating dollars" unanchored to a particular commodity may be misspent is strong, but in the documents on the Recovery Programme presented by the Administration to Congress in January, 1948, there is at least a reference to the possibility of America intervening to encourage multilateral trade in Europe.

Nevertheless, a dollar fund to provide the backing for a European compensation agreement remains an expedient. The only lasting cure is a restoration of European productivity and the restoration to local currencies of their capacity to buy the goods other nations need. Every ton of coal dug out of British mines restores the value of the pound sterling, every yard of textiles, every machine produced, every extra man-hour thrown into the production drive restores the possibility of economic equilibrium and the possibility of re-establishing in Europe a system of convertible currencies, with a fixed value in relation to each other and to the currencies outside. This restoration of productivity is the first step to any more ambitious schemes of complete customs unions or complete financial union. But once it is more or less achieved, many different possibilities can be explored. For instance, for eight years before the war the Sterling Area provided an international financial system of great stability and flexibility. Not only the Commonwealth, but many of the nations of Europe, including Portugal, Scandinavia, and France, were members. The basis of the system was the decision of the various nations to do most of their foreign trade on the basis of sterling. Their own currencies had a fixed ratio in relation to sterling, they converted their earnings of foreign exchange into sterling and held their reserves in London, knowing that they could at any time convert sterling into whatever foreign currency they might require for their foreign trade—including dollars. An important area of what may now become a Western Union thus had virtually a single currency before the war.

During the war the sterling area survived, even though sterling was no longer convertible, and most of the members outside the British Commonwealth withdrew. The remaining members followed the example of Britain in imposing exchange control and paid into London their earnings of hard currency (principally dollars). Thus London held the dollar pool for the whole Commonwealth— except South Africa—and a number of other countries as well. These dollars were then, in consultation with the member governments, spent only on the goods most needed for the common war effort. The end of the war left the framework of the sterling area intact, but in the last two years the whole area's demand for dollars has been so urgent that in spite of great economies in dollar expenditure, not only in Britain, but in the Dominions as well, in March, 1948, the exhaustion of the last dollar and the last ounce of gold was in sight.

The device of a regional currency pool on the lines of the Sterling Area can be the basis of financial unity in a Western association on two conditions, The first we have seen—the restoration of productivity and, through increased production, the restoration to each individual currency (and to sterling in particular) of its purchasing power. There is no short cut, no way round this basic need. If a nation's productive powers fall, that fact can be expressed by lowering the value of its currency, since that currency will no longer buy so much. But devaluations and other financial mechanisms cannot cure, they only adjust. Behind all adjustments in the value of European currencies, in the rates of exchange established and the ratios fixed, one fact remains. They will be worth what they can buy and without production to match them they will have no value at all. Currency stabilization, convertibility, the establishment of a single currency system such as the Sterling Area will follow, not create, the restoration of production.

The second condition concerns not so much the internal working of European economy, but its relation with its greatest trading partner, the United States. It is time to recall the startling fact with which the detailed study of the Recovery Programme was brought to an end—the fact that in 1951 Western Europe may still be buying nearly $3 billion worth more goods in the United States than it can manage to sell there. Such a deficit would be enough to disturb any arrangements made for the creation of financial unity in Western Europe. The old dollar drain would begin again and with it the weakening of local currencies and the spread of financial disequilibrium. Thus before any more hopeful blue prints for future financial stability are drawn up, the basic problem of Western Europe's likely dollar deficit has to be squarely faced.

What measures can be taken to meet it? The need to seek alternative sources of supply and to create new areas of exploitation in Africa and Asia has been mentioned briefly. Here one more necessity—an unpalatable necessity—must be considered. It is this. The nations joining the Western association cannot afford in the next four years to spend the dollars they earn on anything but necessities. To the people of Britain, inured to austerity and used to the most careful rationing of dollar expenditure, this statement presents no difficulties. But in other countries, in Belgium, for instance, or in Italy, or to some extent in Sweden, a great measure of freedom has been restored to individual traders and they have been free to earn dollars by exporting machines or lumber and to buy Cadillacs and fur coats in return. But in a Western Europe seriously determined to re-establish economic independence and to pay its way, some control over dollar expenditure is essential. It is here, perhaps, that the wartime experience of the Sterling Area may be useful. For a period, Western Europe could adopt exchange control for dollars and establish a central dollar pool under the Continuing Organization. Into this pool each nation would be required to pay the dollars earned by its trading and to the Organization's other functions of allocating and distributing raw materials in scarce supply, would be added the task of allocating and distributing the scarcest of all commodities—the dollars needed for essential imports. It might be possible to temper the severity of this programme by leaving traders some dollar bonuses as incentives, but it cannot be doubted that without central control over the main flow of dollars, Western Europe will not even begin to look like balancing its dollar budget by 1951. At the same time, nothing could so knit together and integrate the economic and financial policies of the different nations as the decision to pool their dollar reserves. Few tests of sovereignty could be as sharp. Few could, if successful, give so much assurance of the continuance of economic unity and financial co-operation.

Yet even though financial agreement on these lines may be one of the keys to European co-operation, it is unhappily necessary at this point to repeat an earlier warning—that dollar saving measures concerted by the Sixteen, however essential they may be to European stability, will be exceptionally difficult to explain to the United States, where they will appear to be inexplicably hostile acts directed against Europe's chief benefactor. An example of this attitude has already become apparent in American hostility to the Sterling Area. To America it appears a sinister conspiracy to prevent its members from buying goods in the United States. When the Australians or the New Zealanders or the Egyptians announce that they have only a limited supply of dollars to spend because no more have been "allotted" to them by the authorities in London, the Americans instantly believe that the British Government is holding back dollars in order to cripple American trade or drive American commerce out of the Middle East or to achieve a hundred other unsavoury objectives. What is completely forgotten is the fact that whether Egypt, Australia, New Zealand or Britain itself pay their dollar earnings into a common pool (as they do under the Sterling Area agreements) or spend them separately (as do other nations such as France or Italy or Greece) no difference whatsoever is made to the amount of dollars at their disposal. That figure is decided by one thing alone—the amount of dollars made available by American purchases abroad or by American loans. The Sterling Area's dollar funds are simply made up of the dollars that each nation can earn, and the only difference made by the existence of control from London is that, on the whole, the dollars allocated within the Sterling Area tend to be spent on essential imports such as rolling stock and machinery, whereas dollars outside the Sterling Area may be spent on pulp magazines, and nylons, or salted down in Greek banking accounts in New York.

Admittedly, the producers of less essential goods in the United States—of mink coats and jewellery and perfumes—may complain that they are the victims of discrimination. But if the United States is serious in its desire to reconstruct world prosperity and world stability, the rationed dollars of the Sterling Area give them far greater political dividends than the unrationed dollars spent by other nations. And since in both cases the amount of dollars is identical—only American bodies, public and private, can make dollars available to Europe—it would surely seem that the American prejudice against the Sterling Area is one of the most tragic examples of prejudice and ignorance current in the world to-day. In its distrust of British "double dealing," the United States is helping to undermine one of the few factors of stability left in international financial and commercial exchange.

A similar suspicion clouds American thinking on what happens to a dollar once it has been spent abroad. The United States is embarking on a programme to give, without strings or conditions, some 17 billion dollars to Western Europe in the next four years. No American would regard it as unreasonable to ask that, in return, the dollars should be spent in the United States and few Americans have realized that ultimately a dollar, however many the transactions it may pass through, must of its very nature return to be spent in the United States. The suspicion remains that unless the dollars are spent directly upon the purchase of American commodities, they are in some way "lost" to the United States economy. The tendency is therefore to argue that all Marshall aid must be spent directly in the United States and the reason why many Congressmen have been hostile to the idea of "offshore purchases"—that is to say, of permitting dollars to be spent in other countries, for instance, on grain in Canada or Argentina— is because they think that the dollars then go irretrievably into Canadian and Argentine pockets and forget that the Argentines and the Canadians—or their customers—finally spend the dollars in the United States all the same.

This anxiety about the use Europe will make of its dollars is increased by two factors. The first became apparent even during the war, when the Americans would not permit British exports, made out of Lend-Lease material, to compete with American exports in foreign markets. For instance, if Britain made tractors from Lend-Lease steel, the Americans did not wish those tractors to be sold in competition with International Harvesters Inc. in Argentina. In other words, the Americans were unwilling to supply raw materials for goods which might later compete with theirs, even though American exports were spreading into more and more of the world's markets. This difficulty has now arisen over the Marshall Plan. Congressmen are asking whether the Sixteen should be allowed to use materials provided under Marshall aid to fabricate exports for foreign markets in competition with the United States. In the debate on ERP in the Senate, some Senators opposed the idea. As Senator Connally put it:

"If England asked for steel on the theory that she needed it for her own economy and then sold steel products to someone else, it would be a classic case for the Administrator to say 'You don't get any more of anything, Mr. England.' "

The second difficulty has been enhanced by the Communist *Putsch* in Czechoslovakia. Hitherto, the American administration has recognized Western Europe's need to buy goods beyond the Iron Curtain and thus reduce its dependence upon American supplies. But with each fresh evidence of Communist provocation, the tendency grows in America to regard trade with Russia and its satellites as a method of strengthening a potential aggressor. The Mundt amendment to the Recovery Bill compels the Administrator to refuse materials to the Sixteen if these materials might be used to export to certain (*i.e.*, Communist) countries goods for which America already refuses an export licence. This amendment might well become a demand that Western Europe should cut down its trade with Eastern Europe—in which case one more possibility of securing independence from dollar subsidies will have been cut off.

The most difficult case of all is clearly when America provides the required commodity—say tobacco or cotton—at a cheaper price than that of any non-dollar supplier. Is any American tobacco grower likely to understand why the dollars he has voted are to be spent on non-American tobacco more expensive than the goods he himself provides? Will he accept the position in which he votes the money which enables other nations to discriminate against him? Yet if none of Marshall aid may be used to work up alternative non-dollar sources of supply, the Sixteen Nations will end the four years as dependent upon the United States as they are to-day. This is the dilemma. Is there any way out of it?

Only a profound and determined programme of education and enlightenment can put across to American public opinion the fact that the material which is of all materials the scarcest in the world is—dollars. Only when that fact is grasped can it be explained why nations may seek to buy in non-dollar markets cotton or tobacco or machinery which, though more expensive than the American article, can, nevertheless, be bought for non-dollar currencies. Only then can it be made clear that there are only two ways of curing the disequilibrium from which Europe suffers: one is planning and regulation on the European side to discriminate directly against American products and thus reduce Europe's dependence on dollar supplies. The other solution lies, not in Europe's hands, but with the Americans (or Canadians or Argentines) themselves. It is quite simply to buy abroad as much as they sell.

If this willingness can be induced by clear proof of the permanent disequilibrium following on any other policy, then it is possible to think of ways and means of establishing American-European economic relations on a more stable basis. For instance, might it not be possible to envisage a quite new type of commercial treaty between the United States and the Western Union in which each side binds itself to even out all economic disequilibrium not by cutting imports—which is the method to which Western Europe is likely to be reduced if America will not modify the rules of non-discrimination—but by increasing imports instead? Let us suppose that in 1951 Europe's deficit is a billion dollars. Under present conditions all Europe can do to remedy the lack of balance is to buy one billion dollars' worth *less* goods in the United States—to everyone's disadvantage. But under the new type of commercial agreement suggested here, the United States would undertake to buy one billion dollars' worth *more* goods from Europe. There are obvious and formidable difficulties in the way of such an approach, since American producers and manufacturers might oppose the influx of foreign goods on grounds of competition. Yet if an American population, rising steadily above the 145 million mark, is to continue for a decade in full employment with an annual income of over $200 billion a year, it is difficult to believe that 1/200 of this figure might not be comfortably absorbed and might even be used, with anti-inflationary effect, by increasing supplies in corners of the market threatened by excessive demand. And even if all the difficulties of this method are admitted, it nevertheless offers better hopes for the future than the slashing of imports, the halving of foreign trade, the progressive and contagious impoverishment of nations which followed the application of "orthodox" measures in the Great Depression.

The Western nations cannot by themselves bring about the happy outcome of an agreement on the stabilization of foreign trade between Europe and America, but they can at least pave the way by concluding such agreements with each other—as a preliminary to full union—and by applying them to their trading relations with other partners. Once the idea had found concrete embodiment, the United States might of its own initiative apply the experiment to its own foreign trade.

CHAPTER XVIII

POLITICS OF UNION

The preceding pages have not attempted to give anything approaching an exhaustive list of the possibilities of economic integration in Western Europe. Not a word has been said of the work that can be done by organized economic groups—trade unions, chambers of commerce, co-operatives—to concert their policies across national frontiers and to knit together by hundreds of private purposes and agreements the economic fabric of Western Europe. Little has been said of efforts—in co-operation with such bodies as the International Labour Office—to create comparable conditions of work and comparable living standards for the same type of workers in different national communities. Nothing at all has been said of the possibilities of bringing together planners and administrators engaged in the same activities, to exchange experience and to work for a time in each other's organizations. If a Western European economic union can be formed, the possibilities of joint work within it should be as wide as the openings for co-operation within a national community. Indeed, they should be wider, embracing a far greater variety and richness of experience and leading to new and creative developments in every field. To list them all would not serve much purpose. To describe them in detail would go far beyond the scope of one short book.

In any case, there must be some readers who feel that the space devoted to economic integration has already taken up too many pages. If, they may argue, it is true, as we were told at one stage, that political decisions are ultimately the most important, is it not curious that all the emphasis so far has been placed upon economic possibilities? Is a Western association to have no political forms at all? If so, will it not be the oddest and also the most unstable union the world has ever seen?

The answer to this criticism has already in part been made. Economic possibilities have been stressed because they offer the severest test of sovereignty, and the willingness of States to co-operate fully in the political field can best be proved by the extent to which they are prepared to pool their economic sovereignty. Another deterrent to the elaboration of political forms and constitutions lies in the great variety they may assume, yet another in the unprecedented nature of the union the Western Nations propose to undertake. An association between the oldest nation States in the world, nations with unbroken traditions of sovereignty running back a thousand years and with keen separate historical memories for ever plaguing statesmen and people alike, is not likely to accept overnight the federal forms which, for instance, cover the domination of Uzbeks and Khazars by Moscow or were appropriate to thirteen newly sovereign States in America on the morrow of the War of Independence. Constituent assemblies, universal Western European franchise, presidential democracy—such notions would at present divide more than they would unite. For the next ten years, at least, the political forms of Western Union should be both more modest and more practical.

A possible line of advance was suggested recently by a statesman of international repute, M. Spaak, the Prime Minister of Belgium. He proposed that, in the first place, simply to exchange views and to gain a clear picture of each other's policies, the Prime Ministers of the interested states should hold a conference. M. Spaak's suggestion was for a limited, purely exploratory gathering, but something more regular, more formal and more binding could be made to grow from this unsensational beginning. Each Prime Minister would represent the supreme point of sovereignty in his own community and thus a reunion of Prime Ministers would come as near to the creation of a single European cabinet as can be devised without new and cumbrous constitutional machinery. The secretariat of such a conference would exist, ready made, in the permanent organization set up to administer the Recovery programme and in the organs of military cooperation established under the defence treaties. Thus, for the questions which are generally the concern of a federal government—defence, foreign policy and certain major economic problems—a staff would be in being, seized of all the relevant questions and ready to provide the conferring Prime Ministers with the material and advice they needed for their decisions. At first, these decisions would need to be referred back to the separate governments, but they would go with the weight of an agreed recommendation and the presence of the Prime Minister on the deciding body would usually be a guarantee that the conference's resolutions would, in fact, be carried out. At the same time, the Prime Ministers' conference would, when the times were ripe, be the appropriate source of any initiative in the direction of a formal political constitution to express and maintain the common purposes of Western Europe.

It is difficult to see how more rapid and ambitious steps would help the cause of political unity. But the very formlessness of the enterprise imposes upon those who engage in it an especial obligation to keep the great objective of union in sight and to allow no cross winds of uncertainty or misunderstanding to turn them from their purpose. The seas they have to cross are largely uncharted and all the guide they will be given is the far shore of unity towards which they have set their course. And since neither stars nor charts, nor a well-marked passage, will be there to keep them fixed on this true course, they will be in danger with every current and eddy and contrary breeze of losing their sense of direction and turning aimlessly round while one pulls the tiller, another lets out the sails and yet a third harangues the crew. Only vision and a certain greatness will keep their eyes raised above the perplexities of the voyage and show them the course through shoals and sandbanks to their distant port.

It is this need for a great and overriding purpose that helps to explain why the policies pursued by Britain are likely to be decisive in the next ten years. Essential though it undoubtedly is that the pursuit of unity in Western Europe should be undertaken by nations equal in status and consideration, not dominated by one of themselves or by anybody else, the fact remains that leadership rests with the British to this extent—that if they are not prepared to join and work within a Western association, such an association stands no chance of coming into existence. The reasons are complex. France would hesitate before making any agreement with the Germans unless forty-eight million British stood by its side. The Italians still have reservations about French power and policy in the Mediterranean unless balanced by British interests there. The Low Countries still have memories of Louis XIV and of Napoleon, and look for some counterweight if they are to unite their destinies to those of France. But the chief reason is strategic. In Britain is the protected arsenal which gives the fringe of Europe the hope that the whole of European resistance will not be overcome by one sweep of armies from the East and in Britain,

too, is the link with the United States and with the Commonwealth which ensures not only that Europe's defence will be the
defence of the whole free world, but that forces gathering from
all over the globe will find a foothold in Europe from which to
make their counter-attack effective. It was from the coasts of
England that the great invasion of 1944 was mounted and those
coasts remain the base line of any Western European system of
defence.

In less tangible ways as well, the co-operation of Britain is
decisive. Whatever its present economic embarrassments, the contribution of British mines and mills and factories to the European
recovery programme is tremendous and on such crucial sectors of
British industry as coal, iron and steel, mining machinery, and
agricultural machinery depend to some degree the revival of its
neighbours as well as does its own. The restoration of British production can also offer Western Europe the underpinning of a stable
financial system on the lines of the old Sterling Area, and in the
vital field where economics and politics interlock, the British
experience in maintaining social unity and political peace, in drawing the trade union movement into a constructive role in the State,
and in experimenting with the techniques of planning, make a
vital reserve of political and economic experience upon which
other nations can draw.

But the reasons which give Britain its special position—its
protective waters, its links with the Commonwealth, its unique
relationship with the United States, its economic resources and
political stability—also offer it a special temptation. The words of
André Siegfried may be repeated here—Britain is "a ship moored
in European waters, but always ready to sail away," and it is
precisely when the outlook in Europe is confused and perilous
that the attraction of breaking away from the European mooring
is felt with particular force. It is the whole argument of this book
that the choice between closer association with Europe or continued isolation no longer exists for Britain. It is either association
or decadence. The reasons for this need not be set out once again.
Here the relevant point is the extent to which Britain by uncertainty, by hedging, by coming forward and then drawing back,
can impede the creation of a union which its firm support alone
will bring into being. Since the crises of 1947 and Mr. Marshall's
response to them created the first practical opportunities for more
co-operative action, it has been to Britain that the lead has in-

evitably and almost unconsciously fallen. Mr. Bevin's lightning
reaction to the Marshall offer brought the Paris Conference into
being. The persuasive leadership exercised there by Sir Oliver
Franks shaped the writing of the Paris Report and his exposition
in Washington did much to mould American plans. Once again in
January, 1948, Mr. Bevin warmed the hopes of neighbouring
countries by declaring that the time for Western consolidation was
now ripe, and in March the lead he gave at the Second Conference of the Sixteen helped to initiate practical action to carry
out the recovery programme.

Yet while on this general field the British lead has been sufficiently clear, there are two questions to which only the development
of the Plan can give the answer. The first is whether the British
are sufficiently committed to the practice as well as the theory
of Western Union, the second is whether their influence will be
as positive, constructive, and unequivocal in the third year of the
programme as in the first. On these points, the evidence is incon-
clusive, but not altogether reassuring.

It is a fact that in the first nine months of discussion since the
Marshall offer, British leadership has been clearer in the general
field than on particular practical issues. In such matters as the
drawing up of schemes for a European compensation agreement
or the preliminary discussions on customs unions, the continental
representatives have had clearer views and bolder concepts than
their British colleagues. Again, when the question of Western
European defence was first discussed, the first British reaction was
to offer the old outmoded Dunkirk Pact with its limitation to the
case of German aggression, and only the Communist *coup d'état*
in Prague persuaded the British to accept the contention of the
Benelux states that defence arrangements would be useful only if
they covered all possibilities of aggression from without. In all
this, there is at least a possibility that the British impulse towards
closer association may falter because not enough concrete preparation has been made to work out practical ways and means of
bringing the association into being.

Even more serious would be any suggestion, at any stage in the
development of the programme, that the British Government were
giving its adherence with reservations, as a temporary expedient
for getting out of a particularly awkward situation—an expedient
to be dropped the moment better times returned. The European
nations, feeling in their bones the record of British incursions into

Europe, which in the last four hundred years have always been followed by an equally speedy exit, will be peculiarly sensitive to any sign that the British delegates are preparing once again, as so often in the past, to fold their tents. An injection of this kind of uncertainty could split the proposed association wide open and destroy that fundamental need of any lasting association—the confidence of the partners in each other's loyalty and staying power. A Western association must, in the nature of things, meet difficulties and come upon conflicts of interest vital enough to endanger the whole structure. A half-hearted Britain, ready at the first breath of adversity to attempt a withdrawal, will ensure that in every other nation the first response to difficulty will be a policy of *sauve qui peut*. No one can tell to-day what the dangers and troubles of the West are likely to be in the next decade. They cannot be predicted. They cannot be guarded against in advance. All that the Powers can do in taking the first step towards association is to commit themselves to co-operation, whatever the difficulties and whatever the cost. And it can be laid down as an axiom that if the British are not prepared for such a commitment, not one of the other Powers will be ready to run the risk. These are the real intangibles of leadership—not the great speeches on the great occasions, but the calm, sustained and patient dedication of the national will to pursue a certain policy and to pursue it to the end.

The long survey is finished. Perhaps enough has been said to suggest that, provided the determination of the Western nations is equal to the task, unity in Western Europe can be achieved, first as the framework of a general recovery programme, and then as a political organism existing of its own right and yearly strengthening its inner cohesion. The existence of such a union would offer at least a promise of solving many of the most tragic and most urgent problems hanging over the Western world to-day. As an economic unit of considerable internal prosperity it could hope to conduct a profitable exchange of goods with the United States without falling into debt or economic dependence. As a stable political order on the Atlantic coast, it could expect to forge ever-closer political links with the New World and with the British Commonwealth and stand with them, inside any future world organization, as the party of freedom and Western civilization. At the same time, the principles of its association would be economically so advantageous and politically so flexible that it is not necessary to consider the present division of Europe as a permanent division, but on the contrary, to hope that, with the relaxing of Russian fears and the demonstration that Germany can be made a pacific member of a Western community, other nations might in time withdraw from Soviet tutelage and attach themselves to a union which in politics and culture is more in tune with their own traditions. Such a consummation may not be possible, but at least if Czechs and Poles are ever to throw off Soviet control, they must have some alternative to turn to. At present, no such alternative exists, but with an integrated yet flexible Western association it would come into being.

Internally, too, a functioning Western Union could hope to overcome some of the desperate economic and social problems which at present tear asunder European society. The aim of the Marshall Plan is to restore the European standard of living, even in Western Germany, to something not far removed from 1938, and although such a standard is not high enough, it is a reasonable starting point for that concerted effort to raise production which would be one of the permanent aims of the economic Union and for which, with its internationalized sector of industry and its central planning authority, the Union would have the necessary machinery. But it is not enough to raise output. Europe to-day is torn and divided, not only because wealth has diminished, but also because its distribution is still grossly unfair. These pages have been mainly concerned with foreign policy and with the external problems facing the Powers, but a word must be said—however brief—on the extent to which the stability of Western Union will depend upon achieving internal economic democracy. It is hardly necessary to repeat that for the last hundred years the position and status of the worker have been the Achilles heel of Western society. The starting point of Marxism was that exploitation of the workers which Marx saw all around him and the entry point for Communism has always been the misery of the poor. There is little chance of a stable union in the West unless it can transcend social and economic evils which at this very time have given the allegiance of a quarter of the electorate in Italy and France to the Communist Party and would lead millions more to seek violent solutions if the misery of the masses were to be still further increased.

The first step is obviously to increase the wealth of the community. But growing prosperity is not the whole answer. Its distribution over wider sections of the community must be assured and its flow must be preserved from violent fluctuations. It has been suggested that the creation of internationalized corporations in heavy industry and transport and the introduction of the conception of planning for capital expansion and the maintenance of some central control on financial policy can provide the machinery for attaining a high and stable level of capital investment. At the same time, these measures would go far to satisfy some of the principal demands contained in the various working-class political programmes in Western Europe. But to set up a general structure of international planning is hardly enough to accomplish the difficult and challenging task of drawing the working class completely into the social and political community of modern society. The experience of recent years suggests that two other objectives should be immediately accepted by the member states of the Western Union. The first is to adopt as a basis of policy a concept now increasingly accepted and established in Britain—the concept of a Social Minimum, of a level of subsistence below which no economic misfortune will allow a man or his family to fall. This concept of social security, coupled with family allowances and minimum wage legislation, may sound cautious enough in Britain. In other countries it would have a revolutionary effect. The minimum rates of wages and benefits could probably not be uniform at first, but the trend should be in that direction so as to ensure, little by little, a general raising of European standards towards that of the Union's wealthiest member States. Such a policy would have the incidental advantage of evening out competitive differences owing their existence to poorly paid labour; it might also simplify in time the problem of freedom of movement within Western Europe.

But the worker is not only concerned with economic benefits. The second objective must be to give him a sense of his true position in society. The evil of nineteenth-century society was, as we have seen, to deprive him of his status and his *raison d'être*—or rather to fail, as he emerged to education and political consciousness, to discover what should be his place in the new social order created by industrialism. Politically, by receiving the vote, he became a responsible citizen. Economically and socially, he remained a unit or a hand. There are two immediate ways in which this lack of status can be remedied in a Western Union. The first is by integrating the non-Communist trade unions into the machinery of consultation and planning established at the centre. Great Britain has learnt the inestimable advantage in terms of stability and social peace of drawing the trade unions fully into the machinery of economic planning for the community at large. A similar attempt should be made within the Western Union. The determination shown in the spring of 1948 by the unions favourably disposed to the Marshall Plan to come together to discuss the Plan and at the same time to compel the Communist-dominated World Federation of Trade Unions to take cognizance of Europe's recovery programme is a measure of their interest in the Plan and of their desire to play a part in its development. The desire is one to be encouraged by every means in the various Governments' power.

The second method is one which cannot easily be laid down by some central authority and imposed from above. It is a method which must grow and spread, industry by industry, and factory by factory. It is no coincidence that at the beginning of 1948, in both Italy and Belgium, the chief demand of the trade union movement was for management and production committees in the factories to enable the workers to be drawn into the processes of decision and policy making, and also to enable them to see how their activity and production fit into the pattern of the industry as a whole. Now there is much in this movement that is irresponsible and demagogic. The Communists, in particular, are more interested in forming "Committees of Action" to take over the factories than "production committees" to help them run. But the movement can be a genuine and serious effort to associate the worker with his factory and his industry, just as he is associated with the political machinery of his country at the local and national level. Here, again, British experience can be of some assistance. Not all the Joint Production Committees set up in Britain during the war were a success, but those which were can be a model of a new technique in industry, and in so far as the central authorities of a Western Union are permitted to decide upon industrial policy in such detail, the encouragement of industrial councils as a means of drawing the worker into a genuine industrial community with management should be one of their aims. In the internationalized sectors, they should become a matter of course.

CHAPTER XIX

"WHERE THERE IS NO VISION"

A Union conceived on these lines would not necessarily be the tidy paradise of a planner's dream, but it would stand a chance of being a prosperous, vigorous community with expanding living standards, political freedom, and a growing sense of economic democracy. It would be an infinitely more attractive place than the present wretched and dislocated Western fringe and it might reasonably be expected to offer more attractions than the federation of sovietized police States upon its borders. But is this all that is needed to launch and develop so great a venture? When men speak of Western civilization and of the preservation of its way of life, are they thinking of no more than international steel, a European electricity grid and the spread through Western Europe of Joint Production Councils? When Mr. Bevin spoke of "Western Union," were these the only images to stir in people's minds? And were they moved to consider a great sacrifice of sovereignty, an audacious step into the unknown, an incalculable act of faith simply in the hopes of reaching by 1951 the living standards of 1938? The questions have only to be asked for the inadequacy of all that has been said hitherto to be apparent. Men do not embark on a venture as far-reaching and challenging as that of the union of a dozen sovereign States in a single community simply through economic interest or a sense of political propriety. It is right that economic possibilities and practical policies and factual precedents should be studied first, but all these things—which have admittedly made up the substance of this book—will remain, as in Ezekiel's vision, a valley of dry bones unless there is a spirit to inform them and bring them together in the mighty army of a living faith.

This need for vision and a high ideal would exist whatever the circumstances attending the search for Western unity, but even the most ingrained cynics can hardly deny the need for faith when, looking across the frontiers of Western Europe, they see Communism at work, inspiring many and dragooning many more to a new vision of man and society, a vision which is in part the heritage of the West, and in part its complete denial. For Communism does not content itself with plans and strategies. It combines the most calculated and ruthless practice of power politics with a demand of a religious loyalty and the promise of a visionary and apocalyptic future. To suppose that so effective a combination of immediate action and ultimate reward can be withstood and not only withstood, but defeated and driven back, by nothing more elevating than the prospect of a European electricity grid is to betray a shattering ignorance of the laws of ordinary psychology. Where there is no vision, the people perish and with them all the plans and policies and projects ever drawn up in their name.

What in this last and most vital sphere of all are the prospects for Western Europe? First of all, it must be admitted that in searching for its soul, the West is in a far more troublesome position than its neighbours beyond the Iron Curtain. It cannot, as the Communists do, announce and impose its dogma. It has realized in painful centuries of persecution and religious war what it should no doubt have realized from its origins—that spiritual truth can be conveyed by attraction, inspiration, and conversion, but not by violence. There is no question, therefore, of a Western ideology. The essence of the West is to have none. Beliefs, truths, principles—these are the core of the Western mind, but where the attempt is made to impose them by physical force—as they were in covenanting Scotland, or in the early American colonies, as they are still in Spain to-day—their spiritual vigour leaves them. They become, as Communism has become, one more instrument in the armoury of the tyrant-state. The weapon of religious and cultural uniformity is thus one which a Western Union cannot of its very nature take into its hand. It must be ready to accept and even welcome confusion and contradiction of opinion and belief and yet find ways of holding them together in a reasonable measure of social harmony. In the short run, every advantage is on the side of the totalitarians. Nevertheless, one of the fundamental affirmations of Western faith is that in the long run truth, whether of religion or philosophy or politics or the social order, is great and will prevail without the watchful assistance of a Commissar of Popular Enlightenment.

Another difficulty in assessing the West's reserves of faith and spiritual strength lies precisely in this lack of dragooning and direction of Western opinion, for its very wealth and variety make a precise analysis of the Western spirit exceptionally difficult. It appears beneath the religious idealism of one, the scientific humanism of another, the sceptical benevolence of a third; yet, even in the same minds, Marxist dogmatism or fierce religious intolerance or utter inability to distinguish between the general interest and narrow personal advantage deny the Western spirit as strenuously as the other attributes exhibit it. One has only to think of the shades of opinion represented, say, in a single parliament in Western Europe to realize the incredible and often contradictory variety of ideas and reactions and beliefs and dogmas that go to the making of a forum of Western thought.

Yet through all the variety and apparent contradictions, there run the recognizable threads of a Western pattern of thought, the unmistakable quality of a Western spirit. It is not enough to say that "freedom" is its distinguishing mark. The term is too general to define a particular state of mind, even though it is true that the pursuit and realization of freedom has been the noblest political activity of Western men. But freedom as it has existed in the Western world is not a simple concept. For instance, in individual behaviour, freedom has not been equated with licence. The ideally free man is the man who without external compulsion chooses the good and the true and rejects the unworthy. The libertine, the wastrel, the debauchee are not, in the Western sense, "free" men. Freedom has also been indissolubly bound up with the question of moral responsibility. The Western mind has not in the past accepted the concept of men totally conditioned and preordained to act in certain ways—by environment, by class or, as in an earlier age, by the envy and vengeance of the gods. The free man can choose. This, too, is of the essence of freedom. Again, liberty in society in the Western world has not been a matter of anarchy but of the definition and defence of rights, of the citizen against the State, of the community against the individual. Freedom has been a question of "liberties" in particular, rather than of liberty as an abstract concept. We must therefore go behind the idea of freedom and ask from what foundations it has grown in Western society and what ideas have shielded its growth.

The first foundation of Western freedom is one that has been the support of every great civilization until our day—of Chinese and Indian, of Egyptian and Roman—the belief that underlying the ebb and flow of historical events and human happenings there exists a moral order of right and wrong, and good and evil, which transcends every particular interest and which, far from being created by men and events, is the yardstick by which they are judged. The justice of laws is judged by it as well as the goodness and rightness of men's actions, and it is precisely because it is beyond the reach of human interests and cravings that it is the guarantee of an objective system of law and at the same time of the rights of individual men and women. When the great medieval lawyer, Bracton, wrote that the king (in other words, the State) was below God and the law, he laid down a principle of inestimable importance for Western political liberty, for in his maxim is contained the idea of the legal limits of State action and the denial that government has unlimited sovereignty over the individual citizen. But trace his statement back to its origins and it will be found to rest in the fundamental belief of Western society that an eternal law, a natural law, exists beyond society and is the source, within society, of justice and of right and hence of freedom.

It is possible to illustrate this belief from the sphere of scientific law. Certain laws—of gravity, of thermodynamics—underlie the structure of the universe and the behaviour of material things demonstrates their existence. Similarly the great thinkers until our own time believed that the laws of justice, of right and wrong, of good and evil, are embedded in the same way in the very nature of the universe—the only difference being that man, endowed with a free nature, can choose or not to obey the moral law, whereas material things have no choice in conforming to the laws of matter and energy.

This conception of free choice and of responsibility is another foundation of the Western idea of freedom. We forget, perhaps, because we are so accustomed to it, how rare in the tremendous span of human history has been the notion of a free, autonomous, fully responsible human being. In most of the societies which preceded the Greek city states, the individual was as nothing compared to the community or the State. But in Western civilization, built on the twin foundations of Greek philosophy and Christian faith, there emerges for the first time the concept of man as a supreme being, unique in his personality, absolute in his rights and standing at the head of all creation. It was this revolutionary conception of human personality that succeeded, little by little, in establishing the no less revolutionary doctrine that government existed for the citizen, not the citizen for the all-powerful State. The sense of the unique character of each human spirit reinforced the notion of his rights derived from a superior natural law and was the driving faith behind the origins of modern democracy. From it was also derived the belief, hardly found outside the brief span of Western society, that men should be associated with their own government and should achieve true freedom by being governed, in so far as government was necessary, by themselves.

It can perhaps also be argued that the deep sense of the necessary limitations of government, which Western society has usually exhibited, springs from another fundamental concept of the Western world—that man is fallible as well as magnificent and that the dignity of the human person is only equalled by its capacity for sin. And if men sin, why suppose that they, acting collectively as the State, will fare any better? And what folly could be greater than to leave tyrants who are only men like others, the absolute power they ask for on the grounds that the general run of men are not fit to govern themselves?

These ideas—of man's unique greatness, but equal sinfulness, of his fundamental human rights and of the necessary limitations they impose on government, of the existence of an order of right and wrong, and good and evil, from which these rights are derived and which transcends man and society—these ideas have been among the principal ferments in Western society, making it the most rich and expansive and dynamic society mankind has ever seen. In particular, these ideas have been the very stuff of the freedom which is the West's most fundamental contribution to human greatness and probably its chief power of continued attraction in the modern world.

If this is so, it is surely clear that the challenge presented by Communism goes to the very roots of Western society. On the one hand, Communism being a child of that society adopts its aims and phrases. It speaks of the true people's democracy, it speaks of the rights of the masses and it draws upon the indignation and remorse felt by men at the injustices and the violation of fundamental human rights which have occurred and still occur in Western society. Yet while upholding these aims and ideals, Communism destroys each of the beliefs upon which the Western concepts of law and freedom and democracy have been based. It destroys the belief in an objective order of right and wrong and the idea of a law which transcends particular times and interests. On the contrary, Marxist theory, as we have seen, maintains that "the economic structure of society always forms the real basis from which, in the last analysis, is to be explained the whole superstructure of legal and political institutions as well as the religious and other conceptions.[1]

It destroys the belief in the morally responsible and autonomous human being. Man, as such, his character and personality, hardly puts in an appearance in Marx's pages. He appears in the guise of capitalist, exploiting the masses according to his predestined economic role. He appears as a poor devil of a proletarian, exploited by the same destiny. In time other iron laws will raise him in revolt and submit him to "liberation" by his own dictatorship, the dictatorship of the proletariat. But of his own individual beliefs, responsibilities, and actions, there is not a word. And since man is simply the raw material of a new type of society, it is not surprising that there should be no attempt to define the rights he may enjoy there and the limitations the dictatorship of the proletariat may impose upon itself in the interval before fading away. In any case, by what criterion shall the proper time for disappearance be judged? Since there are by definition no possible standards of criticism beyond society, no objective concepts of good and evil, no ideas of justice or of law existing above and beyond all temporary political convenience, the danger is for tyranny once established to become the unquestioned norm. Faced with such possibilities, few will deny the lethal effect of Communism on the fundamental beliefs of Western democracy and if some still doubted in theory whether the divergence between the two was so great, the methods with which Communist minorities have, in practice, liquidated the remnants of political democracy in such a country as Czechoslovakia, must surely have suggested that in a world run by men who have no truth beyond Marxist truth, no justice beyond Communist justice, and no loyalty beyond their commitment to a Party, democratic society as it has been known in the West must cease to be.

Yet Western democratic society was the soil in which Marxism first took root. How can this paradox be explained? Surely, by the extent of Western society's own apostasy. It was not only Marxists who in the last century were abandoning their belief in a universal law and in the unique nature of human personality. Scientists and rationalists showed Marx the way and continued afterwards to extend their scepticism to more and more of the old

[1] Frederick Engels: *Anti-Dühring*, p. 32.

values of society. Marx after all was only one in a great army of "debunkers" who gradually undermined the tremendous certainties of the Victorians and set in their place the doubts and questioning of the following age. Anthropologists discovered the roots of faith in fear and magic, psycho-analysts discovered the dark grounds of motivation in the unconscious drives of biological man. Determinists of all sorts showed man a new picture of himself—a mere link in a biological chain, bound internally by his instincts, externally by his place in an economic and social environment conditioning his every response. Man who had believed himself to be "little lower than the angels" found himself to be only a little higher than the ants and apes.

But the chief apostasy lay more with the practitioners of society than with its critics, for as we have seen, the nineteenth and early twentieth century were times during which man built up an inhuman economic system, sanctified it in the name of Christian values, and protected it by the dogma of private property. One may blame the debunkers for defining religion as the means of ensuring a docile working class, but all too many of their contemporaries were prepared to use religion in precisely that way. Thinkers might still deny the validity of determinist thinking and continue to claim a unique value for each individual soul, yet in factories without end, in long working hours or later in the mechanization of the conveyor belt, men were, in fact, being degraded to the status of cogs and units, and it was almost as though, while the Marxists and rationalists thought out the politics of the new ant state, the practical men of business were putting it into effect. And this new collectivist society of immense conglomerations of social property in the shape of capital and vast industrial armies of men herded together in the ant heap of industrial towns and among the din of machines in the factories, had not even the advantage of offering the workers status and security. It was not *their* society. Society belonged to the bosses, to the profit makers, to "Them," the distant owners for whom the mass of workers simply worked, understanding neither their job nor the industry of which their job was a part.

Now this may appear an exaggerated picture and it certainly is not true of all industrial activity, but such conditions prevailed over a sufficiently wide field to make understandable the sweep both of Marx's indignation and later of the following he gained. Communism did not come to write the sentence on Western industrial society before it had all but written it itself. The mass of men could hardly remember their unique personality and responsibility in an environment which hour by hour was deadening both. They were hard put to it to believe in an objective order of truth and justice when their justice was the meagre justice of a skin-flint wage packet, the sudden sacking, the agonizing years of unemployment. They could hardly realize their sovereign rights as citizens when government did, in fact, seem to be in the hands of a hostile class. Out of such a society the old belief in democracy began to seep away. Communism only hastened the process, but disillusionment and despair would in any case have completed the undermining from within, and when despair reached breaking point, it was not to Communism that the masses looked. In one country at least, the Germans seized at something more destructive and more terrible than any dictatorship of the proletariat when in Hitler they found the incarnate spirit of violence and unreason.

If this analysis—brief and inadequate though it undoubtedly is—expresses anything like the reality of the Western situation, it follows that the task of discovering the spiritual basis of a Western association is more challenging and more formidable than any of the undertakings in the economic and political field that have been considered so far. Not only must the outward forms of union be created in the political and economic and social field, but into those frames must be breathed a renewed faith in the values and principles which have been for the last two thousand years the creative force in Western civilization. And the renewal of faith demands not only the reaffirmation of certain principles, but the vigorous determination to tolerate nothing in society that makes them a mockery. The first point is perhaps to remember that any attempt to revive the spirit of Western civilization calls for what is in every sense an affirmation of faith. No scientific proof will establish the unique value of the human person and no observation will prove the fundamental equality of human souls. That ideas of good and evil and right and wrong transcend the social order which embodies them cannot be deduced with mathematical certainty, nor can it be argued that the laws of probability are outraged when government violates the rights of the sovereign citizen. The fundamental affirmations of Western society are all matters of faith and it is an historical fact that the faith in which they were grounded and from which they derived their deepest strength, has been the Christian faith. It was as children of God that men received their title to sovereign inalienable rights. It was as immortal souls that they claimed a unique and equal status, it was in the will of God that they saw enshrined the laws and the rights which no government might transgress, it was in comparison with His perfection and with the demonstration of it in the person of Christ that Western man realized his own frailty and drew from it first the humility and then at last the tolerance for lack of which the concentration camps are filled to-day. It may be possible to believe that the richness and the beauty and the incredible flowering of the Western spirit could have occurred apart from its Christian root and environment. It may be possible to believe that the rededication of the Western world to its old ideals can come about without a recovery of its ancient faith. But the only lesson that history gives is that Christianity and democracy grew up so closely intertwined that the languishing of one may well mean the failure and the decadence of the other.

But one cannot draw up plans and blue prints for a religious revival any more than one can legislate for the springing of an oasis in the desert. The test of the fidelity of a Western association to the greatest traditions of its civilization will lie, for Christians, for humanists, for all men of good will, in the extent to which the new society they build enables ordinary men and women to realize their capacities for freedom and growth in a social order stable enough and prosperous and gracious enough not to frustrate them, not to condemn them to the "quiet desperation" which has so often been their lot. All the practical plans and proposals put forward in this book amount to no more than this. There is no other aim in economic and industrial effort, no other purpose worthy to be written into the constitution of a new Western society. Indeed, the only justification of the whole immense labour of transcending the limits of the single nation State is the fact that in Western Europe the well-being and security of ordinary families can no longer be secured by the unaided efforts of a single national community.

Naturally, the new ordering of society will not spring into being on the morrow of creating political union. The process must be a long, but if possible, a steady growth. Nor can we yet foretell what will be this new society's most appropriate economic and social forms. But we can say now and with complete certainty that unless the pursuit of justice and the practice of brotherhood are the first purposes of the men of the new union, they will fail to build their city, just as, for all their material prosperity, their grandfathers failed before them.

One thing at least the Communists may accomplish for a Western Union, and perhaps the men of the West will one day be grateful to them just as, in their daily lives, they are sometimes grateful for the pains and sorrows that have given them strength. So long as Communism, with its apocalyptic appeal, its vision of a classless society, its cry of brotherhood, its claim to offer a society based, not on exploitation, but justice, stands on the very frontiers of the West, there can be no respite from its challenge. The West is offered the choice of fulfilling the promise inherent yet still unrealized within it of creating a free, good, and just society. Or it will fail all the more speedily because of the chasm between its pretensions and its practice. These are the stakes. Who will say they are not worthy of the supreme effort of free men ?

INDEX

3.75